The American Protest Essay and National Belonging

THE AMERICAN PROTEST ESSAY AND NATIONAL BELONGING

Addressing Division

BRIAN NORMAN

STATE UNIVERSITY OF NEW YORK PRESS

Cover: A portion of "The Ohlone Mural: The Capture of Solid, The Escape of Soul," Oakland, California. Printed by permission of the muralist, Rocky Rische-Baird.

An earlier version of chapter 3, "The Addressed and the Redressed: Helen Hunt Jackson's Protest Essay and the U.S. Protest Novel Tradition," published by the *Canadian Review of American Studies* (*Revue canadienne d'étude américaines* 37, no. 1, 2006) is printed here by permission.

Published by
STATE UNIVERSITY OF NEW YORK PRESS
ALBANY

© 2007 State University of New York

All rights reserved

Printed in the United States of America

No part of this book may be used or reproduced in any manner whatsoever without written permission. No part of this book may be stored in a retrieval system or transmitted in any form or by any means including electronic, electrostatic, magnetic tape, mechanical, photocopying, recording, or otherwise without the prior permission in writing of the publisher.

For information, address
State University of New York Press
194 Washington Avenue, Suite 305, Albany, NY 12210-2384

Production, Laurie Searl
Marketing, Michael Campochiaro

Library of Congress Cataloging-in-Publication Data

Norman, Brian, 1977–
 The American protest essay and national belonging : addressing division / Brian Norman.
  p. cm.
 Includes bibliographical references (p.) and index.
 ISBN 978-0-7914-7235-4 (alk. paper) — ISBN 978-0-7914-7236-1 (pbk. : alk. paper)
 1. American literature—20th century—History and criticism. 2. Protest literature, American—History and criticism. 3. American literature—19th century—History and criticism. 4. Politics and literature—United States—History and criticism. 5. Dissenters in literature. 6. Identity (Psychology) in literature. I. Title.

PS228.P73N67 2007
814'.009355—dc22

2006101381

10 9 8 7 6 5 4 3 2 1

CONTENTS

List of Illustrations   vii

Acknowledgments   ix

Introduction   1
CONCERNING DIVISION:
ALLEGIANCE, RENUNCIATION, AND NATIONAL BELONGING

Chapter One   13
TOWARD AN AMERICAN PROTEST ESSAY TRADITION

Chapter Two   41
NEW DECLARATIONS OF INDEPENDENCE:
THREE FEMINIST RE-VISIONS OF A FOUNDING DOCUMENT

Chapter Three   71
THE ADDRESSED AND THE REDRESSED: HELEN HUNT JACKSON'S
PROTEST ESSAY AND THE PROTEST NOVEL TRADITION

Chapter Four   87
THE ART OF POLITICAL ADVOCACY:
JAMES BALDWIN, AMERICAN PROTEST ESSAYIST

Chapter Five   117
IDENTITY POLITICS, COLLECTIVE FUTURES,
AND THE CROSS-ESSAY CONVERSATIONS OF AUDRE LORDE,
ADRIENNE RICH, AND ALICE WALKER

Chapter Six 139
June Jordan and Transnational American Protest

Conclusion 155
Why the Essay?

Appendix 159
Printings of the Combahee River Collective,
A Black Feminist Statement (April 1977)

Notes 161

Bibliography 185

Index 215

ILLUSTRATIONS

Figure One   52–53
"A New Declaration of Independence,"
Mother Earth 4.5 (July 1909)

Figure Two   55
Mug shot, Emma Goldman, 1911

Figure Three   76–77
Letter from H. Price, Commissioner of Indian Affairs
to Helen Hunt Jackson, October 16, 1882

Figure Four   89
James Baldwin and Marlon Brando at the
March on Washington, August 28, 1963

ACKNOWLEDGMENTS

Scholarly projects of any kind quickly accumulate a list of persons to whom the author is indebted in no small way. At the top of this list is Marianne DeKoven who served as director of the project at its dissertation stage, and who also continues to play the complementary roles of intellectual companion, political analyst, professional mentor, movement veteran, and dear friend. Her astute direction, generous nurturance, and unfettered endorsement are a superlative model of collegiality and friendship, a model that guides my own career. Hillary Chute's friendship as a fellow young scholar serves as a reliable beacon, and I trust her professional judgment and suggestions.

Other colleagues and friends also gave generously of their time, interests, and expertise. Cheryl Wall's measured and incisive guidance at key moments helped me bring the concerns and insights of African American literary traditions to an ambitious Americanist project. My colleagues at Idaho State University helpfully and persistently questioned my sense of protest aesthetics. My upper division and graduate students at ISU created lively forums to discuss the richness of the writings I hold so dear, especially members of my seminars in modern/postmodern America. Wesley Brown, Ed Cohen, Cora Kaplan, and Kurt Spellmeyer worked with me in the early stages of the project. Michael Warner's canny assistance in shaping my dissertation helped provide a direction for the ensuing book project, even though only one chapter survives from the original. Channette Romero offered key support during our search for our first jobs, and she continues to model this profession at its best. Members of the 2003–2004 seminar on citizenship at the Center for the Critical Analysis of Contemporary Culture at Rutgers University taught me what it can mean to participate in a bounded scholarly community. For support of the project and careful attention at every stage, I thank my editor, Larin McLaughlin, and all the folks involved at SUNY Press—Michael Campochiaro, Laurie Searl, and Rosemary Wellner. The reviewers for SUNY Press provided terrific revision suggestions, and I am indebted to them for giving of their expertise so freely. Other scholars and friends helped during specific stages, including especially: James Albrecht, Brian Attebery, Jennifer Attebery, Linda Bosniak, Ethel Brooks, Tom Campbell, Terry Engebretsen, Angeline Henrickson Underwood, Margaret Johnson, Linda Keller Kerber, Cristina Kirklighter, Beth Kraig, Brian Lamarche, Anthony Lioi, Lisa Marcus, Leslie McCall, Nick Monk, Joycelyn Moody, Erica Rische-Baird, Piper Kendrix Williams, Carolyn Williams, Jessica Winston, and Brent Wolter. My debts to them are too specific to mention here, but they were all invaluable to this project.

Research for this book was partially supported by a fellowship at the Center for Cultural Analysis at Rutgers University and by Grant No. FY2005-2 from the Humanities/Social Sciences Research Committee at Idaho State University, Pocatello, Idaho. I also extend my gratitude to Candace Falk and Barry Pateman at the Emma Goldman Papers Project at the University of California–Berkeley, Jerry Randall at the Tutt Library Special Collections at Colorado College, and to the staff at the Schomburg Center of the New York Public Library.

An earlier version of chapter 3 was published in the *Canadian Review of American Studies*. Thank you to Percy Walton and the anonymous reviewers for suggestions on that article.

Finally, my partner Greg Nicholl somehow put up with me during my time as a graduate student and then as a new assistant professor. He delivered patience, love, exasperation, support, and sometimes a necessary kick in the pants.

Introduction

Concerning Division: Allegiance, Renunciation, and National Belonging

---

> "I'm saying let's make it 84 percent turnout in two years, and then see what happens!"
> "Oh, yes! Vote! Dress yourself up, and vote! Even if you only go into the voting booth and pray. Do that!"
>
> —Bernice Johnson Reagon and Toni Morrison
> on the 2000 presidential election

When James Baldwin's essay *The Fire Next Time* (1963) became an enduring national bestseller, the United States witnessed the full flowering of an important literary tradition. In order to respond to the founding of an American republic that declares inclusion and enacts exclusion, many celebrated literary figures and activists turn to what I call the American protest essay. In the protest essay, writers bring the experiences of those lacking full social status into the public arena by directly addressing a divided audience, documenting with journalistic fervor representative instances of injustice, and citing state promises of full social participation for all. I titled this book *Addressing Division* because the protest essay is well-suited to attend to a deeply divided citizenry who nonetheless share a commitment to universal visions of national equality. Yet the American protest essay is eclipsed by the more famous protest novel tradition and it suffers from a general underappreciation of the essay form itself—what G. Douglas Atkins goes so far as to call the essay's second-class citizenship.[1] This book treats American debates between integration and self-determination or unity and separatism as manifestations of a long-standing dilemma in protest writing, especially in the essay form: an acute recognition of social divisions potentially undermines an ultimate desire for collectivity.

This book considers essays by Gloria Anzaldúa, James Baldwin, Vine Deloria Jr., W. E. B. DuBois, Ralph Ellison, Emma Goldman, Langston Hughes, Helen Hunt Jackson, June Jordan, Audre Lorde, Norman Mailer, Adrienne Rich, Henry David Thoreau, Gore Vidal, Alice Walker, Richard Wright, and others. Let me caution at the outset that I do not intend to construct a totalizing and all-encompassing overview of American protest essays. The writers and social contexts I am able to cover, even in a book-length project, are necessarily selective, which inevitably omits many writers and essays that belong in the tradition. So, I select texts that illustrate key characteristics common to protest essays, or particular moments in the tradition's continual engagement with narratives of national belonging, and I sometimes point to other writers or essays for which the text under discussion stands.

American protest essayists aspire to national unity by addressing, not repressing, divisions within the citizenry. Identifying this strategy is not a particularly new insight, but the way the essay form delivers on that project merits attention. The essay as a form is known to trust experience over abstract truth, which offers protest writers a forum to test out national stories of belonging. While personal essays generally turn inward to reflect on individual experience, protest essays bring experiences of exclusion to divided publics. Protest essayists may begin in factions or personal dissent but often move toward collectivity. Because they underscore lines of social division, protest writings hazard dismissal for being ultimately factionalizing, too polemical, or merely ephemeral. Within the U.S. context, writers can invoke an official project of building a democratic republic, which allows them to cite national promises—and often state documents—that announce full social participation for all. They offer their divided audience a reinvigorated national "we" that can account for division within that "we." For these writers, the protest essay's gestures of antagonism engender, rather than hinder, collectivity. Whereas the dominant story of national belonging invokes official pronouncements of equality dating back to the Declaration of Independence, American protest essayists recount experiences of exclusion from full social participation. In doing so, they use the essay to foster substantive, not aspirational, stories of national belonging.

This project comes from reading the hopeful and incendiary essays of Baldwin, the conversational essays of Anzaldúa or Walker, or Vidal's serious engagement with U.S. history in his essays. Perhaps the idea originated the first time I read Frederick Douglass's still-relevant speech "What to the Slave Is the Fourth of July?" (1852) in which he uses his status as escaped slave and free black to address an audience of northerners, abolitionists, and political figures in Corinthian Hall, but on behalf of slaves toiling away on southern plantations who Douglass poses as the rightful heirs of the holiday's emphasis on liberty. I began to see essayists replicate Douglass's ability to move among a fiercely divided audience and to claim official promises of equality as his own. The project solidified when I picked up a little pamphlet of three essays called *Patriotism and the American Land*. In response to what Terry Tempest Williams describes as a "hollow patriotism"[2] following the attacks of September 11, 2001, two literary figures and a cultural anthropologist turned to the essay to bring substance to the project of democracy. Williams explains, "Those who raise questions are told to raise American flags instead. . . . But America is still a democracy and a strong one. We do have people with vision. We do have a history."[3] Williams points to Rachel Carson as a patriot in that history, and I note that the essay form allows her to ask questions of America because in that form she can explore experiences—hers and others', including Carson's and the land's—that give substance to her questions about democracy and national belonging. Her essay joins a long history of literary figures who turn to the essay for their political advocacy, and the distribution in pamphlet form recalls Thomas Paine's *Common Sense* (1777) or, in later eras, mimeographed leaflets at protest rallies.

This book joins decades of scholarly attempts to reconcile the stark and often brutal contradictions between lofty promises of equality pronounced—sometimes by bullhorn—by the U.S. nation-state and its practices of inequality, exclusion, and violence perpetrated against many groups within and beyond U.S. borders. This is not a new observation; indeed, this contradiction has been at the heart of American studies and American ethnic studies since their inceptions. This contrast also infuses debates between liberalism and radicalism in most American social movements. To long-standing concerns that U.S. democratic narratives do not match practices, this book offers a better understanding of the unique way the protest essay can account for these contradictions without jettisoning an inclusive national vision. While those occupying seats of power have tended to argue that the way to overcome injustice and inequality is to paper over social division, protest essayists insist that the path to real social equality requires that we address—indeed, underscore—experiences of inequality. These writers work from the premise, to echo Jürgen Habermas, that modernity's project of bringing liberty, equality, and democracy to all is a great idea, but that the idea remains elusive in practice for many groups.

Protest essayists respond to foundational narratives of freedom and democracy not by ceding lofty state promises to mere charges of hypocrisy but instead by seeking full participation in the national community. A nation-state that announces already achieved unity and equality necessarily suppresses awareness of the divisions and inequities within its political community. That is why African American and multicultural studies, following thinkers from literary scholars Toni Morrison and Wahneema Lubiano to legal scholars Charles Mills and Judith Shklar, insist that experiences of oppression are not mere aberrations from or oversights of founding declarations of equality for all. Rather, many argue that announcements of freedom and democracy only gain meaning alongside and against those who are not free, not full members of the democracy. In her study of the American nation and the figure of the foreigner, political theorist Bonnie Honig asks, "Does democracy have a genre?"[4] Honig suggests that the gothic romance, especially the female gothic, is most able to address foreignness. In turn I suggest that the American protest essay is particularly well-suited to address division within a citizenry that likes to think of itself as equal.

The ability to simultaneously claim and critique the nation's inclusive promises comes to full flowering within a genre that is able to connect state proclamations and individual experiences. My investments are in unearthing a tradition of American writer-advocates—some well known, others less so—whose work may have previously been overshadowed by more dominant strands of the essay form on one hand, and by a default attention to protest novels or poetry on the other. As a result, this project is both an aesthetic and a cultural study of common characteristics of the form, some of its key practitioners, and illustrative moments in the tradition's development. Such an approach risks overlooking many important instances of the protest essay, especially in favor of writers whose work has not historically defined the essay genre. It is my hope that future scholars are inspired to do further work by placing other writer-advocates into the protest essay tradition I have identified.

CITIZENSHIP OATHS

A brief look at a recent controversy involving the U.S. citizenship oath can illustrate the dominant narrative of national belonging to which protest essayists must respond. American protest essayists navigate treacherous waters to survive the Scylla of chauvinist patriotism, without sinking into the Charybdis of identitarian politics. In the oath, entrance into full membership in the nation-state via naturalized citizenship requires a simultaneous oath of allegiance and renunciation. Prospective citizens swear off past ties to home countries as they swear to honor—and defend—their host country. Entrance into the nation-state requires exit—ideological more than geographic—from the newly naturalized citizen's former home country. Allegiance to the new country requires a simultaneous renunciation of any past ties to other nations or peoples. This assumption of uniform allegiance and renunciation of past allegiances came to a head on September 17, 2003 (Citizenship Day), when the United States was to adopt a new version of its Oath of Allegiance.[5] The updated version would modernize the oath by removing cumbersome words like "abjure" and anachronistic references like "potentate." Thus the oral recitation would become more meaningful—and more manageable—for the millions of immigrants eligible for naturalization. The revised version, however, was quickly dropped following a controversy in which many decried the perceived attack on a "timeless" document and a weakening of the military obligation that is the foundation of entrance into American citizenry.[6] The Heritage Foundation, for instance, issued an executive statement against "the Department of Homeland Security's misguided attempts to make U.S. citizenship more 'user-friendly' for those who want the benefits of our country, but don't care to accept the responsibility."

The thwarted attempt to make naturalization procedures more welcoming arose at a curious time. The potential revision coincided with vigorous efforts to shore up national boundaries after September 11, 2001.[7] The newly formed Department of Homeland Security now oversaw citizenship services and disparate border policing programs, which consolidated the long-standing scrutiny of immigrants—especially those considered not-white—for their ideological commitment and adherence to the going national ideals. In the yearly proclamation designating September 17 as Citizenship Day, President Bush cited national defense and citizenship as a means toward internal unity: "In the wake of those [terrorist] attacks, we have renewed and strengthened our commitment to a more perfect Union and common defense to justice and domestic tranquility, to the general welfare and the blessings of liberty."[8] In this model of national belonging, naturalization procedures require a uniform recitation of unhesitant adherence to official doctrines—and a stated commitment to fight and die for those ideals. Citizenship Day inaugurates Constitution Week in order to connect the signing of the constitution to "Americans who strive to uphold the duties and responsibilities of citizenship."[9] This move lends historical legitimacy to citizenship procedures that tether war and loyalty, exclusion and inclusion.

While naturalized citizens perform allegiance publicly, birth-right citizens (whether by *jus soli* or *jus sanguinis*) are presumed to possess a natural allegiance that precludes multiple ties to ideologies, projects, or potentates outside national borders. This book looks at writers who challenge the doctrine of natural allegiance when it means unthinking citizenship amid gross practices of exclusion. If naturalization procedures demonstrate how the figure of the immigrant undergoes rigorous scrutiny and thus defines the bounds of American citizenship,[10] the specter of the immigrant also serves as an exculpatory device for preexisting inequities because it obscures internal divisions on display in the protest essay tradition. Writers and political advocates who question the inclusive rhetoric of the nation from within its borders are often subject to accusations of treason, factionalism, or disloyalty in some form, a situation the citizenship oath explicitly seeks to preempt. Though scholars of diaspora and cosmopolitanism dislodge the total decisiveness of the nation-state in the arena of citizenship, official American articulations of citizenship place the nation at the center of stories of national belonging.

In addition to the example of the allegiance–renunciation pairing in the citizenship oath, we can turn to other examples in which national belonging and dissent are in opposition: Emma Goldman's deportation to Russia in

1919 that some women's liberationists would signal as the end of the First Wave of a revolutionary feminism, or the odd favor with which the exit plans of Garveyites and their predecessors have been received. Or how Thoreau's blueprint in his foundational essay "Civil Disobedience" pairs protest and political *withdrawal*, a move that bolsters the notion that dissent necessitates a *retraction* from the nation, and perhaps collectivity itself. In my study, however, there is another option: protest writers offer collectivity in the face of division. This begins to explain the power of another essay in *Patriotism and the American Land* in which Richard Nelson cites Thoreau and Chief Joseph to propose a new patriotism with the American land at the center. To do this, Nelson "express[es] my growing sense of allegiance to this living nation"[11] and then delivers a sort of alternative oath list of the components of the American land to which he swears allegiance and accepts the duty to protect.

WE THE PEOPLE AND PARTIAL CITIZENS

The U.S. citizenship oath gets at a dominant story of national belonging that informs the American protest essay tradition. Many remark that the paradox of inclusion via exclusion means that any articulation of a "we" requires a simultaneous "not-we." Like the citizenship oath, founding documents have the unusual status of being simultaneously hyperpolitical and therefore nonpartisan.[12] The Oath of Allegiance demonstrates and insists that the constitution of a bounded polity in America emphasizes external difference in order to create the semblance of an internally homogeneous "we." Thus arises the potency of national documents and stories that announce equality amid a decidedly unequal social order. These narratives provide the ring of broad inclusion for what Rogers M. Smith calls "civic myths": ideals of full equality that politicians and other leaders cite enthusiastically without necessarily worrying about their veracity for the everyday lives of the citizenry.[13] In this way, founding documents carry a unique ability to bring together factions within the nation under the umbra of a collective "we." W. C. Harris demonstrates how ideals of inclusion, especially in the constitutional idea of *e pluribus unum*—out of many, one—inform nineteenth-century American literature grappling with the twin pulls of unity and diversity.[14] So, too, by addressing experiences of exclusion, protest essayists wish to make the inclusive story promised by civic myths true in actual practice.

If the citizenship debates reflect dominant narratives of national belonging, we can see how protest essayists work within and against this narrative, especially when they position themselves as what I call *partial citizens*. Many protest essayists turn to national utterances of equality to simultaneously claim and critique the idea of a national "we." The essayist threatens the fragile story of a finished "we" based on uniform allegiance. I choose the modifier *partial* to describe the speaker's relation to citizenship because, more so than two-tiered notions of "second-class citizenship," *partial citizenship* is able to account for varying degrees and different forms of citizenship in claims for full equality. Legal scholar Linda Bosniak explains that citizenship comprises contingent, overlapping, and sometimes competing dimensions, including legal concepts of formal status and political membership, republican community participation, liberal rights and obligations, and even identitarian concepts of cultural or world citizenship.[15] Therefore, if citizenship at its most basic denotes membership in a bounded political community, different individuals and groups may have claims to some concepts of citizenship, but not others. In fact, anyone who claims some belonging to the American nation can be considered a partial citizen, though this should not diminish the importance of attending to the unacceptable status of official second-class citizenship.[16] It is important to think about partial citizenship because American protest essayists are able to identify these multiple and sometimes competing concepts of citizenship in order to move between different groups' claims to national belonging.

The partial citizen speaking—from experience, on behalf of others—and addressing the real divisions within a national audience is able to simultaneously claim and critique the inclusive pronouncements of the American Republic in order to make them real. Protest writers use their partial citizenship to gain a toehold on the viable, but unfinished, project of full democracy for all. By claiming the essential Americanness of their projects, protest writers position their visions as the fulfillment of previous national promises. In her study of foreigners' critiques of America, Honig shows how "[Foreigners] make room for themselves by staging nonexistent rights, and by way of such stagings, sometimes, new rights, powers, and visions come into being."[17] In this study, I discuss similar "stagings" by those already *inside* presumed national borders who have been denied full access to, or enjoyment of, civic, economic, and/or social rights. Protest essayists stage stories of equality by claiming preexisting rights by, for, and on behalf of voices that were never meant to speak such civic myths as truths. Whereas some concepts of citizenship aspire toward the universal (e.g., natural rights or human rights) and others insist more on the particular (e.g., group rights or cultural practices), the partial citizen moves among these competing dimensions in a literary tradition able to imagine excluded groups or individuals as full citizens. That is, an essayist like Harlem-born Baldwin can claim the full citizenship of African Americans in territorial and sociological definitions of national belonging in order to protest their second-class citizenship in the legal and political arenas.

Protest writers occupy the outposts of real publics that can deliver the elusive social equality of the modern democratic state. Here, those whose very citizenship is in question are the ones to sift through the promises of the nation-state and hold them against the evidence of experience—their own and those for whom they speak. Participation in the state is more than adherence to a preexisting set of political practices and ideas. In the epigraph, Toni Morrison would just as soon have us enter a polling station to pray as to vote; so, too, protest writers demand hope amid despairing situations of inequality. Their projects may unveil inconsistency between state promises and the experiences of subsets of its citizenry, but these writers do not reside in a balkanized vision of internal group equality more easily achieved. Instead, they argue for an equitable state in which a comparison between promises and experience will not inevitably lead to charges of hypocrisy, broken contracts, and state deceit. Protest essayists turn to inclusive national promises not as mere cant, but as a viable model to pursue in actual practice.

OUTLINE OF THE BOOK

Chapter 1 sketches a protest essay tradition concerned with addressing divided publics, as well as with the speaking self central to the personal essay tradition. In this way I augment understandings of the essay rooted in the writings of Michel de Montaigne by suggesting that the American protest essay also has roots in American political oratory. I trace illustrative moments in a tradition that grounds twentieth-century protest essays in the writing and oratory from earlier American social movements like abolition and appeals for Native American justice. The chapter identifies six common stances adopted in protest essays as a way of addressing a divided public by speaking simultaneously to national promises and experiences of exclusion. Whether they invoke collectivity for unrepresented groups or advocate dissent from unjust national practices, protest writers take seriously the promises of American democracy where "we the people" is a viable, but unfinished, project. Though some writers like Baldwin, Walker, and DuBois are widely praised as master essayists, a fuller understanding of the protest essay tradition can better account for many more writers who use the essay for political advocacy.

The second chapter further explores American protest essayists' relation to the nation by examining specific strategies of engaging founding documents to protest exclusions in inclusive national narratives. Chapter 2 examines three revisions of the Declaration of Independence from various moments and wings of the American feminist movement: the fight for women's suffrage, Emma Goldman's feminist anarchy, and women's liberation in the 1970s. Drawing on Adrienne Rich's concept of re-vision and Henry Louis Gates Jr.'s theory of signifying, I demonstrate how the speakers of these new Declarations draw on the authoritative power of the inclusive national "we" and how they recognize the possibilities inherent in the Declaration's flexible, universalist national collective. By assuming the platform of an authoritative national voice, these speakers address inequalities in their present society while imagining an equitable future that carries the imprimatur of the state via a document of freedom and equality held dear across factions and ideologies.

If the American protest essay is available to writers who engage in political advocacy, what is its relationship to the much more famous protest novel tradition? Writings in the protest mode, even those by established novelists, are often considered nonliterary on the grounds that they are too polemical, ephemeral, or earnestly partisan. Chapter 3 examines the case of Helen Hunt Jackson, whose protest novel *Ramona* (1884) was a wild commercial success and spawned a mythology of New California that persists to the present day. But the novel has its origins in *A Century of Dishonor* (1881), a dense protest essay published three years prior, in which Jackson seeks justice in a direct appeal to U.S. Congress on behalf of American Indians. Jackson's overlooked essay version of *Ramona* provides an instructive case study of how protest essays may better perform the political work often sought—but not always found—in the protest novel tradition. Whereas literary studies often relegate protest essays to secondary status as nonliterary, merely political, journalistic, or in some way position them as satellites, my project places such work at the center of a literary tradition deeply concerned with the fulfillment of the inclusive promises of the nation.

If we are to fully appreciate the protest essay tradition, it is important to identify its key practitioners. Baldwin is the most prolific and successful example of a literary writer who adopted the role of political advocate and turned to the essay for that pursuit. Baldwin's celebrated essays constitute the core of his legacy more so than his considerable work in fiction, drama, and other genres. Yet critics often pit political advocacy against literary merit, even in Baldwin's case. Chapter 4 examines Baldwin's essays to propose that his political advocacy in essay form represents the full flowering of his artistic talents. Baldwin carefully crafts a personal, experiential speaking self who offers representative anecdotes that bring clarity to national debates about race, nationality, and injustice within an integration vision. Because Baldwin so masterfully adopts the stance of representative speaker, his shifting reputation tells us a lot about the cultural status afforded protest essayists. This is why I attend to debates over Baldwin's cultural and literary status in the context of his meteoric rise to fame upon publication of *The Fire Next Time*, his attendant saturation in national media as racial spokesman, and ensuing attacks on him by various factions across the political spectrum. Baldwin's changing cultural status may reflect shifting political currents, more so than a change in literary merit.

Protest essays are vulnerable to charges that their attention to particular groups and experiences threatens their collective or national aspirations. Even more so than debates about Baldwin as racial spokesman, the identitarian concerns of later twentieth-century social movements amplify suspicions about the relationship between the speaker and the spoken for. Chapter 5 examines the cross-essay conversations among Audre Lorde, Adrienne Rich, and Alice Walker as one response within the protest essay tradition to suspicions about collectivity, especially regarding charges of racial exclusion in the universalist project of sisterhood in Second Wave feminism. These essayists speak from personal experience but strive for collectivity across identitarian lines, both in the present and through their efforts to build an inclusive literary heritage. Their cross-essay conversation provides one model for how to solve *the problem of the one and the many* central to the American democratic project. The chapter places their model of generating a collective "we" across essays in dialogue with the long-standing choice between individual dissent or collective protest. They join other routes to the collective "we" in essays and sister genres, including especially the collectively authored manifesto, such as the Combahee River Collective's *A Black Feminist Statement* (1977).

Before the conclusion asks why the essay is so well-suited to address concerns about collectivity and exclusion, the final chapter tests this book's basic assumption: the United States houses a distinct tradition of the protest essay. Around the close of the twentieth century, many announced—with glee, consternation, or fear—the sunset of the nation-state in a transnational era. Debates about whether the United States is a global empire or about the viability of cosmopolitan citizenship require us to return to the nation-state as a key reference point in the American protest essay tradition. Many protest essayists harbor transnational concerns, and many protest essays beyond U.S. borders engage American ideals. The protest essays of June Jordan, a West Indian immigrant active in the Black Arts movement and a persistent advocate for the oppressed around the globe, addresses a transnational audience within the framework of the U.S. nation-state. Since becoming the first black woman to publish a book of her own essays with *Civil Wars* (1981), Jordan belongs in the American protest essay tradition sketched in this book, but she emphasizes how that tradition can speak to transnational concerns, too. Jordan draws on founding national documents and promises of equality and she claims those promises on behalf of disenfranchised peoples both within and beyond current U.S. borders.

THE PROTEST ESSAY IN AMERICAN LITERARY STUDIES

How does this sketch of a protest-oriented tradition of the essay fit within American literary studies? A better understanding of the protest essay can help us sort through at least three concerns about American political writing in literary genres: the place of writers from historically disenfranchised groups in preexisting literary traditions, the possibilities and limits of political advocacy in literature, and what constitutes a national literary tradition. This project builds on foundational work on how specific genres such as the American jeremiad, sermon, or protest novel inform the national literary imagination, and the newest work in American protest literature.[18] Scholars are reconsidering the purchase and limits of using the nation as the key frame of reference for literary traditions. Americanist scholars now propose a transnational approach[19] in response to groundbreaking work that questions the primacy of the nation-state.[20] My project demonstrates how a certain set of American protest writers consciously draw on national traditions and founding documents, and I place minoritarian figures like Baldwin at the center of this essay tradition. I work primarily within Americanist, feminist, multiethnic, and African American literary criticism, though I also I draw heavily from cultural studies. This project may also interest concerned citizens who are inspired by the moving essays of these artist-advocates.

This book also augments how we understand the essay form, especially since the essay is largely under-examined in literary criticism. Few currently available works offer book-length treatments of the form,[21] probably because, as Atkins suggests, the essay "resists our vaunted attempt to describe or define the form";[22] no book-length studies examine a specifically U.S. strand of the essay. Atkins and Alexander Butrym represent the best work on the essay as a form, Martin Stabb and Cristina Kirklighter deliver key work on the Latin American essay, and other important studies look at identitarian traditions of the essay, such as Ruth-Ellen Boetcher Joeres and Elizabeth Mittman's work on the feminist essay or Gerald Early and Juanita Rogers Comfort's work on the African American essay. Scholars tend to focus on particular practitioners of the essay, most especially Montaigne for the personal essay,[23] Joseph Addison and Richard Steele for the periodical essay,[24] or Thoreau, Thomas Paine, and Ralph Waldo Emerson for the American philosophical essay.[25] Other nonfiction prose forms have received book-length treatments, such as the manifesto,[26] the Afro-American jeremiad and protest pamphlets,[27] and the African American sermon.[28] Further, the abundance of popular anthologies (especially Philip Lopate's *The Art of the Personal Essay*) evidences an interest so far largely untapped by literary criticism.

Studying the protest essay fits well within the turn in American literary criticism toward the publics addressed by politically oriented literature. Scholars are reassessing the relationship between the literary, the national, and forms of belonging, especially in terms of citizenship and the public sphere.[29] These studies employ a similar approach: study the relation between divided publics, authors, and the causes on behalf of which they speak. Linda Grasso's study on anger in black and white women's literature is representative in that it works within a relatively short period (1820–1860) and attends to a period before the twentieth century. Grasso's project is also representative of an important trend in Americanist criticism that crosses identitarian lines to view American literary traditions from the vantage of social movements.

Activists and historians are also following suit.[30] And scholars working within identitarian traditions are rethinking dominant understandings of literary traditions across short periods.[31] Finally, Americanist literary and social critics are beginning to analyze the aesthetics, as well as the cultures, associated with protest moments in American history.[32] For instance, T. V. Reed provides one of the first comparative studies of the cultures of twentieth-century social movements that look at "the important but vague and still unfulfilled promises of 'freedom' and 'democracy' announced in the revolution's best known manifesto [Declaration of Independence], and given them more reality, more substance, and wider applicability to the majority of people—women, people of color, the poor—who were initially excluded from those promises."[33] In line with Reed's focus, this book traces a particular essay tradition available to successive American social movements, a tradition on which literary figures who become political advocates are able to draw.

Protest is a widespread term in literary studies. It crosses genres, periods, vocabularies, political affiliations, and critical schools. Yet beyond the protest novel, *protest* defines a formal tradition in its own right. Much the same can be said of the prevalent, but under-theorized, American essay tradition. My project demonstrates how the term *protest* can best account for the scope and history of a distinct strand of the American essay. Protest essays and related forms are often charged with the paradox of being too specific to historical incidents and experiences and too wedded to an impossible utopia. Far from speaking only to a particular moment, however, protest essays enter a venerable tradition of simultaneously claiming and critiquing the promises of a democratic republic. Further, within the protest essay there is another possibility beyond collectivity: from Thoreau to Norman Mailer, individual dissent as divestment or social retraction. The currency of the protest essay is evidenced by its availability to writers with seemingly incongruent political agendas.

Many argue that modernity itself presents a paradoxical subject wherein inclusion is signified so that exclusion may be perpetrated; where "we the people" provides an intoxicating promise of temporary inequality with no real contractual obligation for fulfillment. Protest essayists, however, solicit urgency in order to demand realization of past promises of future equality in the present. Nevertheless, inequality continues to exist despite—or some argue because of[34]—official doctrines of equality in stories of national belonging. There is ample evidence to support such a picture of the inherent failure or duplicity of modern democracy. So, it can be argued that protest essayists are naïve to buy the Republic's trick of empty rhetoric. But these writers reject pessimism and take the promises of the nation-state at face value. They choose a profound optimism. When protest essayists articulate a "we," they continue the legacy of the incomplete projects of American social movements like abolition, Civil Rights, women's liberation, the student movement, and perhaps of American democracy itself.

Chapter One

Toward an American Protest Essay Tradition

> But, to speak practically and as a citizen, unlike those who call themselves no-government men, I ask for, not at once no government, but *at once* a better government . . . I quietly declare war with the State, after my fashion, though I will still make what use and get what advantage of her I can.
>
> —Henry David Thoreau, "Resistance to Civil Government," 1849

> By comparison, black writers seem always involved in a moral and/or physical struggle, the result of which is expected to be some kind of larger freedom. Perhaps this is because our literary tradition is based on the slave narrative, where escape for the body and freedom for the soul went together, or perhaps this is because black people have never felt themselves guilty of global, cosmic sins.
>
> This comparison does not hold up in every case, of course, and perhaps does not really hold up at all. I am not a gatherer of statistics, only a curious reader, and this has been my impression from reading many books by black and white writers.
>
> —Alice Walker, "Saving the Life That Is Your Own," 1975

American protest essayists participate in a tradition anchored both in the personal essay originating in Europe and in American political oratory rooted in social movements. As Henry David Thoreau and Alice Walker attest, the role of the essayist in America—especially when speaking on behalf of those excluded from the nation's loftiest promises of equality—is commensurate with the role of a curious, thinking citizen. Whether the response to injustice is to retract from unjust national practices for Thoreau, or to gather and celebrate the voices of the oppressed for Walker, writers invested in addressing national division often turn to the essay. In doing so, they create a distinct strand of the form: the American protest essay.

When W. E. B. DuBois ushered in the twentieth century by identifying the "problem of the color line," his announcement pointed to crises of racially policed boundaries in literature as well as to the sociological and historical significance of color in America. Writers must then ask: How to address division without reinscribing it? For DuBois, querying the burden of race in America required a diverse cache of forms: sociological survey, elegy, historical sketch, fable, political treatise, and ethnographic study, to name some of the most prominent forms in *The Souls of Black Folk* (1903). Hazel Carby notes the importance of *Souls* to African American culture, and as a model for racial spokespersons, or Race Men. Carby describes the book as "a series of tightly bound ideological contradictions"[1] in which DuBois speaks to a national community through the specificity of racial experience. In *Souls*, Carby argues, "it is the descendants of African peoples who are proclaimed the legitimate inheritors of the principles of the Declaration of Independence, and DuBois inscribes the symbolic power of nationalism directly onto Black bodies."[2] To effectively protest and examine the persistent problem of race in the aftermath of Reconstruction, DuBois requires a form in which his speaking voice can address the fomenting racial divisions defining America. In *Souls*, DuBois assumes a speaking position that inhabits, and crosses between, both sides of the racial veil. The essay, for DuBois and many others, provides a form—Gerald Early suggests the African American essay can even be a "pulpit"[3]—in which divisions among a citizenry are made visible, while still remaining a problem.

It is important to consider DuBois's place in the essay tradition because, even more so than the sorrow songs and lyrics adorning each chapter, the essay is the grand form holding his important book together. But this poses a problem because the essay itself is a curiously under-theorized genre despite its prevalence across periods, geographies, and ideologies. Like DuBois, most major writers have penned something akin to an essay. Yet the essay remains known as the most formless of forms. O. B. Hardison explains, "Of all literary forms the essay most successfully resists the effort to pin it down."[4] In turn, Graham Good attempts an encyclopedic overview of the essay, but wonders, "How can the essay's elusive multiplicity of forms and themes be contained within the systematic scope of an encyclopedia?"[5] Perhaps this is because the essay is, as Cheryl de Obaldia suggests, a "literary hybrid" able to incorporate classical elements of lyric, drama, and epic.[6] Though individual essays elude strict formal description, scholars persist because, as G. Douglass Atkins contends, we are not content to think of the essay as a "mere lump." In key early work on the essay, Theodor Adorno and George Lukacs praise it as the most undogmatic of forms. Most critics follow their lead and praise the essay's independence, or what de Obaldia calls an "essayistic spirit" of free inquiry. The essay tradition, for most scholars, begins with the work of Michel de Montaigne and includes important writers like Francis Bacon, Ralph Waldo Emerson, Thoreau, Virginia Woolf, T. S. Eliot, E. B. White, perhaps more contemporary essayists like James McPhee or Annie Dillard, and sometimes writers from minoritarian literatures like James Baldwin.[7]

DuBois's essays in *Souls* are paradigmatic of what we recognize as key traits of the genre following Montaigne: open-ended, digressive, tentative, experiential, and occasional. In topical essays whose titles directly echo Montaigne, like "Of the Meaning of Progress" and "Of the Passing of the First-Born," DuBois moves among different occasions, both national like the creation of the Freedman's Bureau and personal like the death of his son. He also moves among different locations, both integrated like the literary realm or some New England schools and segregated like the Black Belt or a Jim Crow car. He crosses cultural traditions such as British literature and African American sorrow songs. DuBois can also connect different experiences—both his own and others like Alexander Crummel's. DuBois's embodied movement evidences how essays value experience over abstract truth, especially as the essayist uses various anecdotes to deliver meditations on philosophical or political questions. DuBois also creates intertextual conversations by transporting the words of others into the essay such as in his extended dialogue with key black leaders and the Declaration of Independence in "Of Mr. Booker T. Washington and Others." In these personal meditations, DuBois invites readers on a trip with him through the segregated nation because, as Atkins explains, in the essay "you talk about something by talking about yourself."[8]

DuBois fits well in the company of esteemed personal essayists, but that tradition does not fully capture his project, especially his urgent political concerns about inequality for black people. For instance, the speaking self is not always the cornerstone of DuBois's essays, especially as he documents the unjust experiences of others, like in his fable of the two Johns who represent the exclusion of African Americans from the promises of the nation. In this way, DuBois's essays waver at a key orientation usually prized in the essay tradition: the desire to move beyond the immediate or the particular and toward the enduring or the universal. Atkins suggests that the essayist must unite "immanence and transcendence" to "deriv[e] meaning in, of, and through experience" in a meandering, even "sneaky" approach to universal truths.[9] But for DuBois, and as we shall see for most American protest essayists, particular experience is not solely the pathway to the universal; in fact, it is often in direct conflict with universalist utterances of equality. Even though DuBois famously avers, "I sit with Shakespeare and he winces not," he does not leave behind pressing political concerns as he enters the literary pantheon, nor does he prematurely announce the unification of a divided citizenry.

In his constant movement across—but not erasure of—the color line within individual essays and in epigraphs that bind African American spirituals to European cultural texts, DuBois dwells on lines of social division at a moment in U.S. history when Reconstruction failed to enfranchise black folks. Good argues that even though the essay resists definition, there is a unifying factor: "At heart, the essay is the voice of the individual."[10] But DuBois argues for the urgency of immediate change to bring value to black folks generally, not to himself. In this way, DuBois's urgent address to a starkly divided nation risks falling from the vaulted realms of the literary. Yet de Obaldia suggests that "the divide between the literary and the extraliterary operates within the province of the essay itself."[11] And Butrym praises the essay's "formlessness, which allows us to speak beyond ourselves—or beyond persons much like ourselves—scatters the essay so broadly that it sometimes seems marginally effective as literature."[12] While this may be generally true for traditional conceptions of the essay, DuBois also exemplifies the under-recognized American protest essay strand of the essay tradition.

This opening chapter traces some common stances of the American protest essay as it develops into an available tradition able to combine the open-ended formal conventions of the essay and the urgency of political oratory to address a divided national audience. Like DuBois's color line, literary debates in the first half of the twentieth century often sought to distinguish literature from mere race literature. Further, Jerry Ward explains, "In twentieth-century usage, 'protest,' a word inextricably associated with 'race,' might be taken as pure product of America. Protest was a code word for work of inferior artistic accomplishment."[13] Most famously, in "The Negro Artist and the Racial Mountain" (1925), Langston Hughes argues, "But this is the mountain standing in the way of any true Negro art in America—this urge within the race toward whiteness, the desire to pour racial individuality into the mold of American standardization, and to be as little Negro and as much American as possible."[14] Much the same can be said of problematic appraisals of women's literature, or between literary and political advocacy. The protest essay is particularly vulnerable to these distinctions, especially since, as Cheryl Wall contends in her study of Walker, "Indeed, I would make the case that Walker, despite her reputation as a novelist, short story writer, and poet, has done her best work in the essay, a genre that has at present little critical currency."[15] Wall's astute account of Walker's reputation can be said of most literary figures who also serve as political advocates, and who often choose the essay for that enterprise. In response, we need a better appreciation of the form and function of the American protest essay tradition.

DIVIDED CITIZENS AND
REPRESENTATIVE SPEAKERS:
A SKETCH OF THE AMERICAN PROTEST ESSAY

Protest essayists address a deeply divided American citizenry and seek to bring together that citizenry, or at least a portion of it. They provoke anxiety about social exclusions that jeopardize national unity and question promises of full participation for all. Therefore, the American protest essay concerns itself more with the publics it addresses than the speaking self. That is why it is important to recognize its roots in American oratory in addition to the personal essay tradition of Montaigne. Personal essays connect individual experiences and ideas to the world beyond, which leads to what Atkins and Phillip Lopate refer to as the possibility of the "stench of ego."[16] American protest essays, however, seek a "we": a collective space to speak among and across lines in a divided audience. This "we" is often more interested in the experience of others, especially as those experiences test the veracity of dominant narratives of national belonging. In this way, the American protest essay veers far into the terrain of political oratory, especially oratory allied with social movements.

The dual heritage of the American protest essay—the European-born personal essay and American political oratory—necessitates a dual approach: formalist attention to some of its dominant conventions and historical attention to an essay's specific audience and context. In this section, I identify six common rhetorical "stances" available to protest essayists in the U.S. context. Because the protest essay's elements of oratory are less studied than the formal elements of the personal essay, this sketch will emphasize the former over the latter. This emphasis also informs my selection of representative texts: I choose writers and orators who may not yet be fully celebrated as practitioners of, or precursors to, the essay. At the outset, let me caution that this sketch will not provide an exhaustive account of the protest essay, nor will it exhaust a literary discussion of each representative text. Instead, I illustrate common stances that allow essayists to position themselves between the representative experiences they recount and the divided citizenry they address. Further chapters explore some examples of how key practitioners adopt and adapt these stances as appropriate to their historical situations.

STANCE I: COLLECTIVITY AND THE PARTICULAR READER

> Remember that you are THREE MILLIONS.
> —Henry Highland Garnet, "An Address
> to the Slaves of the United States of America"
> (Rejected by the National Convention, 1843), 1848

Protest essayists stand among deeply factionalized audiences, while pointing them toward inclusive national promises. American protest essayists, then, inhabit a stance between particular readers and collective ambitions. In doing so, they endeavor to give voice to a group, more so than an individual, amid the earnest goal of achieving the loftiest promises of the nation. That is why some scholars nod to the democratic aspects of the essay, such as Cristina Kirklighter's work with the essays of Thoreau and Emerson as progenitors of a politically minded Latin American essay tradition.[17] In the U.S. context, we must place the creation of, and identification with, particular audiences at the center of our understanding of the protest essay. At first glance, the most obvious starting point for a project about American protest essays might seem to be Thoreau's "Civil Disobedience" (1849) as a precursor to Martin Luther King Jr.'s "A Letter from Birmingham City Jail" (1963), or a political pamphlet like Thomas Paine's *Common Sense* (1777) as a precursor to essays by Gore Vidal that also question conventional political thought. But this approach might draw attention away from the audience in the protest essay's desire for substantive national belonging amid practices of exclusion. So, black feminist writer June Jordan's response at the end of the twentieth century to Thoreau's foundational essay better shows how protest essayists stand between collectivity and the particular reader, and the protest essayist's debt to political oratory.

Thoreau's essay, originally titled "Resistance to Civil Government," inhabits a posture of individual dissent from his present government as a path to a better government in the future. In part, this essay fits well within a personal essay tradition since, as in E. B. White's essays, Thoreau's space of solitude—be it Walden or Concord jail—allows him to mull over personal experience as a means of questioning accepted beliefs and accessing experience-tested larger truths. But solitude and collectivity come into direct tension as Thoreau veers into the terrain of the protest essay. In response to state-sponsored activities that he finds disagreeable (the Mexican War, the fugitive slave law, public taxes supporting clergymen), Thoreau indicts citizens' unthinking adherence to the state. For Thoreau, this obeisance threatens "the progress toward a true respect for the individual" (Thoreau 245). He publicly urges a general reader to question the state from a position of privilege: the individual should choose not to support unacceptable state-sponsored activities by claiming a tradition greater than the immediate state (of natural rights, of democracy, of revolutionary independence), which leads to total refusal of civic participation via taxation. In short, Thoreau embraces the individual and advocates divestment or retraction from official collectivity. When he left Walden to walk through the town of Concord, he ended up in the town jail, which affords him a unique vantage—at once removed from and at the center of town—through which to see American society. Thoreau poses individuals in opposition not only to the government but also the collective public, both of which are ultimately coercive.

Nearly a century and a half later, Jordan, whose work I explore more fully in chapter 6, explicitly rejects Thoreau's posture of retraction; she instead advocates entering into collectivity. In her essay, "Waking Up in the Middle of Some American Dreams" (1992), she questions the safety, and the privilege, of Thoreau's individualist stance. Thoreau's dominant vision of political (non)participation holds up the individual as a "higher and independent power" over the state. In her examination of the Reagan–Bush era through the perspective of African American experience, Jordan explicitly inhabits Thoreau's space of solitude and finds a "willful loneliness" when she borrows a cabin on her "pseudo-Walden Pond."[18] Throughout the essay, she rejects American myths of individuality; she also builds on mid-twentieth-century social movements to show that coalitions form the basis of true democracy.

The danger of Thoreau's stance of isolation and divestment becomes clear when Jordan inserts her particular black woman's body into the philosophical space of the traditional essay. Jordan recounts how, while writing alone in her rented drawing room, she is raped. As she considers the meaning of this violent personal event in the public form of an essay, Jordan explains, "Someone had insinuated himself into that awkward, tiny shelter of my thoughts and dreams. He had dealt with me as egotistically as, in another way, I had positioned dealing with anyone besides myself. He had overpowered the supposed protection of my privacy, he had violated the boundaries of my single self" (14). For Jordan, if we focus solely on the individual speaking self in the personal essay and value divestment from society, we rip the speaker from her world, not unlike the experience of sexual violence. Jordan's feminist strategy of politicizing rape calls attention to the privileged space of an essayistic speaker who can retract from the public sphere. Only those who already hold power to give up that participation are allowed the luxury of Thoreau's social divestment strategy.

As she questions the isolationist pull of a Thoreauvian protest essay, Jordan offers an alternative stance: collectivity. To do this, Jordan builds on the unrealized dream of American democracy by embracing the people at the center of the democratic project. Jordan explains, "*Demos*, as in democratic, as in a democratic state, means people, not person" (19). Jordan wakes up from the American dream of individualism and strives for the "civilized metropolis that will validate the democratic state" (19). Collectivity, not divestment, is the rightful heir of American democracy. Jordan's essay narrates her reconnection with other state subjects. The speaker at the heart of her essay becomes a collective "we." It is only upon her return from her space of isolation that her American "dream" will materialize. Further, "we" appears in the essay, but it can only be made real when accepted by a *demos*, a readership.

Nevertheless, divestment from an unjust state remains a powerful narrative in the American protest imaginary. Thoreau writes, "Under a government which imprisons unjustly, the true place for a just man is also prison"

(235). However, even this space of extreme divestment is not as individualist as it might first appear. Thoreau presents prison as a cross-cultural site of interaction not unlike Jordan's *demos*: "It is [in prison] that the fugitive slave, and the Mexican prisoner on parole, and the Indian come to plead the wrongs of his race, should find them; on that separate, but more free and honorable ground, where the State places those who are not *with* her but *against* her—the only house in a slave-state in which a free man can abide with honor" (235). Thoreau risks fetishizing prison and blackness like Norman Mailer would do a century later in "The White Negro" (1957). Yet it is important to underscore that the essay form allows Thoreau to connect his individual speaker to other partial and non-citizens under the state's thumb. In allegiance with these figures, Thoreau swears unallegiance to the state: "When the subject [not citizen] has refused allegiance, and the officer has resigned from office, then the revolution is accomplished" (235). Thoreau removes himself from a collective stance because he "'do[es] not wish to be regarded as a member of any incorporated society which I have not joined (236).'" Thoreau offers thinking allegiance as an alternative, but he still emphasizes non-participation. For instance, with gentle sarcasm, he states, "If I had known how to name them, I should then have signed off in detail from all the societies which I never signed on to; but I did not know where to find a complete list" (237–38).

With Jordan's revision of Thoreau in mind, we can turn briefly to King's influential Civil Rights essay, "Letter from Birmingham City Jail," to see that it builds on Thoreau, but also that it belongs in the collective-minded tradition of Jordan. Whereas Thoreau addresses a general citizenry, King specifically addresses eight progressive white clergymen anxious about the strategy of civil disobedience. From his own Thoreauvian jail cell, King speaks on behalf of a disenfranchised black citizenry because "we were the victims of a broken promise,"[19] and he speaks to the nation through the conceit of the clergy audience who are "men of genuine good will" and whose "criticisms are sincerely set forth" (King 289). By presenting his divided audience this way, King delivers an open letter to a deeply, violently divided nation within a form that prizes reasoned, experiential, philosophical treatises on how the nation can live up to its best promises. King connects celebrated figures like Thomas Jefferson and Jesus to the experiences of the dispossessed who are locked in an "'I-it' relationship" (293) with white citizens. King crosses lines of segregation to invoke a national "dialogue" among co-citizens (292). He argues, "Now is the time to make real the promise of democracy, to transform our pending national elegy into a creative psalm of brotherhood" (296). Though King writes from an isolated jail cell, he imagines—and in the process of doing so, may help create—collectivity outside the cell.

If King and Jordan depart from Thoreau's model of individual dissent, and also from the personal essay's focus on the individual speaker in favor of a collective "we," to what roots can we best locate their concern with the particular reader and national collectivity? In addition to the essay tradition, the American protest essay is steeped in the rich American oratory tradition from the Puritan sermon to the speeches of King and Malcolm X.[20] Therefore, in addition to Montaigne, the American protest essay tradition can trace some of its roots to the Christian Indian preacher Samson Occom. In 1772, Occom delivered an execution sermon upon the public hanging of a fellow Indian (Moses Paul) for killing a white man. He addresses consecutively three distinct factions—whites, Indians, and Moses Paul—though each faction is present to overhear Occom address the other segments. Michael Warner and Myra Jehlen describe the yoking of three audiences in one address as "something of a rhetorical feat."[21] With the sermon's publication, Occom became the first American Indian in English print culture. The scene of address and the circumstances of publication are especially stark illustrations of the stance adopted by protest essayists to address factions simultaneously as co-citizens, or at least co-audience members. In a protest tradition where divisions within a national public are a given, the presence of—and ability to address—a heterogeneous audience is fundamental.

In its printed form, Occom's sermon provides a key early example of the protest esssayist's stance between particular readers and collective aspirations. Occom begins in a generalized "we" related to "mankind" who are joined by a common experience (or threat) of death. At the rise of the U.S. nation-state and its attendant doctrine of individual/natural rights, Occom carves out a position beyond the particulars of race, by which he means nations. Drawing on Christian traditions that supersede social divisions, Occom speaks in a "we" that can speak to and for "Negroes, Indians, English, or of what nation soever."[22] There is also a rhythm in the sermon: Occom shifts between a general "we" and a particular "we" or "you" as he moves between segments of his audience, and as he yokes Indians and whites together then splits them apart. Occom first calls his audience an "auditory in general" (653) then differently addresses "sirs" (i.e., white men, 656) and "my kindred" or "my brethren" (i.e., American Indians, 657).

Upon conclusion of his tripartite address, Occom appends a moral ostensibly directed to his "poor kindred" (Indians) but also applied without difficulty to the white audience. He exhorts, "O let us reform our lives, and live as becomes dying creatures, in time to come. Let us be persuaded that we are accountable creatures of God, and we must be called to an account in a few days. You that have been careless all your days, now awake to righteousness, and be concerned for your poor never-dying souls" (658–59). On the surface, Occom seemingly condemns nonwhites and non-Christians, but his strategy of speaking also to the unaddressed allows him to protest actions by whites that do not live up to the ideals of Christianity and nationalism. Rather than simply excoriating non-Christians as heathens, Occom also protests the killing or displacement of Indians in the birth of the nation. The public hanging offers Occom a platform to address a divided American public, and his sermon also allows him to bring together fellow Indians in public witness. As the whites in the audience overhear Occom's diatribe against an increasingly ambiguous need for reform, Occom dexterously groups under "us" and "we" the indirectly addressed white audience, whose "never-dying souls" are in danger if ever they become accountable to the standards of justice—whether Christian or national—they created. In turn, Occom's *demos*, like Jordan's, stands as the true inheritor of justice.

By anchoring Jordan's and King's essays in the example of Occom as well as Thoreau, we account for the dual heritage of the modern American protest essay, especially its emphasis on divided audiences and collective desires. When essay scholarship places Montaigne almost exclusively at the head of the tradition, we privilege American writers who fit well within the personal essay tradition, from Thoreau and Emerson to White and Ralph Ellison, but we deemphasize protest essayists who are also indebted to American political oratory. In fact, historical research on Montaigne is beginning to uncover elements of oratory and urgent desires for social change, which might make Montaigne look a bit more like Occom. For instance, George Hoffman explores oral aspects from Montaigne's dictating some essays to his secretary,[23] and in her study of Latin American essays Kirklighter explores some of the historical contexts of Montaigne's essays to demonstrate his engagement with the immediate political world.[24] Nevertheless, the nearly universal starting point in Montaigne assumes a cultural history (sixteenth-century Europe) that might miss the full context of American protest essays. For example, Michael Hall provides an important historical study of the essay as he traces a tradition based on a "common attitude" of Montaigne, Francis Bacon, John Donne, and Sir Thomas Brown: "a spirit of exploration," which he locates in the Renaissance idea of discovery.[25] He explores how European gentlemen employ the essay in "the examination of received opinions, to search for inward truths as well as outward."[26] From their drawing rooms, these writers reflect upon world-shattering discoveries of empiricist scientists and New World explorers, and they respond to the *idea* of discovery with a new genre. The essay allows these writers "to put their world back together, to reestablish relation and coherence" in the face of newness itself.[27] The form, then, embodies a colonial or imperial relationship between the essayistic speaker and the new subject matter to be explored and made familiar.

In the American context, however, the essay emerged after the European era of discovery and the initial conquering of the Americas. The American protest essay developed during the rise of the modern nation-state, and it responds by underscoring and questioning divisions within newly formed publics. Practitioners like Thoreau and Emerson adapted Montaigne's model for their transcendental meditations on American identity and democracy.[28] In his influential study of mass printing and eighteenth-century America, Michael Warner tracks the rise of a print-mediated public sphere.[29] For Warner, print culture triggers the creation of a *public* where readers imagine themselves existing among different people reading the *same* text. His later work extends this insight to *a* public, publics, and *counter*-publics.[30] With the rise of print-mediated publics, new kinds of individuals are invented: individuals who understand themselves as represented by print culture in the modern state. But for Warner, the rise of the public sphere creates a complex fraud of civic subjectivity based on "the pretense that representational democracy derives its legitimacy from the people and their law, when in fact it performs what it claims to describe."[31] The protest essay uses American print culture and oratory stances to perform the democratic public for which they call. Further, they simultaneously employ and question the tenets of representational democracy and universal citizenship because they insist that we acknowledge the presence of excluded bodies and audiences within the public sphere.

American protest essays invoke urgency as they incorporate the immediate context of their divided audience in print form. To move among this audience, protest essayists must be able to speak as full, partial, and noncitizens. Print culture allows this because, as Warner explains, "Print discourse made it possible to imagine a people that could act as a people and in distinction from the state."[32] For Warner, the text creates a public distinct from the state, and his later work suggests that *a* counter-public distinguishes itself from *the* public. Further, many of the texts I label *protest essays* are speeches later written down and published. The publics created by printed oral texts like Occom's incorporate a direct correlation to a present audience. These American protest essays are excellent examples of Warner's republican print culture: "He or she now also incorporates *into the meaning of the printed object* an awareness of the potentially limitless others who may also be reading. For that reason, it becomes possible to imagine oneself, in the act of reading, becoming part of an arena of the national people that cannot be realized except through such mediating imaginings."[33] Occom does not address an amorphous national people; his differentiated audience serves as a power map for his readers, who can no longer innocently imagine themselves part of a homogeneous national people. In order to imagine a nation at all, they must place themselves within Occom's trisected audience. Depending on where readers map themselves, they imagine lines of citizenship as inclusive or exclusive of themselves, the speaker, the accused, and the addressed.

A brief look at another protest speech distributed in print form—this one by the free black abolitionist Henry Highland Garnet—provides a final example of how political oratory shapes the protest essay's stance between collectivity and particular readers. In his 1848 address to the slaves of the United States (an address rejected by the abolitionist movement on the grounds that it was too "war-like"), Garnet uncovers the tension between the idea of a national people and those particular groups excluded from the benefits, or even status, of citizenship. Garnet does this by employing state-sponsored discourses of natural rights alongside the basis of slaves' exclusion from citizenship: their race (if not individual members of his audience) was born in Africa. Garnet exhorts, "Think of the undying glory that hangs around the ancient name of Africa:—and forget not that you are native-born American citizens, and as such, you are justly entitled to all the rights that are granted to the freest."[34] In his address ostensibly directed at slaves, Garnet uncovers disparities in freedom and presents them as contradictory to the idea of common humanity on which abolitionists based their political stance. European origins are shed in the unification of a national people; African origins, however, persist to exclude slaves from citizenship. For Garnet, national pronouncements of equality lead to an inequitable citizenry, which he places in the shadow of African glory. Whereas Benedict Anderson shows how literature creates nations as imagined communities,[35] Garnet works within factional lines to address *particular* communities acutely aware of the presence of real division amid national pronouncements of unity, homogeneity, or equality.

Garnet generates a print-mediated collective seeking justice, and he does so along factional lines. Throughout the speech, Garnet addresses a "you" that purposefully lacks a definitive referent. Garnet follows Occom's model by partially yoking slaves and citizens, northerners and southerners, freemen and abolitionists, blacks and whites under the umbrella of a national people. Garnet underscores lines of division within a national community in order to provoke abolitionist horror at hypocrisy: the practice of slavery exists within an official democracy! As a partial citizen able to move among his divided audience, he gradually shifts the "you" to denote slaves in particular. By increasingly addressing slaves exclusively, Garnet displaces those whose citizenship is not in question (white abolitionists) and shuttles power across lines of exclusion to those of African origin. Garnet ends with the refrain, "Remember that you are THREE MILLIONS." Garnet creates and identifies with a faction inscribed within the national body. His incendiary call is not simply a reminder of injustice and hypocrisy. In the printed speech, Garnet remembers collectivity; he reforms the diaspora slavery created. Whereas Occom's printed sermon recreates the original audience, Garnet's address creates a public that supersedes the largely northern abolitionist audience of his initial speech. Garnet's call aligns freemen with slaves and it serves as a threat overheard by those *not* included in the three millions he seeks to convene.

Stance II: Representation and the Spoken For

> Only the BLACK WOMAN can say "when and where I enter, in the quiet, undisputed dignity of my womanhood, without violence and without suing or special patronage, then and there the whole *Negro race enters with me*."
>
> —Anna Julia Cooper, A Voice from the South, 1892

In the epigraph, Anna Julia Cooper poses as *a* voice of a black woman, *a* voice from the South. This stance as a simultaneously personal and representative speaker is another means of accessing collectivity by addressing particular readers. Writing in 1892, Cooper is acutely aware of the tremendous disparity between the highly popular subject of race, slavery, and Reconstruction on the one hand, and the virtual absence of black women participating in that national conversation. Cooper uses her voice as a crowbar to pry open a space for the silenced voices spoken *about* but rarely spoken *for*. Mary Helen Washington reprimands this representative stance: "Clearly, [Cooper] sees herself as the *voice* for these women, but nothing in her essay suggests that they existed in her imagination as audience or peer."[36] Washington is responding to feminist debates about the category "woman," and she reasonably worries that Cooper fails to represent authentically the experiences of *all* black women of the South. Washington worries that Cooper fails to invoke a real community of black women that did not exist in her immediate literary and teaching circles, or to seek out the actual voices for whom she stood. But it is important to distinguish the speaker of Cooper's essay from an autobiographical speaker. Joel Haefner argues that the (personal) essay genre presents a speaker "not as personal expression but as social discourse."[37] This is especially true for Cooper since she inserts a speaking voice of *a* black woman into a national discourse that left no such space. Washington concludes, "Her voice is not radical, and she writes with little sense of community with a black and female past,"[38] but I place Cooper's work in a robust protest essay tradition. Like Garnet's relationship to current slaves, Cooper uses her relative position of privilege to speak on behalf of those who could not speak publicly for themselves.[39] Cooper's voice is neither *the* voice of black women of the South, *nor even her own voice*. Rather, Cooper uses the essay to speak *on behalf of* those silenced bodies denied full citizenship and participation in national conversations.

From privileged positions in front of national audiences, protest essayists speak not for themselves, but on behalf of those they seek to represent. In fact, some do not speak at all from personal experience. For instance, Hughes wrote the short essay "Emmett Till, Mississippi, and Congressional Investigations" (1955) for the *Chicago Defender* to bring Till's murder to a national audience. On August 28, 1955, while visiting Mississippi from Chicago, Till was lynched by two white men for allegedly whistling at a white woman. The notorious acquittal and the widely circulated image of his mutilated corpse helped to galvanize the early Civil Rights movement.[40] Like Occom's response to the occasion of the public hanging, Hughes uses the lynching and the acquittal as an opportunity to inhabit the perspective of the violently vacated place of the lynchee. In response to the threats and violence that stopped many African Americans from voting, Hughes argues, "If such intimidation of the United States . . . is not un-American, I don't know what is. Yet I have never as yet heard or read of the House Un-American Activities Committee (HUAC) investigating such activities."[41] Hughes speaks not from his own experience, but from the experience of the lynching victim whose brutal murder is not included in Joseph McCarthy's official rhetoric of un-Americanness. To create a *demos*, Hughes's speaker seeks allegiance with the violently silenced lynchee, the intimidated voter, or any African American scared speechless. Further, Hughes joins a long protest tradition of black leaders demanding official inquiries into police brutality, extending to Rev. Al Sharpton's demands on the New York Police Department.

Hughes underscores racial divisions among the American citizenry in order to argue for the inclusion and importance of African Americans in the national imagination. Acts of lynching directly contradict elected officials paying lip service to American ideals:

> It would seem to me nice if the white politicians in Washington would now repay those distinguished colored Americans who have sworn and double sworn their allegiance to democratic ideals, by investigating JUST A FEW of the white folks who hang fourteen-year-old boys to bridges and throw them in rivers and who frighten and intimidate colored voters away from the polls—not to speak of those who continue to segregate the public schools, uphold Jim Crow on the railroads, and bar not only Negro citizens of the United States but East Indian diplomats from getting a decent meal in a public restaurant. Just one little small investigation of these things, using just a wee tinnychee bit of our mutual tax money, and showing just one lynched body on TV, or forcing just one Southern mobster to take refuge in the Fifth Amendment, seems to me long overdue. (251)

To directly contradict empty political rhetoric, Hughes raises the specter of the lynchee to bring together the dispossessed. More so than the speaker, Hughes places the image of the dead body at the center of a loyal group denied full citizenship. Hughes is not pledging allegiance to empty rhetoric; he almost inhabits Till's dead body in order to pledge allegiance to as yet unrealized American ideals of racial equity, complete with a road map of where to begin. The ventriloquized experience of the lynched corpse, not Hughes's own experience with HUAC, speaks publicly against injustice. Till, not Hughes, is the subject of this very personal protest essay.

Hughes's later, more politically engaged essays are not as studied as his more literary essays. This may be because, by prizing the speaking self, scholars prefer essays that explicitly speak from personal experience. Phillip Lopate argues for a celebration of the personal essay because it is our most approachable and diverting form of literature. Lopate considers the personal essay implicitly democratic: the form signifies dialogue because the essayist recounts personal experiences so that the reader may reflect on the human condition when experience transcends social lines. The personal essayist, for Lopate, presents an honest or unmediated speaker in a pact of "friendship . . . based on identification, understanding, testiness, and companionship."[42] In this vein, scholarly treatments of the essay typically credit Montaigne's role in the birth of the modern individual who speaks from the authority of experience. This speaking self convenes, questions, and sorts through what has come before: texts, doctrines, discourses, experiences, and aphorisms. Far from a self-centered enterprise, Atkins explains that the essayist "represents the self not for its own sake but rather as a crucible in which experience is tried and tested."[43] The personal essay creates a coherent self at the center of a tangle of traditions, texts, experiences, and ideologies. Similarly, in his study of the academic essay, Kurt Spellmeyer describes this patchwork function as "convention": bringing together potentially competing ideas, ideologies, and discourses into one textual space in order to question dominant ideals, or, for Spellmeyer, social conventions.[44] Hall explains that the essay's posture of tentative questioning allows "the reader to experience the movement of the author's mind and to examine the premises upon which his conclusions are founded."[45] Though the *content* of the essay may be received knowledge, social conventions, or any topic, for most essay scholars the *subject* of the essay is a speaking self corollary to the writer's mind.

So, if the aim of the protest essay is not necessarily to create an autobiographical "I" but rather to speak for those bodies denied a public voice, the American protest essay again finds its roots in the oratory of social movements as well as the personal essay. In his widely printed speech "What to the Slave Is the Fourth of July?" (1852), Douglass, like Cooper, does not speak solely— or even mostly—from his experience as an ex-slave, even though one might expect as much from the author of the most popular slave narrative of the day. Rather, on the abolitionist lecture circuit, Douglass speaks "from the slaves point of view"[46] in his complex critique of the fugitive slave law, the hypocrisy of celebrations of national independence, and the racial grounds of exclusion from the spoils of the war of independence. Douglass uses his position as public speaker to bring voice to those silenced by declarations of already achieved independence. Douglass delivers his speech to an audience whose citizenship is *not* in question: Congress and the packed house in Corinthian Hall in Rochester, New York, which serves as a particular index of the American citizenry in general. He asks, "What have I, or those I represent, to do with your national independence? Are the great principles of freedom and of natural justice, embodied in the Declaration of Independence, extended to us?" (Douglass 115). Douglass does not divorce himself from the masses following Thoreau's blueprint. Instead, Douglass draws a sharp line between "us" and "them" while his speaking self stands as representative for a group lacking delegates in Congress.

In this representative stance, Douglass speaks from his precarious position as a citizen only partially included in the rhetoric of democratic freedom. That is why he can move across stark lines of division to address his "fellow citizens" in the ventriloquized voice of slaves. Douglass refers to his personal experience *inasmuch as it embodies the experiences of those he represents*. As a former slave and popular orator, Douglass uses his speakerly privilege to straddle the line of disparity between the national audience and those violently excluded from citizenship. Douglass accuses, "I am not included within the pale of this glorious anniversary! Your high independence only reveals the immeasurable distance between us. The blessings in which you, this day, rejoice, are not enjoyed in common" (116). Douglass insists on particular social locations of "I," "you," and "we" in order to underscore the power and divisions that render fraudulent any declarations of independence. When the speaker vacillates between "you" (addressed citizens) and "us" (slaves, noncitizens), Douglass demands recognition of the inconsistency between past invocations of equality and the present moment.

Whereas the personal essay often concerns itself with the relationship between the speaker and a literary or philosophical community that came before, Douglass situates his speaking self in line with political and religious traditions informing representative democracy. Further, Douglass uses his public speaking voice and its print circulation to protest the quashing of the very voices he represents. In direct opposition to the self-congratulatory master narrative of independence informing his Fourth of July address, Douglass contends, "but, in regard to the ten thousand wrongs of the American slave, you would enforce the strictest silence, and would hail him as an enemy of the nation who dares to make those wrongs the subject of public discourse!" (126). Douglass stands in for a voice that questions the nation's most profound stories of belonging, and therefore must be silenced. As Douglass underscores the divisions between the fellow-citizens he addresses and the slaves he represents, Douglass invites an antagonistic relationship to the audience ("you") since his voice marks the space of enforced silence of the slaves who are absent from the national audience, and he gives language to "the mournful wail of millions!" (116).

If the personal essay convenes the private writer and public world, the protest essay disaggregates the two when writers like Cooper take stands as representative speakers. In his study of Baldwin's essays, James Cunningham distinguishes between writer and essay by distinguishing between the rhetorical "I" and autobiographical experience.[47] Following Cunningham's insight, I am interested in the strategy of offering *others'* experiences in the stance of representative speaker. Even when speaking with an "I," protest essays do not speak exclusively in autobiographical terms. Instead, they speak *on behalf of* the disenfranchised from a relatively privileged position of access to print culture. Protest writers are acutely aware of the power of their platform, and that their access is not shared by those whose unjust experiences they recount. Recognizing their relative privilege and their representative duties, protest essayists seek out specific experiences of exclusion that question general pronouncements of equality.

Stance III: The Particular and the General (Journalistic Influences)

> Some years ago, after the disappearance of civil rights workers Chaney, Goodman and Schwirner [sic] in Mississippi, some friends of mine were dragging the river for their bodies. This one wasn't Schwirner. This one wasn't Goodman. This one wasn't Chaney. Then, as Dave Dennis tells it, "It suddenly struck us—what difference did it make that it wasn't them? *What are these bodies doing in the river?*"
>
> —James Baldwin, *The Evidence of the Things Not Seen*, 1985

In part, protest essays exist to insert details of injustice into a public record that might otherwise ignore them. Therefore, protest essayists stand between specific historical details and universalist national promises, between the particular and the universal. Like Hughes, they dwell in historical detail in order to document real divisions and injustices for an American citizenry prone to discounting those divisions and instances. The essay in general is prized for its ability to dwell in ephemeral details and everyday life while transcending the bounds of the individual and aspiring toward universal, but experience-based truths. Atkins explains, the essayist "directs his attention, mind, and soul to the immediate, the concrete, and the particular."[48] Kirklighter further suggests, "Nontraditional writers find that the essay's qualities of spontaneity, self-reflexivity, accessibility, and truthfulness work well to meet their needs of transcending the personal and political."[49] Paradoxically, the essay must also retreat from, or even disparage, the mundane, the overly specific, or the confining historical moment; essayists recount experience in order to access truths tested by the "crucible of experience."[50] So, when an essay dwells too much in immediate details it may become a lesser form: journalism. In his seminal study "The Essay as Form," Adorno describes the essay as an open-ended form of inquiry that can escape dogma because every essay must start anew and create its own system of accounting for the details (or data) that compose the individual essay. Adorno argues, "But the desire of the essay is not to seek and filter the eternal out of the transitory; it wants, rather, to make the transitory eternal."[51] Nevertheless, for Adorno, the essay must exceed the ephemeral, lest the essayist drown amid the morass of mass culture. That is, essayists must fear the too particular.

The journalistic mode informs the protest essay tradition because the ephemeral is not subordinate to the general, universal, or transcendent. Protest essays typically use occasions of injustice not as mere springboards, but as a way of tracing patterns of exclusion from national promises. They document details of injustice, and these details often contradict, rather than lead to, universalist promises of equality. The epigraph to this section is from Baldwin's last prose work in which he continues his quest to uproot instances of racial violence that the American record forgets, covers over, or outright denies by investigating the Atlanta child murders of 1979–1981. Chapter 4 explores Baldwin's essays overall, but his final, most journalistic essay can illustrate the stance of protest essayists between historical detail and national promises, between the particular and the general. Like much of his later work, the essay was dismissed for its heavy detail—if read at all.[52] Though the publisher describes a journalistic account of "facts and documentary evidence,"[53] for Baldwin the details of the story expose a larger pattern of American racism, historical neglect, and the failures of the Atlanta black bourgeoisie. In the epigraph, the partially covered corpses of unidentified Civil Rights workers are horrific manifestations of the journalistic detail a wandering, open-ended essay can dredge up. If Baldwin were to transcend these details to articulate a more general statement about America, he would risk re-submersing the corpses in the stream of a personal essay allergic to the journalistic mode.

Baldwin's essay documents the murder of these bodies as it uncovers a systemic pattern that might account for their deaths, and those in the Atlanta child murders. R. Lane Kauffman describes the essay as an "unmethodical method" able to move through the "thicket of contemporary experience" because it does not adhere to prevailing ideologies. As a result, the essayist "swerves to explore the surrounding terrain, to track a stray detail or anomaly, even at the risk of wrong turns, dead ends, and charges of trespassing."[54] Baldwin's essay performs Kauffman's geographical description: he explores the terrain around Atlanta and the Civil Rights South, collects evidence, and connects isolated incidents into an analysis of racism, American failures to live up to the promise of Civil Rights, and the willful disregard for the activists floating half-seen in the tributaries of movements for racial justice. Details are not incidental; they constitute the essay.

Well beyond Baldwin, many protest writers became involved in journalistic enterprises. For example, in the latter part of his career, Hughes heeded his own calls for more investigations of injustice as he moved increasingly into journalistic projects. In the 1940s, Hughes began writing regular columns for the *Chicago Defender*, and was commissioned to write the official history of the National Association for the Advancement of Colored People (NAACP), *Fight for Freedom* (1962). Even Gore Vidal, a writer not usually associated with social movements for racial justice, consistently delves into journalistic modes to document the inconsistencies of state policies and practices. In 1961, for example, Vidal reports an incident to *Esquire* in which he witnesses police brutality against black men in an essay titled, simply, "Police Brutality" and later collected in the National Book Award–winning *United States* (1993).

Essay criticism tends to view the journalistic mode as a digression from the traditional essay on the grounds that it is detail-heavy, too purposeful, and too wedded to the present moment and unreflective masses. Or as H. L. Mencken snidely quipped, "A newspaper is a device for making the ignorant more ignorant and the crazy crazier." In a study of early American periodical essays, Bruce Granger worries that little critical attention is paid to the American version of the English periodical essay because American writers are too subjective and lack detachment from the immediate. He argues that central to Joseph Addison and Richard Steele's *The Spectator* (ca. 1711–1714) is "the creation of a persona [Mr. Spectator] . . . essential to the objectivity which periodical essays strove to maintain,"[55] and that American periodical essays do not live up to that standard.[56] For Granger, periodical essays value a "social point of view" that is based on the model of a "foreign visitor"[57] over a journalist overly concerned with documentary evidence of injustice. In this vein, literary studies distrust some basic tenets of the protest essay. In the protest essay tradition, however, the journalistic mode helps to uncover patterns of exclusion and injustice so that universalist promises of equality might one day prove true in everyday life.

Stance IV: Cleaving Experience and National Rhetoric

> How could Mr. Jefferson but say, "I advance it therefore as a suspicion only, that the blacks, whether originally a distinct race, or made distinct by time and circumstance, are inferior to the whites in the endowments of both body and mind?" . . . He goes on further, and says: "This *unfortunate* difference of colour, and *perhaps of faculty*, is a powerful obstacle to the emancipation of these people." . . . For my part, I am glad Mr. Jefferson has advanced his position for your sake; for you will either have to contradict or confirm him by your own actions and not by what our friends have said or done for us.
>
> —David Walker, "Article II: Our Wretchedness in Consequence of Ignorance," 1848

Protest essayists document representative experiences of exclusion so that they can test universalist promises of equality for all. Montaigne speaks from personal experience in order to question received knowledge writ large, and American protest essayists locate received truths in official state narratives of full equality for all. This national scope coupled with a trust in everyday experience affords the protest essayist a powerful position from which to question state promises through experiences that directly contradict national rhetoric of achieved equality. While essay criticism tends to emphasize how the form cleaves *together* discourses, texts, and experience, protest essays also cleave *apart* state rhetoric from certain citizens' lived experience. In his study of Richard Wright, Ellison describes "Wright's most important achievement: he has converted the American Negro impulse toward self-annihilation and 'going under-ground' into a will to confront the world, to evaluate his experience honestly and throw his findings unashamedly into the guilty conscience of America."[58] Though Ellison follows Emerson in literary and philosophical meditations on the nation, he also follows Wright to bring African American experience—and white experience—into the light of national promises. In his famous essay "Change the Joke and Slip the Yoke" (1958) Ellison looks at "both sides of the joke" to see that white images of the Negro and Negro images of white people are both false. "What's more," Ellison writes, "each secretly believes that he alone knows what is valid in the American experience, and that the other knows but will not admit it, and each suspects the other of being at bottom a phony."[59] Because the essay can bring together discourses, writers, texts, and experiences across time, ideology, and identity, it seeks a national story of belonging that will prove valid in the lives of all citizens.

Within the protest essay, visions of equality and national belonging that have gained official currency must be tested against everyday experience. Perhaps the best example of the desire to achieve a synthesis of American history and experience is in Vidal's essays. Vidal's essay "Democratic Vistas" (2002) comments on the rise of American imperialism in the twenty-first century by citing an earlier desire to expand the boundaries of the U.S. democratic project during Reconstruction. Like Jordan's use of Thoreau, Vidal consciously cites not only state discourse but also takes the name of a famous essay by Walt Whitman. In doing so, Vidal simultaneously invests his project with national authority as well as re-imagines a nation that might live up to its best promises of democratic inclusion. Vidal recounts in journalistic detail the nation's activities under George W. Bush, while invoking specters of democratic visions past from Spiro T. Agnew to Grover Cleveland to James Madison, as well as Whitman. Vidal hews toward cynicism in his citation of foundational stories and avers, "Finally, those founders, to whom we like to advert, had such a fear and loathing of democracy that they invented the Electoral College so that the popular vote could be throttled, much as the Supreme Court throttled the Floridians on December 12."[60] By placing his meditation on voting rights and presidential power in the form of an essay originally addressed to a Reconstruction-era national audience, Vidal locates the current event of the 2000 presidential election in a long history of the failures of black enfranchisement. Vidal provokes anxiety between lofty national ambitions for equality and ugly realities of white supremacy in America. He explains that the founding structures of democracy are designed to locate the potentially flexible "we" of democracy in a select few: "We were to be neither a democracy subject to majoritarian tyranny nor a dictatorship subject to Caesarian folly" (*Dreaming War* 5). The "we" of the United States masks the particular at the heart of its universalist construction; its current manifestation fails the litmus test of the everyday lives of the citizenry.

In Whitman's 1871 essay of the same name, he comments on Reconstruction in the aftermath of the Civil War. Expounding on his 1867 essay "Democracy," Whitman—who poses as the voice of the nation in *Leaves of Grass*—worries about the prospect of full inclusion of African Americans into the democratic structures of the post-bellum nation. Whitman contends that the United States is the sole society in history to "have accepted in unwitting faith, and, as we now see, stand, act upon, and go security for [the democratic principles of the Republic]."[61] Having cited lofty national promises, Whitman quickly addresses divisions within the polity by validating the fears of the secessionists and the powerful: "I will not gloss over the appalling dangers of universal suffrage in the United States. In fact, it is to admit and face these dangers I am writing. To him or her within whose thought rages the battle, advancing, retreating, between democracy's convictions, aspirations and people's crudeness, vice, caprices, I mainly write this essay" (Whitman 363). True to the protest essay tradition, Whitman addresses a divided citizenry and concerns himself with those excluded from full participation. But unlike the vast majority of American protest essayists, Whitman separates himself from the excluded and panders to those who fear their inclusion while paying homage to the ideal. Whereas Whitman worries about the future ability to reach such an aspiration, protest essayists demand its realization in the present by insisting on the hypocrisy of the discordance between ideals and practices. Vidal, too, addresses the inconsistency— indeed, hypocrisy—between democratic principles and action, but does so in order to leverage the moral and political authority of the excluded, oppressed, and dispossessed.

The protest essay's stance between experiences of exclusion and national promises of inclusion is especially visible when writers inhabit official state discourse. American political oratory again offers a key precursor to the protest essay when freeborn David Walker brings the words of Thomas Jefferson into his 1848 abolitionist appeal, and he presents the experiences of slaves as a means of questioning official state ideas about achieved liberty and black inferiority. Protest essays often draw directly from the words of the state, especially with readily available documents like the U.S. Constitution and Declaration of Independence. Though Rogers M. Smith may distrust inclusive civic myths of equality for the divisions they mask, American protest writers draw on the legitimacy afforded by such civic myths to foster real union that can live up to promises of democracy without denying or evading experiences of exclusion and disenfranchisement. Smith argues, "Because these stories are meant to inspire as deep and enduring an allegiance as possible, leaders have an incentive to make them true descriptions of the people's common characteristics and the benefits of embracing common civic identity."[62] While this may be true at the official level, American protest essays draw from democratic political traditions to demand—now!—equitable publics and citizenries.

In his militant speech, later circulated with Garnet's address in pamphlet form, Walker explicitly inhabits the U.S. Constitution so that he is able to simultaneously claim the democratic rights it delivers and condemn its racist exclusions. Walker organizes his speech into "articles" and addresses a "Preamble" to "My dearly beloved Brethren and Fellow Citizens."[63] As in the speeches by Occom, Douglass, and Garnet, the groupings "brethren" and "citizens" are not synonymous. By inhabiting a founding document, Walker questions the legitimacy of the original document in the everyday lives of the directly addressed "you": the slaves of the United States of America. Walker cites not only national stories of belonging, but the state document itself that announces inclusion. Walker speaks on behalf of an excluded group that should be included in such pronouncements. Following Walker, the protest essayist can quote state leaders and documents in order to cleave their rhetoric with experience of exclusion.

Walker cleaves experience and state rhetoric not only to expose the hypocrisy of inclusive pronouncements amid exclusive practices, but also to claim those promises for the slaves and free blacks. In his comprehensive account of Walker's life and influence, Peter Hinks suggests that Walker's (black) nationalist ideology demands and imagines a transformed America, not separation along identitarian lines. Hinks traces Walker's attempts to distribute the *Appeal* directly to slaves in the South and he distinguishes Walker's nationalist vision from popular schemes to recolonize Africa with free blacks, schemes that were also being rejected by "a handful of thoughtful whites" who were beginning "to consider other ways for the races to live together."[64] For Hinks, African Americans changed their relation to the nation and "through their change, America would have to change as well."[65] As a model for the protest essay, Walker's brilliance lies in his formal experiment to inhabit the Constitution to demonstrate that a plan for races to coexist as citizens was already written into founding documents.

Chapter 2 discusses a feminist tradition of rewriting the Declaration of Independence that furthers the example of Walker and Garnet. For this chapter, it is important to note that the strategy of unveiling hypocrisy between national promises and citizens' experience brings the protest essay into close alignment with the manifesto. To that end, a brief look at the Port Huron Statement (1962), a key document of the student movement of the 1960s, illustrates how protest writers unveil inconsistency when inclusive states pronouncements fall short of, or in direct opposition to, experience. In doing so, they capitalize on the long-held American distaste for hypocrisy, often speaking in what Douglass calls a "scorching irony." In the introduction to the Port Huron Statement, the Students for a Democratic Society (SDS) claim ownership of state pronouncements of equality by highlighting the failures of those in power to make such pronouncements real: "The declaration 'All men are created equal . . .' rang hollow before the facts of Negro life in the South and the big cities of the North. The proclaimed peaceful intentions of the United States contradicted its economic and military investments in the Cold War status quo."[66] The SDS documents incidents of oppression and inhabits the vantage of the Negro in the South in order to bring states' failures to light. Instead of rejecting state promises, the SDS speaks on behalf of the oppressed as the rightful heirs of pronouncements of equality, pronouncements that are rendered valid or invalid according to the empirical data of African American experience. These state-sponsored promises are powerful sites for writers to claim full democracy as a viable, albeit unfinished, project.

Whereas the Port Huron Statement and Walker's and Garnet's addresses earnestly cite state promises, many essays follow Vidal's more literary cynicism and employ parody when inhabiting authoritative texts. This parody does not lead to self-effacement, meaninglessness, or political ambivalence. Instead, protest essayists reclaim national stories of equality from the vantage of the oppressed. For example, in his early essays, Vine Deloria Jr. inhabits the rhetoric and personae of state documents that police U.S.–American Indian relations. Deloria is a theologian, administrator, and, until his death in 2005, a key American Indian thinker ever since his writings gave voice to the 1970s Red Power movement. As executive director of the National Congress of American Indians (NCAI) in the early 1960s, Deloria argued for grassroots organizing among Indians. In a lesser-known writing from that period, "From the Archives—December 2, 1504," Deloria inhabits not a founding U.S. document but a colonialist field report, and he speaks from the position of a "savage" of the New World. Deloria employs familiar colonialist arguments for the right to displace peoples. In the colonialist form, Deloria is able to write what James Treat describes as an "alternative narrative of discovery."[67]

True to the protest essay tradition, Deloria speaks in a representative voice as he details for "us" (Indians) the curious ways of the newcomers. Deloria reports, "We call them savages since they wear funny clothes and don't know a word of Indian language" ("Archives" 295). Deloria presents the report as an academic paper at the NCAI convention of 1504. In this parody, he inverts social hierarchies so that he can analyze and appropriate state claims of equal citizenship, fairness, or homogeneity. Deloria is acutely aware of the power of the United States to define Native Americans simultaneously as wards of the state, as noncitizens, and as the object of national debates about religion and citizenship, but never as speaking subjects. Rather than quashing Deloria's voice, however, colonialist documents—like Walker and the Constitution—furnish Deloria with a public voice. When Deloria inhabits colonialist ideas about the absence of American Indian culture, he repudiates the argument, but also reverses it to expose the duplicity of colonialist ideas about civilization and savagery that persist into the twentieth century.

Parody is a key component of 1960s literature, which is the decade generally regarded as the beginning of postmodernism and its penchant for recycling older texts, often for humorous effect. The wry humor of parody serves an earnest purpose in the protest essay: organizing American Indians. Deloria sent the *NCAI Sentinel* to "dues paying" Indians and Indian Tribes. By inhabiting the discourse of modern democracy, Deloria reclaims the tenets of democracy as rightfully belonging to those who were written over in dominant stories of the invasion of the Americas and the birth of American democracy. "We have tried over and over to explain democracy to them, with no success," Deloria explains to his fellow Indians confused by the savages' propensity for only marrying Indian princesses. He concludes, "Although we believe all men to be equal, they insist on making differences and so until they mature I guess we will be stuck with this royalty thing" ("Archives" 296). Rather than repudiate the conquistadors, Deloria inhabits official state rhetoric like "all men are created equal" in order to uncover the hypocrisy in the utterance as well as to claim democracy as originated by his fellow Indians.

Deloria's better-known early writing, *Custer Died for Your Sins* (1969), contains an even more direct strategy of inhabiting state narratives. In the book's opening essay, Deloria argues against Columbus's combination of "religion and real estate."[68] Instead, Deloria desires a return to Indian traditions in which religion is not separated unnaturally from everyday life. Deloria assumes the colonialist false dichotomy of white culture/indigenous nonculture in the now familiar critique of the inability of the Western gaze to understand the knowledge of medicine men and mislabel it as the work of the devil. "Above all," Deloria argues, "they overlooked the fact that what the Indian medicine men did *worked*" ("Missionary" 23). Like Walker's rewritten Constitution, Deloria wrote the original version of the essay in direct response to a 1965 article, "The Indian in a Cultural Trap" by Lawrence E. Barry for the Catholic journal *America*. In that article, Barry casts the missionary's presence on reservations as an ordained project to save the uncivilized. Barry argues, "Indian reservations have been chosen—and wisely so—as target areas in the War on Poverty. The good of the country as a whole demands such actions, since these depressed areas can be breeding grounds for crime and disease."[69] In protest, Deloria inhabits Barry's amnesia-prone essay to counter the assumptions of the nation that created the reservation system. Deloria counters, "Missionaries have been chosen—and wisely so—as targets in the War on Ignorance conducted by the Indian people of this country. The good of the country as a whole demands such actions, since these people can be the breeding ground for doctrines of intolerance, arrogance and unwise policies regarding the American Indian" ("Missionary" 284). Deloria delivers a sarcastic and utterly devastating exposure of the hubris in Barry's invocation of the state's need to correct the foibles of the American Indian. Deloria simply reverses the subject and object of Barry's text. In doing so, Deloria claims the country for American Indians and displaces the missionary as the object of national discourse. Like Garnet's address, Deloria uses the dominant script to call for a collective project: the War on Ignorance. But the essay is only a beginning to this war; it is up to his readership to continue the fight.

Stance V: Incitement and Open-endedness

> This document represents the results of several months of writing and discussion among the membership, a draft paper, and revision by the Students for a Democratic Society national convention meeting in Port Huron, Michigan, June 11–15, 1962. It is represented as a document with which SDS officially identifies, but also as a living document open to change with our times and experiences. It is a beginning: in our own debate and education, in our dialogue with society.
>
> —Introductory note to the Port Huron Statement, 1962

Protest essays draw on the open-endedness of the traditional essay, but for immediate political ends: they incite readers to continue their projects, often by ending with questions, plans of action, or calls for a direct response. Adorno values the open-endedness and incompleteness of the essay as he paints it as a key form for undogmatic academic inquiry. Adorno critiques positivist underpinnings of the scientific experiment and suggests that "the essay, however, does not permit its domain to be prescribed."[70] Whereas George Lukacs deemed the essay behind other forms in its "road to independence,"[71] Adorno argues that such an unformed form is a great asset because it is able to provide an open system where old things and ideas are shuffled into a new critical field, a new ordering. As such, the essay delivers the truly open system of empirical inquiry promised by the scientific model, but lost in science's overriding desire to establish and test universal laws. For Adorno, the essay provides a machine for constant renewal, resorting, and reviewing. The epigraph takes Adorno's description to its logical conclusion: it announces a "living document" able to participate in ongoing national dialogues and social change. Like the manifesto, protest essayists look to their readerships and their circulation to deliver the equitable future they imagine.

When protest essays end in direct calls to action they are a literal embodiment of Adorno's open-endedness. From Hughes's demand for meaningful congressional investigation of un-American activities to Garnet's call for slaves to remember they are three million strong, protest essays do not end in resolution since the nation they address remains divided. For a good example of open-ended calls for direct action, we can return to Jordan's essay "Waking Up in the Middle of Some American Dreams" in which she calls for a new American dream of real union. Jordan ends, "I do not believe that these new American dreams of mine mark me as special, or different. In these longings, and in this faith, I do not believe that I am living alone in America. But you will have to let me know: Am I?" (24). This is not a rhetorical question; she expects an answer. Jordan invites a reciprocal relationship with her addressees, and delegates power and responsibility to them. The white space following her closing question simultaneously signals the end of the essay and the *start* of the collective project she desires. The questions that end Jordan's essays leave space for direct participation, which is why, as Ruth-Ellen Joeres Boetcher argues, they veer into the terrain of the polemic "whose principal goal is to incite."[72]

Jordan's questions call for a response as they try (*essai*) to bring about the equitable future she imagines. Jordan draws on the provisionality associated with the essay genre, but as a means of underscoring her essays as unfinished projects to be continued in the political world. In another essay that questions the exclusion of immigrants in chauvinistic English-only policies, Jordan ends with an incitement for her audience to speak, followed by a blank space of hopeful opportunity and despairing silence: "I believe that somebody real has blinded America in at least one eye. And, in the same way that so many Americans feel that 'we have lost our jobs,' we suspect that we have lost our country. *We know that we do not speak the language.* And I ask you: well, what are we going to do about it?"[73] In direct opposition to a dominant narrative that paints America, jobs, and language as the property of a white "we," Jordan conjures a collective "we" that seeks to encompass all those written out of this story. The new language spoken by "we" turns out to be the rightful heir to U.S. democracy. As Jordan reclaims the language of the state, she transforms it. The final vision, though, depends on the "we" to act.

Protest essays are provisional and digressive with direct political consequence. Indeed, by their explicit participation in the sociopolitical realm, protest essays enter formal kinship with manifestoes, position statements, and journalistic op-ed pieces. Like those sister genres, the protest essay's open-ended calls to action can work as warnings, as well as hopeful incitements. For example, Alice Walker resurrects an unforgotten curse unleashed upon the world, and first recorded by Zora Neale Hurston, for an essay that protests the racism, militarism, and patriarchy that threaten our survival. Walker recites the curse and thus unearths the voices buried in the long wake of Western imperialism and expansion. She inhabits the folk tradition prized by

Hurston and cries, "*Only justice can stop a curse*" (*In Search* 342). Walker relays this curse collected by Hurston in the 1920s—"And by then it was already old" (*In Search* 339). Walker's call for justice not only demands a response, it also invests such a call with a long history.

Walker's is only one of many more examples. To end his piece on Till, Hughes employs sardonic humor in a question demanding collective response: "Imagine lynching children! It makes me sick at the stomach. Have senators no stomachs?" ("Emmett Till" 251). The imperative invokes urgency, the interrogative demands an equally strong response. Protest essays not only appeal to national promises of equality, they also call for citizens to continuously question American democratic systems. Therein future protest essayists answer a challenge laid down by orators and essayists from previous social movements.

PROTEST WRITERS AND THE TRADITION OF THE ESSAY

Protest essays engage crucial debates about the validity of American stories professing democracy for all. Yet, if we accept that the essay form is most in alignment with a belles-lettristic or personal essay tradition, we concede at least two important points: (1) that the epicenter of the modern essay is the property of those who already have access to full citizenship; and (2) we neglect a history of writings by and about those speaking from experiences of exclusion, not for themselves alone. Following such a concession, if we want to value contemporary essays by influential writers such as Audre Lorde, Baldwin, Adrienne Rich, Gloria Anzaldúa, or other political advocates, we are left with two equally unsatisfactory arguments: (1) such writers form an entirely *new* tradition; or (2) such writers appropriate the essay tradition; to borrow from Lorde, they simply claim the master's tools.

Joeres wrests the essay tradition from bourgeois roots in her study of radical feminist essays. She explains, "The essay has been through a variety of changes, but historically, at least, it has almost always been a tool of the privileged classes."[74] Joeres explores how radical feminist essayists appropriate its traits for overtly political purposes. Joeres adds, "*The whole issue of form, whether overtly or only obliquely referred to, does indeed play a role in the selection, use, and adaptation of the essay by radical feminists.* The form itself becomes an obvious statement, pressing itself insistently forward into the reader's consciousness, occasionally varying enough from the expected to call attention to itself as different."[75] While I applaud this approach, we can also place radical feminist essays at the center of an American protest essay tradition more aligned with political advocacy and social movements. Indeed, many contemporary protest essayists seek a cultural history to call their own. In addition to Walker's landmark project to recover Hurston and a black women writers' tradition in her celebrated essay "Looking for Zora" (1975), Rich's project to "re-vise" women's writing comes to fruition in the essay form, especially in *Blood, Bread, and Poetry* (1986), and Baldwin's celebrated essays ask us to think about America with a black perspective at the center. By recognizing the American protest essay strand of the essay tradition, we restore these writers to their rightful place at the center of a tradition concerned with America's democratic ambitions and its undemocratic practices.

In literary studies, *protest* remains apart from high literature and too often marked as raced, gendered, or different because it is perceived as too politically driven, partisan, factionalizing, immediate, or polemical. For some, this has required that we jettison literary traditions altogether, for, as Alan Wolfe suggests, "Judge our contemporary culture warriors by the standards of books, and they disappoint: logic, evidence and reason are conspicuously absent. Judge them by the standards of pamphleteering, and they may be doing democracy a favor, reminding our apathetic public why politics matters."[76] I propose that we read protest essays as literature *qua* literature. The relationship between literary merit and protest designs often sits at the nexus of a longstanding dilemma: acute recognition of social urgency invites dismissals that the protest essay cannot exceed its specific location, time, identity, or event it protests. As a result, familiar understandings of literary traditions seem to not quite fit the projects of many protest writers. LeRoi Jones (Amira Baraka) called his 1966 collection of essays *Social Essays* and in 1985 Jordan called her essay collection *Political Essays*. Jones (Baraka) and Jordan push against conventional understandings of the essay, but they stand easily as preeminent protest essayists. The highly charged work of politically engaged essayists requires that we reconsider the essay form that attends both to the urgency of the historical moment and to the artistry of literary figures who turn to the essay for political advocacy.

Protest writers are not latecomers to the essay. They constitute a distinct strand that is often overlooked in our focus on the Montaignean personal essay. A story of the protest essay embedded in both the European personal essay and American political oratory provides a compelling history in which contemporary protest writers can claim foremothers and forefathers. I have, of course, chosen examples of protest essays that neatly embody the specific stance under examination. Including these protest essays in a general study of the essay could simply demonstrate the elasticity of that most formless of forms. But seeing them as a distinct tradition allows for a richer discussion of the relationship between the essays and the divided citizenry they address with such urgency. For, when the essay stretches as far as I pull it, new affinities emerge with journalism, manifestos, sermons, speeches, jeremiads, and general rants. Within this tradition, writers do not jeopardize their art when they assume the mantle of political advocacy. Indeed, for the American protest essay, political advocacy is art.

Chapter Two

NEW DECLARATIONS OF INDEPENDENCE: THREE FEMINIST RE-VISIONS OF A FOUNDING DOCUMENT

I have alerted us to tensions in the stance of the American protest essay: desiring union while speaking as a representative partial citizen who underscores division within the audience. By posing the speaker between universalist promises and specific experiences of exclusion, protest essays lend urgency to long-term goals of social equality. Since many protest essays look to inclusive pronouncements of the nation-state—either in official documents or general ideas about national unity—this chapter examines one tradition of claiming, inhabiting, and rewriting one of the nation's most authoritative documents: the Declaration of Independence. Writers cite this document, what T. V. Reed calls the "revolution's best known manifesto,"[1] in order to protest its exclusions and to achieve the unity it describes.

Rewriting the Declaration is an especially useful example of the general tendency in the American protest essay outlined in chapter 1 to reference state pronouncements of inclusion that contradict practices of exclusion. From the Seneca Falls Convention's "Declaration of Sentiments" (1848), to Emma Goldman's "A New Declaration of Independence" (1909), to women's liberation group Bread and Roses's "Declaration of Women's Independence" (1970), new generations of social movements return to founding documents, especially the Declaration, to articulate a new agenda that addresses inequality and division within an already accepted national story of belonging. When we look at texts that cite the state's words to protest unjust practices, we have to inquire about the stance of the new speakers toward the old documents. Does the strategy perpetuate or undermine the state's authority over its citizens, be they partial, second-class, or full? Do the revisions enforce or question national citizenship? Are official documents effective platforms for providing an inclusive script for national belonging? This chapter especially asks: What does it mean to place rewritten state documents at the center of both a protest essay and a feminist tradition?

This chapter looks at three revisions of the Declaration, each from a different moment and political orientation in American feminism, in order to understand how protest essays build on the resonance of authoritative state documents of equality. Henry Louis Gates Jr.'s influential theory of signifying in African American literature and Adrienne Rich's groundbreaking concept of women's writing as "re-vision" can help us understand the widespread technique of rewriting dominant narratives. For Gates, signifying makes "the written text speak with a black voice."[2] For Rich, re-vision is "the act of looking back, seeing with fresh eyes, of entering an old text from a new critical direction," an act that "is for women more than a chapter in cultural history: it is an act of survival."[3] If historically disenfranchised groups place themselves at the center of dominant texts and traditions, literature must follow suit. For example, Keith Byerman suggests that contemporary African American fiction actively remembers the past, which necessitates "the reconceptualization of black experience as a survivor narrative and thus a rewriting of the American grand narrative" and countering a dominant "story of individual achievement and democratic progress."[4] Most minoritarian literatures question narratives of achieved equality, but protest essayists signify or re-vise founding documents to also claim them, and perhaps make their promises real.

Rewriting the Declaration simultaneously lends legitimacy to a social movement and questions the authority of the un-rewritten document. That is, the re-vision presents itself as *more* authoritative than the original because they are able to address experiences of exclusion and disenfranchisement. The re-visions also endow the speakers with great national authority. In doing so, they question the state's hold on declarations of equality in favor of persons not considered full citizens (i.e., mid-nineteenth-century women), a foreign national (i.e., Goldman), or those concerned with women across the world (i.e., women's liberationists). If the personal essay provides an experiential venue through which to question received knowledge, protest essays that rewrite state documents question not only the dominant national story of already achieved equality, but also who gets to make such assertions in the first place.

INCLUSIVE POSTURES IN THE DECLARATION OF INDEPENDENCE (1776)

Before we look at the three feminist re-visions, I propose that we think of the Declaration itself as a key progenitor of American protest essays because it also creates unity by addressing division within a populace, but by emphasizing separation from the old nation to create a new one. No collective utterance of "we" is more authoritative, well-known, and disputed than those in founding documents. The first "we" of the Declaration appears in the famous opening line: "We hold these Truths to be self-evident, that all Men are created equal, that they are endowed by their Creator with certain unalienable Rights, that among these are Life, Liberty and the Pursuit of Happiness." Throughout the text, the exact referent of the "we" is occasionally very particular: the thirteen United States of America speaking unanimously, the People, the Representatives of the United States of America, the Colonies-cum-Independent States, and the fifty-five signatories. While the "we" shifts among that set of particulars, the movement itself creates a fundamental slipperiness so that future speakers can claim this "we" even if they are not necessarily intended by the original framers.

The Declaration of Independence has attracted a great deal of academic interest in its political authority, rhetorical richness, and oratorical postures. Rhetoricians examine how a small group of elites speak on behalf of a diverse constituency to offer a viable story of national belonging that undergirds the political legitimacy of the U.S. nation-state. In an influential work informing this chapter, Phillip S. Foner looks at revisions of the Declaration across social movements, political ideologies, and locations. In doing so, he provides an historical overview of how various groups have written themselves into the founding document's lofty promises in order to wrest control of that document for their progressive ends.[5] Further, Stephen Lucas looks at the rhetorical sophistication required to persuade an eighteenth-century audience "that the Americans were justified in seeking to establish themselves as an independent nation."[6] Wilbur Howell examines the historical context to see the Declaration as a brilliant exercise in logic and argumentation,[7] while William Smith approaches it as an excellent example of eighteenth-century polemics.[8] And Elizabeth Renker traces the writing process to show how Jefferson and other founders consciously presented their speaking selves as able to collectively announce the arrival of an independent nation.[9]

I defer to those studies for thorough discussions of the historical, political, and rhetorical context of the Declaration. Here it is important to notice two aspects that open the possibility for, or even invite, feminist re-visions: the flexible, inclusive *we* and the implied *not-we*. Critics return to the historical context of the Declaration, which seems to belie its loftiest promises and its ostensibly national gaze, especially given the practice of slavery. For instance, Jacqueline Bacon examines how African American abolitionists such as David Walker use the Declaration's own words to levy new interpretations that address hypocritical practices and include slaves within the document's aura of inclusion, revolution, and independence. She argues that African Americans "confidently appropriate American Revolutionary rhetoric in their discourse, assuming their rights as given and chastising

Americans for violating them."[10] Further, in one of the most influential studies of the Declaration's authoritative status, Leo Huberman traces immigrant history to assess how many of America's inclusive promises remain unfulfilled, especially through the pause of a comma between "we" and "the people."[11] Finally, Michael Walzer suggests that American pluralism works because it functions as ethnic pluralism where unity and division reside in the public and private spheres, respectively, in order to solve the paradox between the one and the many written into *e pluribus unum*.[12]

If the doctrine of natural rights is self-evident and not conferred by a certain government or religious entity, then *any* speaker with a claim to natural rights—either within the jurisdiction of the nation or beyond—can claim those rights, along with the collective public voice the Declaration creates. Lucas argues, "As the phrase 'one people' implied much more than it actually said, so 'the opinions of mankind' veiled the many layers of audience . . . the Declaration was also meant for posterity."[13] While certain segments may have felt specifically addressed by the "we"—English sympathizers, the Spanish and French, British subjects in the American colonies—the Declaration wraps its collective "we" in an ambiguity that future speakers can exploit for their own purposes. The Declaration offers a platform from which to reshape, borrowing from Homi Bhabha, the nation it narrates. While scholars point to how the Declaration becomes a living document not necessarily tied to its historical moment,[14] feminist re-visions address particular exclusions in the original document by insisting on the legitimacy of women to be included in its universalist aspirations. Feminist re-visions thereby participate in what Amanda Emerson identifies as the movement from equivalence to equity in the life of the Declaration, a trajectory perhaps purposefully embedded by "deliberately vague" terms like *men* and *we*,[15] which "managed the entailments of a myth of equality in ways that ensured its continued efficacy as an abstract term of unification and affiliation, while also adopting its significations to include such counterintuitive formulations as 'separate but equal.'"[16]

Feminist re-visions make visible the "not-we" at the heart of the Declaration's cleavage of the American people, and at the heart of collectivity itself. The notorious utterance of "we" in the Action of the Second Continental Congress (the technical name of the Declaration) stands in direct opposition to a "He" (King George III)—repeated no less than nineteen times in the short document. In contrast, "we" appears only eleven times. In the final entry in the list of wrongs done by "He," the Declaration submits, "He has excited domestic Insurrections amongst us, and has endeavoured to bring on the Inhabitants of our Frontiers, the merciless Indian Savages, whose known Rule of Warfare, is an undistinguished Destruction, of all Ages, Sexes and Conditions." "He" is the totally external *not-we* that casts a shadow over divisions internal to the emergent nation, such as the indigenous inhabitants of the new nation's land. The Declaration specifically names the "Indian Savages" as external to the factions "amongst us," about which the Declaration is conspicuously silent. Domestic exclusion is both central and buried in the act of creating the unanimous declaration. It follows that for each feminist re-vision, the goal is to recalibrate the *we* and *not-we* so that it encompasses those subjects for whom the rewritten version is meant to speak. Therein arises the question of who each feminist re-vision will include and exclude, especially concerning national boundaries. By contesting the lines of "we" and "not-we," these new feminist Declarations re-vise the national story of belonging, and they seek to extend rights and obligations to a new set of citizens historically denied access to the privileges and duties doled out by the state.

Like most American protest essays, the Declaration is rarely seen as a literary document in its own right. Critics favor approaching the Declaration as a solely political piece, and many have traced in minute detail its political roots. Carl Becker provides the most influential study of its political philosophy,[17] and many scholars have built on his study to diligently trace the rhetorical ancestry of the document within various strands of political philosophy. Most see the Declaration as closer kin to political speechifying than to the essay. Americanist Edwin Gittleman is the exception when he approaches it as Jefferson's slave narrative, "deliberately disguised however as a state paper,"[18] alongside other eighteenth-century literary documents. To that end, Gittleman traces the successive drafts from which Jefferson's references to slavery were excised, and he notices literary devices like metaphor (in the extension of war imagery to slavery[19]) and metonymy (in the repetition of "HE" to invoke a ritual incantation to exorcise the demons of a foreign power[20]). So, by placing feminist re-visions in the American protest essay tradition, we can further understand how protest essayists draw upon political oratory and statist discourse, in addition to personal essays, or even political essays following Paine.

DECLARATION OF SENTIMENTS AND RESOLUTIONS (1848)

One of the most famous feminist re-visions is the Declaration of Sentiments and Resolutions from the 1848 Seneca Falls Convention, a touchstone event of First Wave feminism. Directly inhabiting the authoritative and familiar words of the original, the Seneca Falls re-vision declares, "We hold these truths to be self-evident: that all men and women are created equally; that they are endowed by their Creator with certain inalienable rights; that among these are life, liberty, and the pursuit of happiness; that to secure these rights governments are instituted, deriving their just powers from the consent of the governed."[21] Elizabeth Cady Stanton and her co-authors[22] built not only from their political experiences in the abolition movement,[23] but also on the rhetorical model of Frederick Douglass, David Walker, and Henry Highland Garnet who recognized the power of revered founding documents whose promises rang hollow for many in jurisdictional earshot. In the re-vision, Stanton et al. underscore the exclusions in the seemingly universal declaration of rights by presenting the category *men* as only describing one "one-half the people of this country" (140–41), or the "family" of man. When they inhabit the famous lines of the founding document, they turn a potentially disinterested liberalism into progressive politics concerned with domestic injustice. In doing so, they turn universalist aspirations into a framework to enfranchise particular groups, and they turn our attention to actual practice as well as lofty pronouncements. By adding "and women" to "man" and "they," they attend to exclusions kept silent in the original document, and they expand the flexible pronoun to address divisions within the national community. Their re-vision expands the circle of "the governed" and insists on a doctrine of "consent" that must now include women.

Stanton et al. rewrite the "we" with which the nation speaks. Drawing on the Declaration's political authority and format, the Declaration of Sentiments enacts the project it describes: full participation by all those included in the re-vised national story of equality and independence. Whereas the original creates and legitimates a newly independent nation, the re-vision participates in that nation so that its promises of equality ring true for women. As the re-vision expanded the scope of the "we," a set of resolutions was needed because women have been "invested by the creator with the same capabilities, and the same consciousness of responsibility for their exercise, it is demonstrably the right and duty of woman, equally with man, to promote every righteous cause by every righteous means" (141). When the Declaration of Independence becomes a Declaration of Sentiments and Resolutions, the test of the government's rightful power depends on how its institutions are perceived by the governed, which now includes women as speaking citizens instead of material property.

The Seneca Falls Declaration is an aesthetically complex document worthy of literary as well as political scrutiny. Most often, literary studies treats this major feminist document like most protest essays: as a secondary text cited quickly for historical context before moving to a more literary text. This approach rightly places Stanton et al.'s re-vision into the abolitionist literature of Douglass, Harriet Jacobs, and Harriet Beecher Stowe.[24] For instance, Stephen Matterson turns to the Seneca Falls Declaration to elucidate the gender acrobatics Jacobs performs as she links abolitionism with a nascent women's rights movement. He argues, "In the complex discourse of *Incidents*, Jacobs makes use of the idea that marriage is a variation of slavery. This coupling of the woman's position in marriage with slavery had been central to the Seneca Falls Declaration, with its assertions that the married woman is 'civilly dead' and 'completely deprived of liberty.'"[25] In a footnote, however,

Matterson reverses the borrowing to observe that the Seneca Falls re-vision draws upon the language of abolition. When we attend to matters of literary tradition, as well as political ideas and historical context, we can understand more fully how the re-vision participates in a protest tradition of partial citizens speaking to and from founding documents.

Martha Solomon Watson examines the rhetorical relationship between the 1848 Seneca Falls declaration and the original Declaration. For her, Stanton et al.'s rewriting of the Declaration, first in 1833 then in 1848, shows how "the process of intertextuality can enrich our understanding of iconic texts" as we see the "dynamic intertextual play" between the re-visions and the original.[26] She finds that the second Declaration of Sentiments directly mirrors the rhetoric of the original, whereas the first Declaration of Sentiments simply borrows the ideas, "with the crucial substitution of 'man' for 'king' as the oppressor and women rather than the male citizens of the American colonies as the oppressed."[27] Watson poses the re-visions as "echoes" or "parallels" of the founding fathers, but also as a two-directional rereading because the Seneca Falls declarations "subtly but significantly enlarged the definition of citizen entailed in the Declaration of Independence."[28] By doing so, "they shifted the rhetorical focus and purpose of the Declaration of Independence to accommodate their own needs and, in so doing, helped alter the public perception of it."[29] This move signals a shift from bellicose to pacifist stances and from individual to group rights.

By re-vising a founding document, Stanton et al.'s central claim is that rhetoric can be empty and even harmful when divorced from practice; they want to connect rhetoric to the everyday lives of the citizenry. As Rich and Gates suggest, the act of re-vision is noteworthy because inhabiting a foundational text is more than an instrumental act. The Seneca Falls writers reinvigorate the national "we" by placing women—their lives, perspectives, and experiences—at the center. Instead of assuming the validity of the state's declarations, Stanton et al. draw upon the essay form's reliance on lived experience to question seemingly settled ideas about equality as they, too, submit facts "to a candid world." The re-vision pays homage to the durability of the nation amid "light and transient" events. Yet it warns, "But when a long train of abuses and usurpations, pursuing invariably the same object, evinces a design to reduce [women] under absolute despotism, it is their duty to throw off such government, and to provide new guards for their future security" (139). The re-vision claims for women the civic duty of governmental dissent, and therefore full citizenship, as it avers, "The history of mankind is a history of repeated injuries and usurpations on the part of man toward woman, having in direct object the establishment of an absolute tyranny over her" (139). Stanton et al. place themselves at the center of the national "we" and displace men onto the tyrannous *not-we* of the original. Whereas the original proposes to replace one unjust government with another, the re-vision suggests a history of gender oppression beyond England and its colonies. Therefore, the nation must be refashioned to live up to its own pronouncements of equality. "This government" becomes a particular example in a universal aspiration for the end of man's tyranny over woman.

To achieve true equality between men and women in the re-vision's aspirational designs, the Seneca Falls writers reach for authority within and beyond the nation-state by drawing on both political and religious authority. Robert Hariman argues that "feminist orators of the nineteenth century such as Elizabeth Cady Stanton and Sojourner Truth so artfully reinterpreted the Genesis creation myths and other Biblical stories, and not merely to neutralize those powerful weapons but to turn them on their adversaries."[30] It is also important to place the re-vision in a feminist tradition of rewriting founding documents. If the doctrine of separate spheres confers sentimental authority to women, then that authority can be used to rewrite the nation. In fact, in the Declaration of Sentiments' long list of "facts" against man's tyranny is an accusation that "He has usurped the prerogative of Jehovah himself, claiming it as his right to assign for her a sphere of action, when that belongs to her conscience and to her God" (140). "He" has misinterpreted the original document and written woman into an object ("her") of the state, and thereby perverted the unalienable rights naturally bestowed upon all. By speaking about "He" and his wrongs against "her" as an affront to the Creator, the Declaration of Sentiments jockeys for the position to speak for the collective nation. If man has disenfranchised "one-half of the people of this country," the woman citizen must construct a national "we" that lives up to the document's inclusive aspirations. More than the lack of suffrage, the re-vision protests how marriage makes a woman "civilly dead" (140) and advocates an inclusive set of political practices.

The re-vision also draws on familial discourse in order to provide women an entry point into state language and to include the whole family of the citizenry. Whereas the original Declaration imagines a universal model of Peoples that can "dissolve the political bands" between them when necessary, the re-vision draws on the language of humanity as "the family of man" (139), which includes gendered factions. Though the familial imagination is conspicuously silent on matters of racial difference, the Declaration of Sentiment's insertion of a particular group into a universalist founding document opens the possibility for other excluded factions to follow suit, even if it fails to do that work itself. Hazel Carby's work demonstrates the central place of racial division in the construction of suffragist positioning.[31] Most famously, Sojourner Truth challenged white feminists' assumptions about inclusion by asking, "Ain't I a Woman?" Donna Haraway explores how Truth's words circulated in multiple versions, thereby enacting a possibly fuller flowering of the ability to address the particular within universalist (humanist) aspirations that do not rely on an origin myth of sameness.[32] I draw on this important work to point out that the feminist tradition of re-vising the Declaration creates a platform for later groups to address their exclusion from national imaginaries and practices.

Though it protests women's exclusion, the Declaration of Sentiments creates a "we" that leaves the "not-we" purposefully silent so that the collective it imagines becomes purposefully manifold. Firstly, the re-vision excises the Indian-baiting in the original. In its stead is a goal of full inclusion for the currently disenfranchised: "He has endeavored, in every way that he could, to destroy her confidence in her own powers, to lessen her self-respect and to make her willing to lead a dependent and abject life" (140). The list of grievances both validates the original's aspiration for equality under the banner of independence and critiques the execution of "this government" because it renders one-half of the family of man dependent. The shift to emphasize full inclusion, however, may have the unintended effect of excluding other groups such as by removing mention of ethnic and racial division altogether. Nevertheless, the re-vision poses the nation-state neither as unified nor as the inevitable boundary of its aspirations for equality. In fact, the re-vision now includes a set of Resolutions that proscribes full inclusion of all factions of a society, not necessarily a society particular to the United States: "Resolved, That the speedy success of our cause depends upon the zealous and untiring efforts of both men and women, for the overthrow of the monopoly of the pulpit, and for the securing to women an equal participation with men in the various trades, professions, and commerce" (142). In this way, the re-vision draws on the flexibility of the original "we" to speak as excluded citizens and to make room for others who advocate for national reform. "Our cause" is simultaneously specific to Stanton, the other writers, participants of the Seneca Falls Convention, suffragists, and any self-elected members of future social movements.

Feminist scholars have long noticed how anti-slavery activities afforded (mostly white, privileged) women the ability to fashion a political voice, breach the separation of the political and domestic spheres,[33] and create a public space of autonomous women speaking.[34] Studies of Stanton, First Wave feminism, and liberal feminism abound, and I defer to them for in-depth meditations on the possibilities and limits of Stanton's feminism. Here I suggest that rewriting a founding document provides a strategic platform on which, to borrow from Mary Loeffelholz, to pose as a woman citizen. In the Declaration of Sentiments, the woman citizen speaking stands in metonymic relation to the particular factions for which and to which she speaks. Feminists wrestle with how leaders like Stanton enter the public arena contrary to the doctrine of separate spheres. In one of the more delightful examples, Lisa Strange and Robert Brown trace the cultural history of the bicycle and Stanton's endorsement of its ability to break feminine gender codes because "If for no other reason, the bicycle posed a challenge to the doctrine of separate spheres by offering women a way to escape the physical confines of the home" and the "'close atmosphere' of the brick-and-mortar church."[35] The Declaration offers a similar technology to ride into the previously off-limits territory of state-building so that women claim unalienable rights, and in the process re-vise the declarations of those rights.

The construction of an open-ended collective manifested as, but not defined by, the nation is important for both the Declaration of Sentiment's specific critique of the separations inherent in the public/private split, as well as for a general history of feminism. Scholars are reconsidering the original Declaration as a transnational document.[36] So, too, feminist scholars now question the transnational scope of U.S. liberal feminism. For instance, Sandra Stanley Holton traces Stanton's European stumping trips in the 1880s and early 1890s in order to show that Stanton was engaged in building "a kinship circle of women"[37] by connecting her movement to British suffragism, Quaker abolitionism, and a radical alternative to U.S. liberal suffragism. This "transatlantic legacy from the abolition movement"[38] brings into relief the political and rhetorical strategies at play when figures like Stanton enter the hallowed ground of founding U.S. documents. If the charge of the Declaration of Sentiments is to overthrow patriarchy (man's "absolute tyranny over" woman) as opposed to the original's goal of severing ties to a specific imperial power, then the nation becomes only one possible container of the collective "we" announced by the re-vision. Future re-visions begin to see even more clearly the transnational possibilities of the original.

A NEW DECLARATION OF INDEPENDENCE (1909)

A 1909 re-vision of the Declaration by anarchist and brilliant political thespian Emma Goldman further stretches the inclusive scope of the original beyond dominant stories of national belonging, and it more militantly claims unalienable rights outside the nation-state without jettisoning the power of the national narrative of liberty and equality. Goldman published "A New Declaration of Independence" in her monthly anarchist magazine *Mother Earth*, then in leaflet form shortly after its initial publication.[39] In doing so, she follows the example of Stanton and many more to come: she simultaneously claims and critiques the authoritative power and pronouncements of the founding document of her adopted country. But she invests the original narrative with a more polemical view of governments and oppression. In her re-vision, Goldman claims the inclusive possibilities of the founding document and writes, "When, in the course of human development, existing institutions prove inadequate to the needs of man, when they serve merely to enslave, rob, and oppress mankind, the people have the eternal right to rebel against, and overthrow, these institutions" (137). Closer kin to Henry David Thoreau than Stanton, Goldman creates a People's "we" that must declare independence from the state.

In her re-vision, Goldman carefully extricates the current U.S. government ("existing institutions") from the national ideals professed by the original Declaration. This is because Goldman speaks on behalf of the People who do not need independence from another people, but from a set of practices that have failed to live up to the original ideals, which she embraces rather sincerely. In fact, even though anarchism typically stands in opposition to the nation-state as a general concept, Goldman uses the language of the original *without irony* to articulate her vision of an anarchist future when humans will be truly free to achieve "life, liberty, and the pursuit of happiness." Goldman wrests those ideals from the province of existing institutions like the nation-state and the Church by describing them as "eternal" rights, not unalienable rights bestowed by a creator. Though Goldman removes the Church, she embraces Enlightenment ideals of natural rights that gave rise to the modern liberal nation-state. Goldman is not seeking to implode ideals of freedom and equality; she embraces them earnestly and claims them on behalf of anarchism.

Goldman achieves two key results in her re-vision. First, she portrays the moment of origin as filled with admirable promise that has been lost. In her famously provocative essay "The Tragedy of Women's Emancipation" from the first issue of *Mother Earth*, Goldman writes, "Liberty and equality for women! What hopes and aspirations these words awakened when they were first uttered by some of the noblest and bravest souls of those days. . . . Now, woman is confronted with the necessity of emancipating herself from emancipation, if she really desires to be free."[40] Throughout her career, Goldman adhered fairly consistently to the polemical structure of denouncing the current practice—but not the original ideal—of a movement, be it feminism, the American or Russian revolutions, or modernity. The second result follows the first: Goldman accuses the existing U.S. government not of illegitimacy per se, but of hypocrisy in not carrying out its original ideals. For example, as she maintains in her essay "Police Brutality" (1906), "If we as a nation were not such unspeakable hypocrites, we should long since have placed a club instead of a torch in the hand of the Goddess of liberty."[41] By basing her critique in charges of hypocrisy, Goldman endorses the authoritative founding document, if not the government laying claim to it.

Goldman poses the People as the true heirs of U.S. ideals. In her introduction to the inaugural issue of *Mother Earth*, Goldman unequivocally embraces Washington, Jefferson, and Paine as the rebels of their day helping to create an America that was "vast, boundless, full of promise."[42] For Goldman, founding statesmen belong to a line of anarchist descent, not to contemporary American patriotism. She writes, "A period of but a hundred years had sufficed to turn a great republic, once gloriously established, into an arbitrary state which subdued a vast number of its people into material and intellectual slavery, while enabling the privileged few to monopolize

A NEW DECLARATION OF INDEPENDENCE

By Emma Goldman

WHEN, in the course of human development, existing institutions prove inadequate to the needs of man, when they serve merely to enslave, rob, and oppress mankind, the people have the eternal right to rebel against, and overthrow, these institutions.

The mere fact that these forces—inimical to life, liberty, and the pursuit of happiness—are legalized by statute laws, sanctified by divine rights, and enforced by political power, in no way justifies their continued existence.

We hold these truths to be self-evident: that all human beings, irrespective of race, color, or sex, are born with the equal right to share at the table of life; that to secure this right, there must be established among men economic, social, and political freedom; we hold further that government exists but to maintain special privilege and property rights; that it coerces man into submission and therefore robs him of dignity, self-respect, and life.

The history of the American kings of capital and authority is the history of repeated crimes, injustice, oppression, outrage, and abuse, all aiming at the suppression of individual liberties and the exploitation of the people. A vast country, rich enough to supply all her children with all possible comforts, and insure well-being to all, is in the hands of a few, while the nameless millions are at the mercy of ruthless wealth gatherers, unscrupulous lawmakers, and corrupt politicians. Sturdy sons of America are forced to tramp the country in a fruitless search for bread, and many of her daughters are driven into the street, while thousands of tender children are daily sacrificed on the altar of Mammon. The reign of these kings is holding mankind in slavery, perpetuating poverty and disease, maintaining crime and corruption; it is fettering the spirit of liberty, throttling the voice of justice, and degrading and oppressing humanity. It is engaged in continual war and slaughter, devastating the country and destroying the best and

20

FIGURE 1

Emma Goldman, "A New Declaration of Independence," *Mother Earth* 4.5 (1909): 20–21. Note the union printing label at the bottom of first page.

Kate Sharpley Archive, Berkeley, California.

finest qualities of man; it nurtures superstition and ignorance, sows prejudice and strife, and turns the human family into a camp of Ishmaelites.

We, therefore, the liberty-loving men and women, realizing the great injustice and brutality of this state of affairs, earnestly and boldly do hereby declare, That each and every individual is and ought to be free to own himself and to enjoy the full fruit of his labor; that man is absolved from all allegiance to the kings of authority and capital; that he has, by the very fact of his being, free access to the land and all means of production, and entire liberty of disposing of the fruits of his efforts; that each and every individual has the unquestionable and unabridgeable right of free and voluntary association with other equally sovereign individuals for economic, political, social, and all other purposes, and that to achieve this end man must emancipate himself from the sacredness of property, the respect for man-made law, the fear of the Church, the cowardice of public opinion, the stupid arrogance of national, racial, religious, and sex superiority, and from the narrow puritanical conception of human life. And for the support of this Declaration, and with a firm reliance on the harmonious blending of man's social and individual tendencies, the lovers of liberty joyfully consecrate their uncompromising devotion, their energy and intelligence, their solidarity and their lives.

MOTHER EARTH

A Monthly Magazine Devoted to Social Science and Literature

10c. per Copy $1.00 per Year

Publisher . . . . EMMA GOLDMAN
Editor . . . . ALEXANDER BERKMAN
210 EAST 13th STREET, NEW YORK

every material and mental resource."[43] Goldman offers a master narrative of edenic origins corrupted by subsequent national practices and capitalist industry that perverted its original promise. Though this move may endorse American exceptionalism, it also shows that the current United States is an exception to its own rules.

Goldman fundamentally disrupts American narratives of already achieved harmony and equality by standing between national promises and actual experiences, and through her increasingly sophisticated use of her speaking self in the essay form. In "A Woman without a Country" from the May 1909 issue of *Mother Earth*, Goldman taunts the United States and mocks the very idea of citizenship: "You have Emma Goldman's citizenship. But she has the world, and her heritage is the kinship of brave spirits—not a bad bargain."[44] She addresses the nation-state directly, and discusses her own person by name, which points to her increasing awareness of herself as an historical figure, citizen, and speaker within the essay. With scathing irony, Goldman lambasts the assumption that "no American citizen can be a very bad man" and proclaims that she is "dreaming un-American dreams" within its borders.[45] Further, in the 1908 pamphlet, "Patriotism: A Menace to Liberty," Goldman argues that one's ability to "love the spot" in which one lives has been perverted into a machine that murders in the name of defending the nation because "Patriotism assumes that our globe is divided into little specks, each one surrounded by an iron gate."[46] In the essay, Goldman is able to escape the "iron gate" of nativist nationalism as she frames an anarchist vision as the "American dream."

Goldman's posture of Americanism in the re-vision is more than mere strategy meant to implode the original from within. She sincerely embraces the ideals articulated in the original. By adopting such a stance, Goldman risks what Linda Hutcheon describes as complicitous critique: she lends credibility to the dominant story of already achieved equality and independence by working within a document with extreme gravitational pull and held dear by many. In fact, Goldman had long cited authoritative national texts (the U.S. Constitution, patriotic songs like "America the Beautiful," the Declaration) in order to show that anarchist activities were in line with original ideals and, in turn, that current governmental practices were out of step with them. Goldman's first citation of the Declaration is in her defense of Leon Czolgosz's assassination of McKinley in "The Tragedy at Buffalo" (1901). In that essay, she paints anarchists as native patriots and the president among "the money kings and trust magnates of this country" who comprise the "small band of parasites who have robbed the American people" and infringed upon their "'Life, liberty, and the pursuit of happiness.'"[47] Goldman reverses the common anti-immigrant images of infestation to pose those in power as moral, political, and legal outsiders ruining the nation for the People.

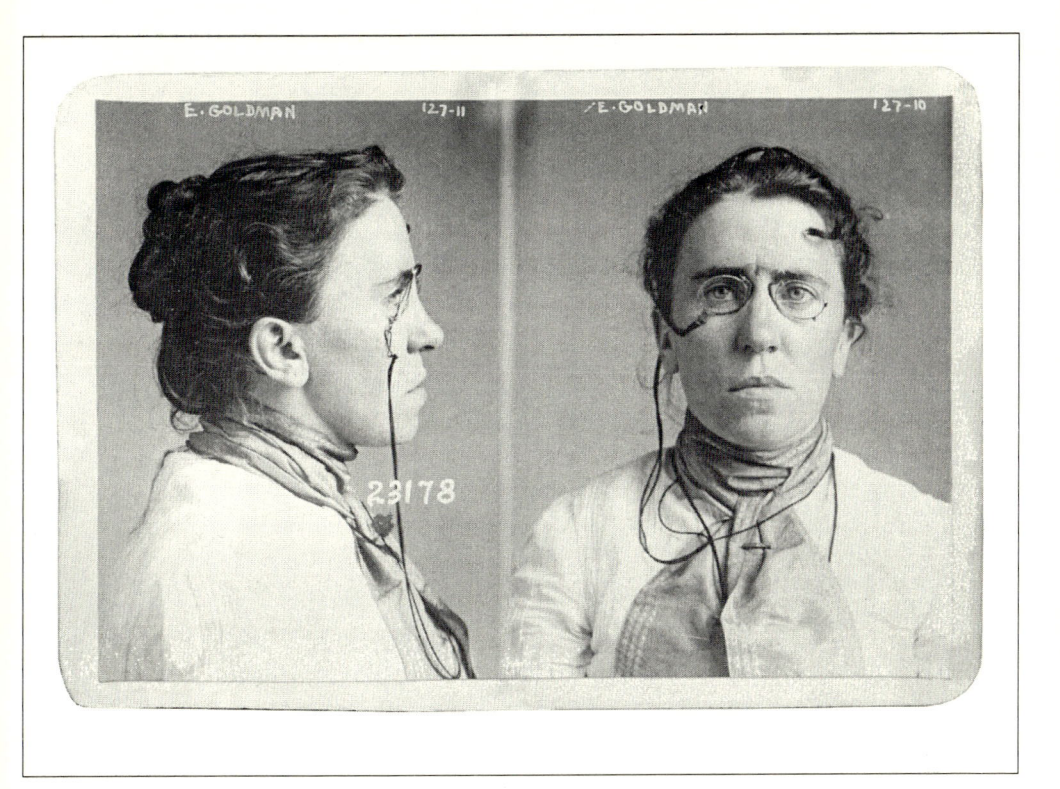

FIGURE 2

Emma Goldman, mug shot, ca. 1911. This undated mug shot points to the government surveillance of Goldman's activities, which lead to numerous detentions, police charges, and eventually to the revocation of her citizenship and her deportation in 1919.

Prints and Photographs Division, Library of Congress.

When Goldman claims the authority to speak as citizen-stateswoman, she counters the prevailing sense in the U.S. imaginary that anarchy is the product of unclean immigrants, a foreign threat to American unity and order. Goldman's patriotic posture—while potentially incongruent with some anarchist philosophy—can be seen as a response to fierce nativism. This nativism, for instance, resulted in the Anarchist Exclusion Act of 1903 in which, as Candace Falk explains, "Congress officially barred entry to alien anarchists—mandating that all immigrants swear upon arrival that their political persuasion was not anarchism. . . . The law was rooted in part in an erroneous belief that assassins were never American citizens."[48] Many anarchists responded by insisting on the organic Americanism of their ideas, as well as the U.S. citizenship of many American anarchists like Goldman and Czolgosz.[49] Because of the overwhelming anti-immigrant sentiment sweeping the nation, Goldman did not take lightly the prospect of endorsing a document of fervent patriotism. Falk explains: "The subjects of patriotism and national boundaries were difficult to address for an anarchist and internationalist like Goldman, who viewed patriotism not as a benign love of place but as a dangerous force charged with the hazardous ingredients of 'conceit, arrogance, and egotism.'"[50]

Goldman's relationship to founding documents is tenuous because she inhabits a space of partial citizenship. That is why Falk argues that Goldman's writings must be understood within the context of her "unusual number" of FBI files because "the mechanisms of surveillance and repression may have been more severe when applied to Goldman, whose politics, gender, ethnic identity, and immigrant status marginalized her and made her more vulnerable than other dissenter to the abuses of power."[51] But, Goldman writes into the re-vision the very social lines that would exclude her or render her vulnerable to nativist rejection. She declares, "We hold these truths to be self-evident: that all human beings, irrespective of race, color, or sex, are born with the equal right to share at the table of life; that to secure this right, there must be established among men economic, social, and political freedom" (137). True to the original, Goldman speaks in a collective "we" espousing the self-evident eternal truth of natural rights, but she modifies the original's homogeneous sense of the People by enshrining race, color, and sex into the founding document. She also invests the document with an inclusive, familial image of a welcome table. By posing the existing government as inimical to the feast of independence and human rights, Goldman disentangles the current government from its own founding document. From that authoritative platform, Goldman grants herself full, rightful citizenship as well as the People for whom she stands. Falk explains, "Although Goldman identified America as the locus of her life's work, the feeling was not mutual."[52] In fact, in the years leading up to her re-vision, the United States deployed agents from the Treasury, Postal Service, and Bureau of Immigration to track, stymie, stamp out, and/or deport her dissenting voice.

Though she speaks from a national platform, Goldman maintains an internationalist stance. This strategy reflects the tension between the universalist aspirations of a doctrine of natural ("eternal") rights and the enshrinement of those rights within a specific nation. Goldman is at pains to reconcile her strategy of claiming the rights to bring about an international anarchist future in a national origin story. Goldman stands between eternal truths and present realities because she writes, "each and every individual is and ought to be free to own himself and to enjoy the full fruit of his labor."[53] The space between *is* and *ought* (here and there, future and now, original ideal and current practice) makes visible the original document's insufficient ability to imagine division within the newly formed People. Instead of an exclusionary patriotism, Goldman imagines a collective based in "harmony" and concludes, "And for the support of this Declaration, and with a firm reliance on the harmonious blending of man's social and individual tendencies, the lovers of liberty joyfully consecrate their uncompromising devotion, their energy and intelligence, their solidarity and their lives" (138). The image of collectivity is not one of a newly created, homogeneous People; rather, Goldman writes division into the founding document because the People come together in solidarity from a diverse set of talents, desires, experiences, and across national boundaries.

The venue in which the re-vision first appeared, *Mother Earth*, also sought a resolutely transnational scope. *Mother Earth* consistently featured articles from a transnational array of important anarchist thinkers, writers, and reports of anarchist events around the globe. Articles on events in Japan, Spain, and Mexico appear at the time Goldman's New Declaration was published. The people on behalf of whom the re-vision speaks are not necessarily circumscribed by arbitrary national boundaries. Like Stanton, Goldman purposefully leaves silent the boundaries of this solidarity. Throughout her writing and speaking at this time, Goldman draws upon a discourse of "harmony" in which governmental institutions, she argues in "What I Believe," only exist "to maintain or protect property or monopoly."[54] Removing government inhibitions to "true social progress and harmony," Goldman consistently argues, will lead to "the spirit of a deeper sense of fellowship, kindness and understanding."[55]

If Goldman imagines a harmonious and endlessly inclusive *we*, then who is the *not-we* in her re-vision? Goldman's persistent internationalism potentially conflicts with a re-vision that locates anarchist roots in a founding document yet resists the nativist patriotism so associated with national origin narratives. Through repeated references to "liberty-loving" People, Goldman paints anyone in opposition in the straw position of liberty-haters, a polemical strategy common to political speech. But such a move jeopardizes the cleavage between *we* and *not-we* at the heart of the original because a People must declare independence from another. For the most part, Goldman does not divest the People from another group; instead, she divests them from government, property, and fear of the Church and public opinion. But Goldman possibly cordons off at least one group because she substitutes domestic tyrants—capitalists—for the external "He" of the original. She cites the few that have taken resources from the many and argues, "The reign of these kings is holding mankind in slavery" (137). Goldman moves the external "He" of the original onto domestic soil, thereby using class division as a possible line at which the people must wage independence.[56] Also, unlike the other re-visions, Goldman's is singularly authored, and therefore risks elevating herself over the People for whom she speaks. But it is important to note that Goldman emphasizes government institutions more so than capitalist kings, and she even compresses the original's list of grievances into one paragraph, which the main leaflet version further submerges into the previous paragraph. This de-emphasis suggests that the re-vision seeks to cast a very wide, possibly universalist, net for the domain of the People.

The move to embed anarchism and an inclusive net into the founding document added fuel to the fire of various government agencies and functionaries who saw Goldman's protest as inimical to citizenship. The government's strategy to silence Goldman involved a decades-long effort to strip her of citizenship, under the idea that dissent is a foreign vice infecting an otherwise unified people.[57] For instance, long before the 1903 Anarchist Exclusion Act, in an 1893 case by the City and County of New York against Goldman for speeches to unemployed workers, a grand jury described Goldman as "an evil disposed and pernicious person, and of the most wicked and turbulent disposition" and it accused her of "unlawfully, wickedly, and maliciously" provoking a crowd of 500, which would "excite the good citizens of our said State and of the United States to hatred and contempt of the government and constitution of the State and of the United States."[58] This charge directly echoes the naturalization oath's promise, in the words of Kersner's 1884 application, "to renounce forever all allegiance and fidelity to every foreign Prince, Potentate, State or Sovereignty whatever, and particularly to the Emperor of Germany." As a woman, Goldman was not required to take the oath, though her pious use of the Declaration can be seen as a sort of oath of allegiance. Nevertheless, Goldman's anarchist stances fundamentally jeopardized her eligibility for continued citizenship.[59]

Anti-anarchist laws and nationalistic jingoism pervade the government's efforts to suppress Goldman during the time of *Mother Earth*'s launch and Goldman's early national speaking tours. The extent of anti-anarchist hysteria is evidenced by the three year prison sentence given to First-Class Private William Buwalda for shaking hands with Goldman at a rally where he "did frequently and repeatedly applaud the said address, and did on its conclusion declare to the said Emma Goldman his sympathy with her and his approval of her remarks."[60] Theodore Roosevelt ultimately granted clemency, lest the Buwalda case "change [the public's] feeling into one of sympathy for the offender."[61] Yet for government officials, anarchism was a disease that could be spread by mere handshake, and a remarkable number of them considered Goldman's dissenting activities to be in direct opposition to U.S. citizenship. For instance, in May 1909 the Chief of the New Haven police asked the U.S. Department of Justice about the legality of his refusal to allow Goldman's activities in his jurisdiction by citing an unpassed law that would "mak[e] it a crime for anyone to speak against the government in a derogatory manner."[62] And in early 1910 the U.S. postal commissioner successfully postponed *Mother Earth* under the premise that Goldman's article "The White Slave Traffic" was obscene and therefore unmailable.

Amid the fury of government suppression, Goldman is seen primarily as an orator and political thinker, not a member of a literary tradition. Goldman maintained ties to many major figures from H. L. Mencken to Theodore Dreiser, worshipped literary figures such as Oscar Wilde in his later writing and Thoreau, and held friendships with literary figures such as Margaret C. Anderson, editor of *The Little Review*. In *Mother Earth*, Goldman's essays appeared with poems by esteemed writers from Victor Hugo to Emily Brontë and reviews of literature by celebrated authors such as Jack London and William Blake, and Mother Earth Publishing published major authors such as Henrik Ibsen. Falk notes Goldman's original "intention to include cutting-edge poetry and fiction alongside political articles" in *Mother Earth* but that vision "never fully materialized" its "lofty visions of becoming a literary radical magazine whose words and ideas would be woven into the fabric of American culture."[63]

The absence of formal approaches to Goldman's work on the lecture platform, in *Mother Earth*, and in her essays leads to an incomplete understanding of how she positions her speaking self in relationship to the national declarations she claims, critiques, and rewrites. Instead, critics follow Goldman's cue and see her writing as extensions of her speeches. Craig Monk portrays Goldman as an orator who uses *Mother Earth* as a lecture platform that gives Goldman "reasonable access to her readership."[64] Though Monk notes that Goldman's aim is "joining art and social commentary," he notes the "literary shortcomings of [Goldman's] anarchist brethren," which results in a "stillborn alliance between art and anarchism" that leads to "*Mother Earth*'s lack of a coherent literary aesthetic."[65] Monk argues, "Indeed, this suggestion that modern writers were growing too concerned with aesthetic innovation and too neglectful of social and political events was made by activists even as literary magazines, asserting their political allegiance, responded to the events of the late 1920s and 1930s."[66] Martha Solomon treats Goldman as a masterful rhetor and argues that her speaking and writing are closely linked since her essays differ little from extant lecture notes and her "natural forum is the lecture platform,"[67] a forum that allowed her to overcome what Solomon perceives as ideological problems "inevitable in anarchist rhetoric."[68] Solomon explains, "Many features of her rhetoric, especially the flaws in her reasoning and her frequently awkward and melodramatic style, would be less objectionable to a live audience caught up in her dynamic delivery than to an armchair reader."[69]

Though her contribution to literary pursuits is largely unrecognized, Goldman's life and political work are well-documented. In addition to her own writings and autobiography *Living My Life* (1931), Richard Drinnon chronicles Goldman's activities,[70] Alice Wexler explores Goldman's personal life,[71] and the work of Falk as Goldman's biographer and editor of the Emma Goldman Papers Project continues to provide an exhaustive, rich, and complex portrait of Goldman.[72] Goldman is most often understood in a political tradition of anarchism and as a prescient feminist who bridges First Wave reform and Second Wave radicalism. In this vein, Goldman refused women's suffrage as a political goal because it would simply add women to a broken set of existing institutions that enslave humans, rob them of their eternal liberties, and drain their potentials for full physical and intellectual expression. Drinnon notes, for instance, that women's liberation group WITCH (Women's International Terrorist Conspiracy from Hell) embraced Goldman's argument that "We don't want to be equal to unfree men."[73] Further, Alix Kates Shulman presented Goldman's essays to a women's liberation audience in order to rescue her from accusations of anti-sisterhood and to paint Goldman as "an indisputable radical feminist" committed to self-determination.[74] For Shulman, when Goldman was forcibly deported to Russia in the red scare of 1919,[75] this marked the end of a radical alternative of First Wave feminism, to be resuscitated fifty years later.

Perhaps the re-vision, when placed in the American protest essay tradition, suggests how Goldman successfully joined her literary and political ambitions. During the run of *Mother Earth*, Goldman slowly becomes aware of herself as a masterful essayist. In her introduction to *Anarchism and Other Essays* (1910), Goldman considers her transition from successful orator to essayist. She explains, "My great faith in the wonder worker, the spoken word, is no more."[76] Finding the lecture platform wanting because her notoriety turned her speeches into mere spectacle, Goldman explains, "I came to see that oral propaganda is at best but a means of shaking people from their lethargy: it leaves no lasting impression. . . . The relation between the writer and the reader is more intimate."[77] Writing, and its circulation, increasingly became a part of Goldman's aesthetic and political vision.

Critics, biographers, and even Goldman herself tend to see her as more arbiter than practitioner of the goal to join art and politics. But it might be useful to think of Goldman as an important participant in the American protest essay tradition. In her essay on *Mother Earth*'s tenth anniversary, Goldman repeats the twofold aim to speak on behalf of unpopular political causes and "to establish a unity between revolutionary thought and artistic expression."[78] Here Goldman conceives of the literary as that which is able to remove itself from the political current, but not in a disinterested way. In her introduction to *The Social Significance of the Modern Drama* (1914), Goldman praises a fusion of experimentalism and social realism. She argues that literature has a unique power to unsettle hardliners—conservatives and anarchists alike: "Since art speaks a language of its own, a language embracing the entire gamut of human emotions, it often sounds meaningless to those whose hearing has been dulled by the din of stereotyped phrases."[79] Goldman seeks a literature that mirrors modern life in a way that bourgeois literature did not and European drama was beginning to do: "They know that society has gone beyond the stage of patching up, and that man must throw off the dead weight of the past, with all its ghosts and spooks, if he is to go foot free to meet the future."[80] Goldman draws on literature's ability to wed the past to the future as she consistently argued that the United States (and soon the Russian revolution) held all its promise at the origins, and that the key to an equitable future lies in living up to the promises of rebellious beginnings. Although she ultimately cedes literary ambitions to her contemporaries' search for aesthetic innovation, Goldman helps redefine the literary and finds the essay as a form best able to join the revolutionary and the artistic.

Even if Goldman never fully thought of her essays as literary objects, a masterful essayist slowly emerges out of the pages of *Mother Earth*. This is perhaps most evident in numerous reports from the field when Goldman writes about her speaking tours, and sometimes implicitly meditates on the purchase of the written word over the lecture platform. In an early issue, Goldman reports on "The Joys of Touring" where she locates her speaking self as a hardened activist always on a moving train because "anyone who can survive twenty years of tossing about in the foul and suffocating air of our railroad cars must indeed be strong."[81] Here Goldman draws on the essay's trust in experience over abstraction as she insists on the bodily experience of organizing, and also invites the readers along her journey through St. Louis, Montreal, London, Cleveland, and Toledo. In doing so, the reader experiences the lecture circuit across disparate lecture platforms, a forum that Goldman finds lacking because it risks being entertainment, not activism. As a result, Goldman and her readers connect ephemeral visits to a general pattern: "In all cities so far visited I have found among the comrades a very live and active interest in our recently organized Federation."[82] The essay form provides a medium for further organizing, as well as a platform for a collective vision and Goldman's print posterity. The essay form delivers Goldman's unique ability to move among the personal and the political, the particular and the universal, the enduring and the immediate.[83]

The "New Declaration of Independence" and Goldman's other writings are much more formally sophisticated than mere speeches rendered in print. Goldman begins to recognize herself as a literary essayist in preparation for *Anarchism and Other Essays*. In her published accounts and in her private letters to longtime lover Ben Reitman, Goldman discusses writing lectures in preparation of the manuscript that would become *Anarchism and Other Essays* (1910). She often describes them as splendidly written masterpieces and she expresses a desire not to turn in something mediocre to a publisher. In fact, while nearly bedridden with a painful broken leg that hindered her work on the manuscript, Goldman writes to Reitman, "You did not like the WS Traffic yet everyone of some literary judgment did."[84] As Goldman contemplates the written word—from its lasting effects beyond the lecture platform to issues of copyright and purchase price while courting a publisher—Goldman quietly begins to subject herself to literary, not just political, terms of evaluation. And her essays evidence an increasingly masterful use of the form. By incorporating her speaking self, the events of the day, and the political currents into her extended meditations on the promises and limits of the United States to deliver an anarchist vision, Goldman connects the immediate to the enduring in a way she finds more satisfying than her earlier lectures. In her essays Goldman uses current political issues—birth control, free speech, the repression of her speaking tours—as springboards into lasting themes of harmonious kinship, anarchist futures, and how to attain the life, liberty, and the pursuit of happiness promised in the Declaration. These protest essays, more so than her speeches, constitute Goldman's lasting influence and her recurrence in later political movements. When Times Change Press reprinted three of Goldman's essays for a 1970 women's liberation pamphlet, the jacket argues, "The historic essay by the well-known revolutionary anarchist Emma Goldman are remarkably relevant to questions being debated within the women's movement today."[85]

The circumstances of publishing the re-vision shed further light on the tension between radical re-vision and reform, and on Goldman's relationship to mainstream ideas. She appends a footnote: "This 'Declaration' was written at the request of a certain newspaper, which subsequently refused to publish it, though the article was already in composition" (137). By embedding the genesis of the re-vision and its rejection by a mainstream publisher into the document itself, Goldman dramatizes its ultimate publishing as an act of self-determination consistent with the original's ideals. Drawing on Goldman's autobiography, Falk notes that Goldman entered—and won—a *Boston Globe* contest to write a new Declaration, but the paper's owners reneged at the last minute.[86] The debacle with the *Globe* illustrates the futility of using existing institutions to bring about an anarchist future, in the same way that Goldman enters the hallowed ground of the Declaration to claim the very nation whose practices she protests. By using the footnote to juxtapose the publication in *Mother Earth* against a mainstream inability to fully critique the original, Goldman insists on the insolubility between her vision and the current U.S. government, each of which lay claim to the Declaration.

Goldman looms large in the U.S. cultural imaginary, appearing in celebrated works like E. L. Doctorow's *Ragtime* (1975), Warren Beatty's *Reds* (1981), Tony Kushner's *Angels in America* (1994), and Howard Zinn's play *Emma* (2002). Future social movements also claim her, from women's liberation to anti-globalization to anarchism. Like the original Declaration, she fashions her own longevity by using inclusive pronouncements and visions to frame current events. Goldman's legacy remains an anarchist whose relationship to the (U.S.) nation-state ranges from suspicion to hostility. Shulman argues, "[Goldman] identified the state with its laws and the church with its morality as agents of women's oppression."[87] She is also seen as "a symbol of conscientious, spirited opposition to societal pressures."[88] Strange, then, that she uses a founding document to articulate her collective vision. Scholars struggle to reconcile Goldman's anarchist postures with her suspicion of collective movements and theories of group oppression. Drinnon, for instance, remarks that "along with most other radicals of the period, Emma had a blind spot when it came to the importance of race" but "even if she remained largely unaware of the complicated interrelationships of racism and nationalism, she had a full realization that patriotic nationalism was poisonous."[89] Strange, again, that Goldman enters the founding U.S. document, a prime location of poisonous nationalism. By placing Goldman's work in the feminist tradition of re-vising the Declaration, and seeing them as American protest essays, we begin to appreciate how the protest essay moves between not only universalist promises and experiences of exclusion, but also between global visions of justice and national locations of substantive rights.

DECLARATION OF WOMEN'S INDEPENDENCE (1970)

Women's liberation followed Goldman by questioning the First Wave's predominant reform goals of inclusion into national institutions. Instead, women's liberation took on the exciting project of questioning social institutions and imaginaries from the ground up, possibly changing the way society itself worked. More so than earlier moments in American feminism, women's liberation imagined a global sisterhood and offered cross-cultural theories of women's oppression, especially in the radical and socialist strands. Within that global project, the Boston-based socialist feminist organization Bread and Roses asked in a 1970 outreach leaflet, "DO WE WANT EQUALITY IN THE MAN'S WORLD, OR DO WE WANT TO MAKE IT A NEW WORLD?"[90] Bread and Roses's radical posture rejects mere reform and echoes directly Goldman's notorious stance against woman's suffrage. The leaflet begins, "Sisters: We are living in a world that is not ours—'it's a man's world.'"[91] The group explicitly poses women as subordinate to, and to be liberated from, a patriarchal society. This potentially separatist stance gained currency in later versions of radical feminism seeking to create a wholly new society in which women could enjoy their full potentials. The propriety of the world itself is at stake in the project to organize women and imagine a more equitable society.

It is curious, then, that the group employs apparatus of the U.S. nation-state by re-vising a founding document the same year they distributed the pamphlet. In "Declaration of Women's Independence," the collective takes up the prose of the Declaration in order to announce a need for "one sex to dissolve the political bonds which have connected them with another."[92] As proof, Bread and Roses proclaims, "We hold these truths to be self-evident," the first of which being "that all women and men are created equal and made unequal only by socialization" (45). Because it inhabits so intimately a founding document, the "we" proclaimed by Bread and Roses may not divest itself totally from the "man's world." By dwelling in a founding national "we," Bread and Roses reclaims the nation as the property of women and women's liberation. The state may be the political form imagined by the Declaration, but Bread and Roses follows Stanton and Goldman by pushing against a unified image of the People. They balance nascent debates between liberalism and separatism—that is, between the collective and the particular—by using the nation as a framework to address internal division. Within their list of self-evident truths, Bread and Roses's re-vision confers the right of dissent "whenever any form of government becomes destructive to the liberty of a sufficiently large group of people, be they a race, class, political group, or sex" (45). If the original Declaration imagined a newly independent People in rather homogeneous terms, Bread and Roses underscores divisions where factional lines become fault lines. Identitarian lines of social division are now self-evident truths housed within a People, along with the rights afforded to them by the state. The dormant dividing lines are always present; they are activated when a segment is rendered unequal by socialization.

Imagining a heterogeneous nation allows Bread and Roses to address division within a universalist project. Contrary to the original Declaration's argument for independence of one nation from another, Bread and Roses's re-vision imagines a totally reinvented society:

> Women must be able to participate in the economy on the basis of equality with men. We believe that the nature of work in our system is demeaning to human beings, and we do not want merely to upgrade women into the alienated jobs that men now hold. However, we refuse to do the low-grade, low-paid, and service work any more. Such jobs must be shared by men and women. (45)

By inhabiting a "we" that encompasses both men and women, while also addressing cemented hierarchies within that group, Bread and Roses reinvests the national "we" with a Marxist platform for economic change as well as a truly equitable collective that recognizes, not quashes, division and difference. The gendered division of labor is a defining issue in women's liberation, and many groups focused specifically on the unpaid labor of domestic work. For instance, the National Organization for Women (NOW) included a demand for child day care centers in their founding Bill of Rights (1967) and a 1969 leaflet by The Feminists explained legal assumptions embedded in marriage and noted, "According to the marriage contract, your husband is entitled to more household services from you then he would be from a live-in maid. So why aren't you getting paid?"[93] In a particularly fun pamphlet, The Campaign for Wages for Housework declared, "The women of the world are serving notice. We clean your homes and factories. We raise the next generation of workers for you. . . . Now we want back the wealth we have produced. WE WANT IT IN CASH, RETROACTIVE AND IMMEDIATELY. AND WE WANT ALL OF IT."[94] By packaging the critique of the unpaid or underpaid economy of women's labor within the authoritative form of the Declaration, Bread and Roses articulates a national program that would benefit all citizens by escaping an alienating labor system that also oppresses male citizens. By speaking as stateswomen, they place women and women's concerns at the center of how and why a nation forms.

The re-vision's insistence on factions corresponds to Bread and Roses's own genesis out of a complex matrix of competing political philosophies and interests within and outside women's liberation. Bread and Roses is among many important national groups that achieved prominence in women's liberation. Bread and Roses was founded in Boston in the summer of 1969 by Meredith Tax, now with Women's World, a global literacy and anti-censorship project, and Linda Gordon, now a feminist historian at New York University. Bread and Roses eventually represented the socialist faction of the movement, and regarded the U.S. nation-state with postures ranging from deep skepticism to outright hostility. While liberal feminism sought inclusion in reformed, but ultimately intact, government institutions, Bread and Roses fostered women's solidarity across political boundaries and they modeled their work on Marxist or socialist efforts to organize the workers of the world. In a social and archival history, Wini Breines explains that Bread and Roses organized female liberation activities in response to "women's subordinate positions in [the new left and SNCC] and men's disdain and arrogance in the face of women's concerns."[95] In her foundational study of women's liberation, Alice Echols describes the group as "politico in orientation,"[96] which can be seen as a response to separatist-oriented female liberation group Boston's Cell 16's initial rejection of Tax and Gordon.[97] In response, Bread and Roses named themselves after a famous 1912 strike by women in Lawrence, Massachusetts, and created a purposefully loose-knit network of small collectives and consciousness-raising groups. Each subgroup, or cell, engaged in its own activities, such as anti-war demonstrations, educational sessions, and various "zap" actions.[98] Bread and Roses lasted until 1973, at which time the currency of politico hardliners generally gave way to a more disparate set of analyses of women's culture and oppression.

Since the Declaration of Independence establishes a new People against the repeated generic pronoun "He," the format lends itself quite easily to a radical feminist position on the primacy of women's oppression. New York Radical Women takes this position and baldly declares in their principles, "We take the woman's side in everything."[99] But Bread and Roses uses the Declaration's formal structure of a grievance list in a way that does not fall easily along preexisting social lines. In effect, they are able to address division and document injustice, yet still articulate a universalist aspiration. The list of grievances, which was so important in making a case for independence from "He," is amenable to the conventions of manifestos, action items, and issue-based position statements so familiar to grassroots political organizing. In their re-vision, Bread and Roses groups their list of grievances into four sections: "The Economy," "Control of Our Bodies," "The Family," and "Education and Culture." Each section describes how women's potentials are undermined, lists specific affronts and alternatives, and forwards an implicit philosophy of equality within a reinvented society. For instance, in "The Family" section, Bread and Roses declares, "The family unit should not be seen as the only economically and socially acceptable unit of society. . . . Any number of adults should be able to make legal contracts between themselves, other than marriage ceremonies, that will concern mutual responsibilities for each other and for children" (46–47). Bread and Roses is at great pains to identify alternative models open to the different groups, both within a sisterhood and within a nation. The image of mutuality described by the re-vision balances the liberal individualism of the original with women's liberation social critiques of women's group oppression.

By moving among the factions they address and the political philosophies they tap, Bread and Roses uses the Declaration's flexible "we" to keep women at the center of their universalist project. They declare, "Women should be able to control their own bodies, to have children if and why they want to, and to refrain from having children if they want to. . . . While we think population control is essential, it must not be substituted for a sharing of the world's resources between rich and poor countries" (46). The re-vision moves among universalist statements of equality, documentation of specific practices of oppression, and particular subject positions. As they argue for an end to eugenics programs, Bread and Roses offers an alternative for how to reproduce an equitable society for all with women's choice at the center. Further, the re-vision itself rallies women to come together to make real the society described by the document.

Bread and Roses do not limit their reimagined society to the preexisting nation-state; instead, they imagine a transnational collective based in international cooperation. They imagine a transnational sisterhood: "The educational system and the media in our country perpetuate undemocratic myths about the nature of women, working people, and black, brown, red and yellow people. They also deny these groups any knowledge of their own history" (47). Always within a transnational frame, Bread and Roses attends to their particular positions within the United States by recognizing the distinction between "our country" and "their own history." Baxandall and Gordon explain that the re-vision appeared as a leaflet for a 1970 International Women's Day demonstration.[100] It is tempting to read this potential incongruence between nationalism and internationalism as testimony to Bread and

Roses's inability to appreciate fully the demands of what Breines identifies as "a kind of 'third worldism' [that] characterized the politics of many late sixties white radicals."[101] Breines explains that Bread and Roses members undeniably "embraced antiracist politics. They were acutely self-conscious of their own status, primarily white, educated, and middle class and attempted to develop programs and strategies that included and recognized difference, particularly by addressing the difficulties facing poor women and women of color."[102] However, Breines contends, Bread and Roses was consciously grounded in a personal politics that kept their own experiences at the center and sometimes risked uncritically endorsing third-world freedom fighters and residing in white guilt.[103] Breines's reflective analysis demonstrates how we can account for seeming contradictions between women's liberation thought and action. Nonetheless, to understand fully how a founding document of the fiercest imperial power on the globe can participate in international women's solidarity, it is important to place the re-vision in the long tradition of rewriting the Declaration that simultaneously claims and critiques the authority of the original.

Besides Goldman, Bread and Roses is not alone in framing the Declaration as viable for an international vision of collectivity. Recent cultural studies look at how the Declaration stakes out a transnational jurisdiction beyond the newly formed United States. David Armitage traces how the Declaration relates to and participates in international legal structures and customs. Pramod Mishra traces ethnic Americans' relationships to both the United States and their countries of origin by arguing that the Declaration is best seen as a transnational document that links Lockian philosophy of governing by consent under natural law and Newtonian principles of universalism, which is a liberal secularism borne out of Locke's travels between crown and colonies. The result of this "transatlantic colonial transaction" of "the contradictory impulses of nationalist and cosmopolitan aspirations"[104] is an uneasy alliance between human rights and the nation-state, which could be applied to those not included in practice: namely, slaves and Indians. Many groups—from academic to bureaucratic to activist—write Declarations of *Inter*dependence to embrace an ethic of connectivity across political boundaries. With these transnational approaches, we can appreciate how and why an internationalist feminist group such as Bread and Roses would choose to employ a tool of the nation-state—a document mired in exclusionary patriotism and nationalism—for a project of global sisterhood.

Bread and Roses's "Declaration of Women's Independence" joins longstanding efforts to reimagine a society better able to live up to its promises. In the feminist debates and backlash of the 1980s, much of the promise and hope of women's liberation has been forgotten or obscured in favor of a rather caricatured version of the movement and its project of sisterhood. Dominant versions of women's liberation might pit sisterhood and the nation-state against one another. In their documentary history, Baxandall and Gordon explain that some of the distortion of women's liberation in the contemporary imaginary is a result of the ephemeral nature of the movement's print culture.[105] In a note on the texts, many undated and unsigned, Baxandall and Gordon explain that the lack of dates and names is "typical of many women's liberation leaflets and posters that were intended for immediate circulation and without self-consciousness about the historical importance of what was being created"[106] Further, liberal feminists and organizations were "more centralized, less outrageous, more focused"[107] than women's liberation. If liberal feminism, such as organizations like NOW and leaders like Gloria Steinem and Betty Friedan, "kept better records,"[108] women's liberation was often "hostile to the idea of intellectual private property"[109] in its more radical or leftist roots. Bread and Roses explicitly distrusted authoritarianism and devised organizational structures that would not reproduce it.[110] Many veteran activists and feminist historians point to this self-imposed "tyranny of structurelessness"[111] to explain the overdue need for archival projects. In my approach, the culture of semi-anonymous authorship is valuable because it fits neatly with the Declaration of Independence, and the protest essayist's stance as representative, not personal, speaker.

A FEMINIST "WE" IN DECLARATIONS OF INDEPENDENCE

Like the Oath of Citizenship discussed in the introduction, the Declaration creates a collective "we" by cleaving to and separating from another group—hence the paradox of the most sacred political document announcing inclusion and equality based in separation and departure. Paradoxes abound within the document, and more pressingly in its ascendance to national ideologies of inclusion amid conspicuous practices of exclusion. That is why so many social movements find traction by unveiling the hypocrisy between state words and deeds. Indeed, in *Declarations of Independence*, populist historian Howard Zinn suggests that hypocrisy is written into the founding document because it addresses the inherent conflict between the government and the governed.[112] Which is to say that citizenship (membership in a bounded polity) carries the potential for hypocrisy between thought and action, even in the classical sense as outlined famously by J. G. A. Pocock: citizenship in classical Greece held that "the citizen is one who both rules and is ruled."[113] Zinn goes so far as to suggest that the Declaration adorning school walls across the country while foreign wars belie its every claims is "more deceptive than [Machiavelli's]."[114] But even under such scrutiny, Zinn's project—not to mention his title—siphons legitimacy from the document he cross-examines. Like Zinn, generations of American social movements recognize the power of founding documents.

So, perhaps the re-visions of the Declaration are attempts to live up to Pocock's classical Greek ideal of reciprocal rule.

Stanton, Goldman, and Bread and Roses participate in an important feminist tradition of re-vising the Declaration to correct the failings of the original to enshrine women's rights. In doing so, they draw on the simultaneously flexible and authoritative national "we" to claim the authority of the state for their respective social movements and to articulate a collective vision that might deliver on the original's promises. Feminist, abolitionist, and other progressive social movements are not alone in using the literary strategy of inhabiting founding documents. For instance, in the aftermath of the Civil War, right-wing individualist Lysander Spooner expressed opposition to the newly reconstructed union not by re-vising, but by debating the U.S. Constitution. In his 1867 pamphlet called "Treason, No. II., The Constitution," Spooner places the first lines of the Constitution in an epigraph and he opens, "The meaning of this is simply: We, the people of the United States, *acting freely and voluntarily as individuals, consent and agree* that we will cooperate with each other in sustaining such a government as is provided for in this Constitution. The necessity for the consent of 'the people' is implied in this declaration."[115] Unlike in the feminist tradition I outline, Spooner substitutes and erases the founding document's inclusive pronouncements to "form a more perfect union, establish justice, insure domestic tranquility, provide for common defence, promote the general welfare, and secure the blessings of liberty to ourselves and our posterity."[116] So, his re-vision of the national *we* serves a procedural critique about states' rights, not a collective vision. Spooner's response to the idea of "the people" is one of disdain for collectivity itself. Spooner shrugs off the national *we* as an impossible idea, rather than an authoritative location to enshrine rights and generate a collective sense of identity. Whereas the feminist re-visions access inclusive visions through particular subject positions, Spooner removes himself from that collective space. He does not inhabit the form, he implodes it so that it cannot withstand a post-secessionist critique.

It is important to look to other refutations of the document in order to underscore what these three re-visions gain for their respective waves of feminism: attention to the rights of the excluded under the authoritative banner of inclusion. Even in the most skeptical re-visions such as Goldman's anarchist distrust of patriotism, the living *we* in the Declaration—and the lofty pronouncements of inclusion in other national narratives—provides a vision beyond cynicism of how to generate substantive union. If Huberman is right that the spirit and practice of the original Declaration separate the nation from the very people that compose it, it is important to note that the *letter* of the founding documents provides a space for future writers and movements to reclaim the document for their own ends. The act of re-vising founding documents whose practices the writer protests risks charges that, in the famous words of Audre Lorde, "the master's tools will never dismantle the master's house."[117] But the re-visions embed within themselves an argument that the founding ideals, if not national practice, belong to the speakers and those for whom they speak. Or, responding to Lorde's dictum, the re-visions claim the documents as their own so that the house never belonged to the master in the first place. Foner characterizes alternative Declarations as seeking to finish the unfinished work of the original, a move that possibly cedes propriety over the original. In these feminist re-visions, we see speakers reviving both the substance and hope of the utterance "we the people."

Chapter Three

THE ADDRESSED AND THE REDRESSED: HELEN HUNT JACKSON'S PROTEST ESSAY AND THE PROTEST NOVEL TRADITION

> It makes little difference, however, where one opens the record of the history of the Indians; every page and every year has its dark stain.
>
> —Helen Hunt Jackson, *A Century of Dishonor*, 1881

> I persist in the simple view that all art is ultimately social: that which agitates and that which prepares the mind for slumber. The writer is deceived who thinks that he has some other choice. The question is not whether one will make a social statement in one's work—but only *what* the statement will say, for if it says anything at all, it will be social.
>
> —Lorraine Hansberry, "The Negro Writer and His Roots," 1959

In 1959, Lorraine Hansberry delivered a manifesto of socially conscious writing that responds to the political demands long placed upon the Negro writer. As the celebrated author of *A Raisin in the Sun* (1959), Hansberry insisted that writers have no choice but to recognize the social implications of their work, which countered some of the dominant literary sensibilities of the day. Writers who accept Hansberry's declaration that all art is social retain the choice of *which* formal tradition best fits their projects. The contested partition between literature and political advocacy in American culture traverses periods, genres, ideologies, and critical schools, and it comes to a head in the protest essay tradition. When accomplished novelists or poets venture into the territory of socially conscious essays and cash in their celebrity in service of social movements, they risk rejection by both literary and political circles. Warring factions in critical and creative circles often debate the merits of writers identified with social movements in a zero-sum competition between literature and politics, between mere policy wonks and artists. The dilemma of the protest essay—underscoring social division threatens the overarching desire to come together—points to tensions between the ineffably literary and the directly political, especially when American writers take seriously the project of representative democracy. In this chapter, I further examine the possibilities and limits of the protest essay to simultaneously claim and critique the inclusive pronouncements of the state. To do so, I compare the form and influence of a protest essay that was also translated into its more famous cousin genre, the protest novel.

In 1881, Helen Hunt Jackson published her protest essay *A Century of Dishonor* in order to chronicle—in overwhelming detail—the already long history of U.S. violence and duplicity toward American Indians, and to appeal for state-sponsored justice in a technique similar to the feminist revisions of the Declaration of Independence. The noteworthiness of her act lay not only in the argument of the essay itself but also in her choice to publish under her own name. Before then, Jackson had established herself as a popular poet and novelist by publishing pseudonymously or under the initials H. H.[1] It was the protest essay, not the novel or poetry, through which Jackson constructed her public voice and political authority. Evoking the legacy of Samson Occom, Jackson engages a political issue and print public by speaking out for persons who lacked full membership in the American polity, but whose destinies and everyday lives were shaped profoundly by the expanding American nation. Jackson's act to publish her appeal became doubly audacious when she sent a copy to each of those whose hands she claimed were most bloodstained: members of the 1880 U.S. Congress.

Protest writing is often viewed as a diversion from, or even perversion of, purer forms of literature. In this vein, the protest mode sullies genres like the novel because it aspires to political immediacy and addresses specific citizens and experiences within a form that seeks to overcome the particular. But when novels are translations of protest essays, we can measure varying generic abilities to address division and engage a citizenry. Jackson's best-selling fiction can in part be understood as novelistic translations of her proximate work in the protest essay. This case study of the American protest essay registers how a white author writing about racial exclusion uses her claims to U.S. citizenship when her civic authority itself is in question following gendered doctrines of the public/private split. When Jackson protests the displacement, genocide, and legal trickery of U.S.–American Indian relations, she must justify her ability to do so in a public venue like the essay. When the essay, rather than the novel, is at the center of a literary protest tradition, we can better attend to Jackson's highly stylized and politically complex means by which she draws upon her relatively privileged but contingent claims to state authority. In the essay, authors are best able to inhabit the dual role prescribed by the protest mode: writer and citizen, subject and spokesperson.

TAKING THE STATE'S WORDS AT FACE VALUE: JACKSON'S STRATEGY OF SHAME

> To write in full the history of any one of these Indian communities, of its forced migrations, wares, and miseries, would fill a volume by itself. . . . All this [history] I have been forced to leave untouched, in strict adherence to my object, which has been simply to show our causes for national shame in the matter of our treatment of the Indians. It is a shame which the American nation ought not to lie under, for the American people, as a people, are not at heart unjust.
>
> —Helen Hunt Jackson, Author's Note to *A Century of Dishonor*

Jackson enters the realm of public protest through the essay. Chapter 1 argues that the awareness of and ability to address divided audiences is the hallmark of the American protest essay. Further, protest essayists draw on the authoritative words of the nation as citizens—either full, partial, or second-class—because they have formal legal status to make official claims on the state. The case of Jackson, a nineteenth-century New England woman writer newly outraged after a tour of the Southwest, illustrates the importance of the state in the protest essay. Upon her return in 1881, Jackson published a diatribe against shameful U.S. treatment of American Indians in a book-length essay. With earnest belief in state promises—combined with a journalistic fervor for a detail-heavy picture of U.S.–Indian relations—Jackson demands that the United States live up to its own grand narratives of equality. In the opening essay, Jackson delineates contradictions between practice and political principles of national sovereignty, natural rights principles of a "right of occupancy," and legal and moral principles of enforcing already written treaties under U.S. law. Nine further essay-chapters tell illustrative stories of displacement, occupation, broken treaties, and massacres of various Indian tribes. Jackson presents neither a consistent plan for honorable action, nor a coherent political theory. Instead, she demands that the United States figure out how to break its history of "cheating, robbing, breaking of promises" (342) and live up to its word. Jackson is aware of a failed Indian Reform tradition to capture not just the hearts, but the political will, of those in power. Jackson presents her voice as a witness who must not go unheard: "There are hundreds of pages of unimpeachable testimony on the side of the Indian; but it goes for nothing, is set down as sentimentalism or partisanship, tossed aside and forgotten" (338). Though she rejects immediate full citizenship for Indians as a "grotesque" (340) solution, Jackson applies the mythic words of the state to those outside territorial national boundaries when she protests "the refusal of the protection of the laws to the Indians' rights of property, 'of life, liberty, and the pursuit of happiness'" (342).

In response to the perceived failure of *Century* to deliver immediate justice to American Indians, Jackson translated her political tract into fictional form in the 1884 best-selling novel *Ramona*. In the novel, Ramona leaves the comfortable mestiza ranch of her adoptive mother Señora Moreno and flees westward with her Indian lover Alessandro, whose village has been plundered by white settlers. In a personal letter, Jackson worried that her essay failed because "it has tried to attack the people's conscience directly,"[2] a charge that Michael Dorris replicates a century later declaring *Century* "unimpressive either as history or as literature" and ultimately inferior to *Ramona*'s "propaganda."[3] Jackson explains that she translated the essay into the novel in the form of a sugared pill, "and it remains to be seen if it will go down."[4] Valerie Sherer Mathes notes, however, "*Ramona* was in print only ten months before [Jackson] died. Since its initial publication by Roberts Brothers in November 1884, however, it has gone through numerous stage and screen versions as well as a score of books written by authors claiming to have discovered the real Ramona, or the real Alessandra, or the real rancho where the story took place."[5] Mathes notes that in literary studies the novel has had more impact in terms of its love story than in terms of its protest designs or reform legacy, so much so that many readers journeyed to California to find the "real" Ramona, not to find justice.

Jackson wrote the novel after her essay did not spark immediate federal reforms. In the meantime, she had been appointed by the Department of the Interior to visit the Mission Indians in California and her understanding of the plight of Indians deepened. Jackson envisioned direct political change arising from her protest novel, even though the protest essay had failed to do so. In a letter to Thomas Bailey Aldrich, Jackson explained, "If I could write a story that would do for the Indian a thousandth part what *Uncle Tom's Cabin* did for the Negro, I would be thankful the rest of my life."[6] At the time, American Indian justice was understood through the history of African Americans and abolition. First in her essay then her novel, Jackson sought to recapture the reformist energies of a previous generation when a woman's sentimental novels could participate directly in national social movements. In her influential reclamation of Stowe's novel, Jane Tompkins argues that "the enormous popularity of these novels, which has been cause for suspicion bordering on disgust, is a reason for paying close attention to them."[7] But I consider the less popular essay form over the sentimental novel. Tompkins describes the protest novel "as a political enterprise, halfway between sermon and social theory, that both codifies and attempts to mold the values of its time."[8] But in her protest essay, Jackson deliberately invokes confusion between the moral and the political by underscoring the basic incoherence and duplicity in the congressional record on American Indians.

Ramona, too, failed to foment direct political change, either in public policy or national sentiment. At the center of the novel's failure lies the question of protest: its appropriate form and the curious space of a writer who seeks redress for those about whom she is writing (American Indians) from those she is addressing (U.S. citizens, Congress). In the novel, Jackson projects the history of systematic displacements, massacre, and forced assimilation through the prism of a miscegenation plot. In the climax to the Reconstruction romance between an Indian and a white New England woman, Ramona discovers a "taint of Indian blood"[9] in her veins. Mathes describes the novel's reception as overwhelmingly missing Jackson's reformist goals: "Jackson failed to create a sympathetic feeling for the Indians among many of her readers, who instead saw only a tender love story."[10] Mathes points to the March 1885 issue of *Overland Monthly*, which "noted that more poet than reformer emerged. It possessed 'no burning appeal, no crushing arraignment, no such book as *Uncle Tom's Cabin.*'"[11] Many of the dismissals of Jackson's novel, not surprisingly, attack on the basis of genre: a woman's novel engaged in political protest inappropriately violates the gendered divide between sentimental authorship and civic participation. Sara Hubbard, writing for *Dial* in 1885 lamented, "Helen Hunt's exuberant fancy and passionate feeling were of splendid service in the realms of poesy and fiction, but proved the worst hindrances when she tried to work in the domain of fact."[12] Jackson was very disappointed in the dismissal of her novel's reformist impulse in favor of the romance story. She wrote to her friend Charles Dudley Warner in 1884, "but nobody except you, & and the N.Y. Tribune critic has seemed to care a straw for the Indian history in it."[13]

If after *Ramona* the reader's attention was directed *away* from Congress in Washington, D.C., and *toward* the newly colonized land of California, I argue that this response is partly a product of genre. Before *Ramona*, Jackson uses the protest essay to stage her first foray into publishing under her own name, and the essay allows Jackson to seek redress from an appropriate source: Congress. The protest essay is able to confer authority to a nineteenth-century New England woman so that she can cash in on her greater, albeit *partial*, access to citizenship and state power on behalf of those who are overwritten by state institutions, which at the time formally excluded American Indians from citizenship. Scholars often look at the phenomenon of visitors to California searching for the "real" Ramona, thereby sparking an industry of Ramona tourism and Ramona-brand commodities.[14] The critics—and Jackson herself—roundly disparage the Ramona tourism industry as a distraction from the actual plight of American Indians. But I suggest that the protest novel *invites* readers to move beyond their white privilege and sympathize with the benevolent American Indian protagonists, which can manifest as the search for the "real" Ramona. The protest essay, on the other hand, requires readers to *employ* their citizenship to petition the U.S. Congress for justice on behalf of American Indians who lack this formal status.

> *Refer in reply to the following*
>
> ## Department of the Interior,
>
> OFFICE OF INDIAN AFFAIRS,
>
> *Washington,* October 16, , *188* 2.
>
> Mrs. Helen Jackson,
>
>   Madam:
>
>   Your letter of the 16th September, to the Honorable Secretary of the Interior, has been this day handed me for reply. The work of selecting a permanent home for the Mission Indians of California, in which you propose to engage, is one of very great importance, and I doubt not under your management, will be productive of very beneficial results not only to the Government, but also and particularly, to a very deserving and heretofore much neglected tribe of Indians. The only difficult question to be decided before answering your letter was, as to how the funds could be provided with which to pay the necessary expenses. You have very generously proposed to give your time to this work, free of charge, and only ask that your expenses, estimated at about $1200, should be paid.
>
>   Congress leaves the Indian Office without adequate means to meet this class of expenditures, but I am now able to say to you that the funds will be furnished you as required, as also for

FIGURE 3

Letter from H. Price, Commissioner of Indian Affairs to Helen Hunt Jackson, dated October 16, 1882, regarding her offer to work on behalf of the Mission Indians of California to secure a permanent home. The final paragraph reads, "I therefore express the earnest hope that your self-imposed and praise-worthy efforts may result in the adoption of some measures for their permanent benefit."

Special Collections, Tutt Library, Colorado College, Colorado Springs, Colorado.

> the expenses of Mr. Kinney, whom you propose to associate with you in this good work. The promptings of humanity, as well as a sense of justice demand that these Indians should be placed in a position where the fruits of their labor will be for their own benefit, and where unprincipled white men cannot in the future, as in the past, deprive them of what is justly their own.
>
> These unfortunate people, once the owners of 365,000 head of horses, cattle and sheep, and harvesting 75,000 bushels of grain in one year, have, in the last half century, been driven from place to place, the victims of unscrupulous adventurers, and seem destined to become homeless wanderers and vagabonds unless the strong arm of the Government is interposed for their relief and protection.
>
> The attention of Congress has repeatedly been called to the condition of these Indians, but up to this time no decisive action has been taken for their relief.
>
> I therefore express the earnest hope that your self-imposed and praise-worthy efforts may result in the adoption of some measures for their permanent benefit.
>
> Very respectfully,
>
> H. Price
> COMMISSIONER

Instead of privileging her fiction, I suggest that we look at Jackson's protest essay on its own. We must avoid the temptation to read Jackson's essay solely as a proto version of a more fully realized novel. Kate Phillips, for instance, describes *Ramona* as a "masked" version of the essay's didactic jeremiad.[15] Rather than read the direct government appeal as an "unmasked" or more pure version of Jackson's reform, it is important to attend to the way the essay shapes Jackson's protesting voice. In the protest essay, Jackson is best able to situate her speaking position in relation to the addressed (the Unites States) and the redressed (American Indians). Along with scrupulously documenting injustices committed against specific groups, Jackson exhaustively cites previous statutes, treaties, laws, and U.S. policies of "the great discovering Powers" to argue for recognition of American Indians' "right of occupancy" (10). More so than the protest novel, there is a specifically addressed audience in the essay. Jackson draws upon her legal ability as a partial citizen to make claims on the state as she cites the words of recognized political experts, and directly quotes the sovereign power: Congress. For instance, Jackson cites an act passed by the California State Legislature in 1850 that requires the white owners of land occupied by American Indians to "permit such Indians to peaceably reside on such lands unmolested" (513–14). Jackson notes that this act was never enforced.

Jackson's protest essay is no less confused about nationhood, whiteness, and justice than the Reconstruction Romance in *Ramona* in which justice filters through the trope of a racially mixed heroine. On one hand, Jackson argues for the autonomy or sovereignty of American Indians, but, on the other, she never argues that their "right to occupancy" necessitates the *withdrawal* of U.S. occupancy. The argument presents a tension between American Indians as distinct noncitizens incorporated by U.S. boundaries and simultaneously as peoples inscribed by U.S. judicial and legislative bodies. In her essay's diatribe against the endless cycle of broken treaties, displacement, and rewritten rules that constitute U.S.–American Indian relations, Jackson explicitly calls for the application of state definitions of justice:

> The question of the honorableness of the United States' dealings with the Indians turns largely on a much disputed and little understood point. What was the nature of the Indians' right to the country in which they were living when the continent of North America was discovered? Between the theory of some sentimentalists that the Indians were the real owners of the soil, and the theory of some politicians that they had no right of ownership whatever in it, there are innumerable grades and confusions of opinion. (9)

In order to seek redress, Jackson claims the very source of national honor that she protests. Jackson's solution is to locate and enforce an already written treaty, and to justify such enforcement through the public words of statesmen.

Jackson's project necessitated not only a practical solution but also a means of rekindling the thrust toward national reform from a generation earlier during Reconstruction. That is, it required both a change in public policy and a reinvented national vision. Because of her work on behalf of American Indians, Mathes places Jackson in a reformist history: "Although *A Century of Dishonor* did not immediately become a bestseller and did not bring about an improvement in Indian affairs, it did lay the groundwork for Jackson's next Indian crusade, that of the Mission Indians of Southern California. . . . This work would prove to be her most lasting legacy."[16] But such gains were not the direct and sweeping federal reform sought by Jackson. Fourteen years before

Jackson's crusade, Thomas Wentworth Higginson announced the end of an era in U.S. history when social problems could explode America's stable national boundaries and ideologies. In an 1867 essay, Higginson insists, "We seem nearly at an end of those great public wrongs which require a special moral earthquake to end them."[17] For Higginson, the national conscience now resided in a palliative fantasy of a nation healed. In his seminal work on nationness, Benedict Anderson observes that the nation is imagined as limited, sovereign, and as a community.[18] Jackson's argument requires the nation to reopen wounds to reform inconsistencies between just pronouncements and unjust practices, and thereby Jackson jeopardizes the integrity of the American nation in a post-Reconstruction age.

Considering the unwelcome reception of Jackson's essay, Higginson's assertion seems vindicated. In one telling review of *Century* published in *The Nation*, the reviewer concludes that even "the warmest sympathizer" would realize the necessity of European and American paternalism and would "repudiate" the "red man's" right to "possession of this continent."[19] According to the reviewer, Jackson's work was dangerously factionalizing because it promoted "disunion" and represented simply "an obstacle to the fair trial of Mr. Schurz's plan" to civilize the Indians.[20] In his introduction to the 1885 edition, Julius H. Seelye remarks, "It will be admitted now on every hand that the only solution of the Indian problem involves the entire change of these people from a savage to a civilized life."[21] In the reception of *Century*, Jackson's confused opening of ideological and geographic borders to incorporate autonomous not-Americans within state-sponsored systems of justice proved untenable for her readers. Jackson's effort to extend honorable nationalist practice to those beyond state boundaries—citizenship was not conferred on all American Indians until 1924—ran counter to the post-Reconstruction soldering of national factions. As a result, reviewers tended to either cite the inevitability of the displacement of American Indians or argue for total assimilation.

THE PROTEST NOVEL AND THE LITERARY DEMANDS OF POLITICAL ADVOCACY

Any study of the American protest essay must address the very familiar, often best-selling, and thoroughly established protest novel tradition. Well beyond Jackson, when American writers seek or accept the task of speaking on behalf of a social movement or cause, they turn to the protest novel as much as the essay. In doing so, they speak as political advocates within a literary form that might resist direct political action and representation. As Jerry Ward explains, protest novelists purposefully cross the "minefields" and "boundaries" between art and sociology.[22] As many protest writers find, to make claims on the state as a citizen does not necessarily align with the demands of writing or reading a protest novel.

A very cursory overview of the U.S. protest novel tradition is necessary to understand the terrain in which the protest essay finds itself, and the literary grounds on which Jackson poses her voice for justice. Very generally, the American protest novel became a full-fledged national form with Stowe's abolitionist novel *Uncle Tom's Cabin; Or, Life Among the Lowly* (1853). More than any other early protest novel, Stowe's characters—including most notably Uncle Tom, Aunt Chloe, Topsy, Eliza and George, Little Eva, and Simon Legree—indelibly mark the American and literary imagination, whether celebrated as instructive social archetypes, vilified as racist tropes, or dismissed as naïve caricatures ill-suited for the task of protesting social exclusion and injustice. After Stowe and Reconstruction, the protest novel entered an age of social realism when authors like Upton Sinclair and John Steinbeck charted the social experience of economic systems operating in America, often writing fiction and journalism in tandem.[23] The tendency to translate protest essays into novel form persists. For example, Thomas Pynchon studied the Watts riots for the *New York Times Magazine* in 1966, which Jeffrey Louis Decker suggests is an analog for the postmodern novel *The Crying of Lot 49* (1965).[24] It may be surprising to some that Pynchon published a novel that is seen as a signal text for postmodernism while on journalistic assignment in Watts in the aftermath of some of the worst urban riots of the century.[25] These sorts of examples provide excellent opportunities to query the relationship between the fictive and the journalistic,[26] and between the protest novel and the protest essay.

Appraisals of the protest novel, by both writers and literary critics, are as contentious about categories of race, class, gender, nationality, and so on, and definitions of the literary as are the novels themselves. After Stowe's novel, backlashes against literary interventions into political affairs were common. These backlashes were not solely a reaction against women entering the public, but also against the idea of author-advocates. Modernism, in this vein, can be understood as a response that carves out a space for literature as a separate, oppositional space in which writers offer readers a means out of the immediate, or the narrowly political. This runs counter to the protest novel's designs, which imagine a direct relationship between the literary and immediate publics so that readers seek redress within real political systems that delve out injustice to fictional characters in novels. Subsequent literary debates weighed aesthetic experimentalism over more earnestly representative modes, especially as postmodern sensibilities became increasingly averse to the social realism of earlier protest fiction.

In the twentieth century, the protest novel is most associated with African American literature. At the beginning of the twentieth century, African American artists increasingly addressed a black audience and constructed identifiably black literary traditions, especially in response to an earlier era of obeying the rules of a white-defined and -dominated literary tradition. For instance,

Harlem Renaissance thinker James Weldon Johnson considered the limits of token black writers in white literary histories, such as Phyllis Wheatley, who, in his reading, adopted white genres and addressed an exclusively white audience. For Johnson, every African American writer faces the dilemma of addressing a racially divided audience. He asks pressingly, "To whom shall he address himself, to his own black group or to white America? Many a Negro writer has fallen down, between these two stools."[27] The challenge for Johnson, or any protest writer, is how to address division without reinscribing it. That same year, Wallace Thurman proscribed a specifically masculinist stance in order to avoid kowtowing to a white readership. As for Wheatly, Thurman argues, "Heretofore, every commentator, whether white or black, when speaking of Phillis Wheatley, has sought to make excuses for her bad poetry.... Although Negro poets objected to the mistreatment of their people, they did not formulate these objections in strong, biting language, but rather sought sympathy and pled for pity. They wept copiously but seldom manifested a fighting spirit."[28] In response, Richard Wright offered Bigger Thomas, a black everyman figure driven to murder (of two women: young white heiress Mary Dalton and his poor black girlfriend Bessie) and to flight by systems of racial exclusion and second-class citizenship in *Native Son* (1940). Chester Himes, especially in *If He Hollers Let Him Go* (1945), further moved the protest novel out of a sentimental tradition toward manly defiance. Hilton Als argues that Himes distanced his writing from the "sensitive men choking on their own alienation" of Wright and Baldwin by depicting "unapologetic and testosterone-driven" urban males who trumpet their marginalization because they do "not depend on the white world for validation."[29] Not unlike Jackson, Himes also turned to the essay while writing protest novels, especially in "Negro Martyrs Are Needed" (1943), which calls for black revolution from the pages of *Crisis* magazine.

In 1937, Wright famously decreed the protest novel *the* appropriate vehicle of African American literature in his proscriptive "Blueprint for Negro Writing," which criticizes black writers who go "a-begging to white America."[30] In that famous essay, Wright rejects the often ambivalent stances of Harlem Renaissance writers, and Zora Hurston's "Negro minstrelsy" in particular.[31] In 1949, Baldwin notoriously dismissed the novels of Wright and Stowe in one wide—and astute—characterization of "Everybody's Protest Novel." According to Baldwin, the protest novel lacks vision because the form can only reflect—and therefore reinscribe—social fantasies of race, sex, and class.[32] Throughout the 1960s, literary critics responded to Wright's call and Baldwin's warning by highlighting the literary merit of works that were otherwise read for sociological insights. For example, David Britt argued in the inaugural pages of the *Negro American Literature Forum*, "Protest fiction is a legitimate, if exhausted, category of American literature" whose literariness resists mere sociological portraiture.[33] As is evident in

Jackson's reception, criticism of the protest novel must always wrestle with the relation between the literary and the social.

By the mid-twentieth century, the protest novel was a vibrant tradition within most historically disenfranchised groups. The protest novel sat at a nodal point between the universal and the particular, the literary and the social, and between artistry beholden to none and earnest political advocacy. When a protest novel fell too far into the latter categories, it risked dismissal as artistically wanting. Critics categorized overly accessible protest fiction as the "the novel of outrage"[34] or "holler books."[35] If the sensationalism and stereotypes of protest fiction were seen as only appropriate for a sociological purpose before 1949, writers after Baldwin's essay attempted to escape the genre entirely so as not to be, as Pearl K. Bell described the problem, "manacled to the racial shibboleths of the 'protest novel.'"[36] The 1960s renaissance in ethnic literatures arose at this time of simultaneous distrust and recognition of the social import of protest fiction. For Bell, writers like Baldwin or Philip Roth did not "set out be 'ethnic writer[s],' but both were forced into pigeonholes by the anger their work aroused among their own kind."[37] The protest novel also moved into more autobiographical terrain, especially following the overlap between Wright's novel and his autobiography *Black Boy* (1945). Other writers also moved easily between the protest novel and autobiography, such as in Piri Thomas's memoir of Puerto Rican experience *Down These Mean Streets* (1967). Following the rise in popularity of writer-advocates, the 1960s witnessed a peak in literary figures sharing platforms with religious and political leaders, as evidenced by the popular 1960s triumvirate of Baldwin, Malcolm, and Martin during the Civil Rights movement.[38]

As they address current social divisions, protest novels and novelists also tend to look back at earlier literary and social traditions, especially by claiming the importance of speaking from the voices and experiences of marginalized groups. For instance, following dismissals of Baldwin's integration stance, Ishmael Reed strikes a pose of black self-determination to refuse the assimilationist stances of Stowe's characters in his parodic novel *Flight to Canada* (1976), which directly dismantles American visions of progress. Reed further imposed masculinist designs on the protest novel with his antifeminist *Reckless Eyeballing* (1986) in which the lynched body of an Emmett Till character is exhumed for posthumous trial by his white female accusers. In the wake of pervasive suspicion and grand dismissals of sentimental protest novels, Tompkins famously rescued women's protest novels as a valuable political and literary site for women to participate in the social, political, and literary nation through domestic fiction.[39] Tompkins argued that Stowe had been unduly dismissed within a narrow conception of the literary. "Consequently," Tompkins explained, "works whose stated purpose is to influence the course of history, and which therefore employ a language that is not only unique but common and accessible to everyone, do not qualify as works of art."[40] After Tompkins's reclamation, in 1989 Hortense Spillers revisited the fraught literary landscape tilled by Stowe's and Reed's novels.[41] Spillers argued that the act of claiming a political voice through literature by a white New England woman in 1852 and a black male writer in 1976 enforces a grammatical silencing of the Chloes of the world.[42] Scholars continue to reconsider the mythic and sexualized struggle between black men and white women in the protest novel tradition and the related silencing of black women and others. For instance, David Ikard reads Himes's depictions of women in *If He Hollers* in the tradition of Michael Awkward's black male feminism,[43] and Lynn M. Itagaki notes the vilification of other ethnic minorities such as Japanese Americans in that novel.[44]

Today, nonfiction journalism that fuses reportage with storytelling seems to perform the social critique and capture the popular imagination in ways that earlier generations of protest novels did. The best—and best-selling—examples are Barbara Ehrenreich's *Nickel and Dimed* (2001) and Eric Schlosser's *Fast Food Nation* (2001). We should note that neither Ehrenreich nor Schlosser intend to translate their work into novel form, though *Fast Food Nation* is now translated into a feature film. Protest novels remain fodder for literary critics who seek political theory in novel form, while the category of the literary remains distanced from the earnestly political. Danielle Allen looks to *Invisible Man* (1952) to understand Ellison's literary intervention into democratic theory with a novel first decried as *not* a protest novel—because it retreated from the public sphere in favor of psychological examinations—and now read as overtly political because it provides a novelistic account of "what it is like, psychologically speaking, to be an individual in a democratic world of strangers, where large-scale events are supposed to arise somehow out of one's own consent and yet never really do."[45] Postmodernist sensibilities continue to distrust sentimental and universalist impulses in favor of experiential subjectivities and decentered narratives.[46] So, earnest protest novels that directly appeal to the nation grow further out of favor. Now that the protest novel is dislodged as the genre of choice for artist-advocates, we can revisit earlier protest novelists, like Jackson, to reappraise their proximate contributions in protest essays.

JACKSON'S PROTEST ESSAY AND THE DIVIDED NATION-STATE

If we are to fully appreciate *A Century of Dishonor*, we must see how her essay works outside the protest novel tradition in a few key ways, especially regarding her audience. As chapter 1 argues, the American protest essay draws on the European personal essay and American political oratory so that its prime concern is the divided publics it addresses and the experiences of exclusion for which the essayist speaks. Therefore, the American protest essay is particularly able to identify—and protest—divisions within a citizenry that likes to think of itself as inclusive and equal. Further, chapter 2 explores how protest essayists do not readily cede their claims to the grand narratives of inclusion proffered by the state. Consequently, they can strategically cite state promises—*and take them at face value*. When Jackson addresses the state itself, she addresses a highly factionalized public of non, partial, and full citizens and she provides a space—a national *we*—to deliver the state's grand promises.

At first it might appear as if Jackson's confusion about American Indian sovereignty and national honor invites rejection by a public impatient with an internally contradictory vision of justice. Yet the explicitly addressed readership of the essay—the target of her accusation of shameful and dishonorable conduct—is not a hopelessly nebulous American readership, as is the case with the protest novel. Instead, Jackson locates the national conscience by specifically addressing Congress. Jackson professes,

> There is but one hope of righting this wrong. It lies in appeal to the heart and conscience of the American people. What the people demand, Congress will do. . . . What an opportunity for the Congress of 1880 to cover itself with the lustre of glory, as the first to cut short our nation's record of cruelties and perjuries! the first to attempt to redeem the name of the United States from the stain of a century of dishonor! (30–31)

If Jackson's cry were simply an ambiguous appeal to an American readership writ large, the politics of shame and honor could easily lose their poignancy. But Jackson's addressee is no literary conceit. When Jackson personally sent copies—bound in blood red—to every member of Congress,[47] she made her imagined audience real. Like Stanton, Goldman, and Bread and Roses, Jackson claims the legitimacy of founding fathers' words as her own. In fact, she adorned the covers of the congressional copies with the words of Benjamin Franklin: "Look upon your hands! They are stained with the blood of your relations."[48] The delicious audacity of her gesture is only matched by its devastating logic: seek honor from official spokespersons of honor.

Without the distribution to Congress, the deep contradictions between assimilation, justice, rigid territorial boundaries, ethnic sovereignty, and national shame could be seen as Jackson's confusion. However, since protest essays directly engage and incorporate their audience into their writing, the confusion shifts to Congress. As each member of Congress opened the page, the contradictions were restored to their origin: the confusion and inconsistencies embedded in national practice. Contrary to the famous scene in the senator's private drawing room in Stowe's novel, Jackson carves out an expressly public space for her appeal to state-sponsored honor. By distributing *Century* to Congress, Jackson's diatribe against her nation's conscience does not require translation of the history of genocide into an ahistorical romance. More than "a local colorist,"[49] Jackson is a writer-advocate working in the public sphere who strategically draws on inclusive state pronouncements on behalf of persons never meant to take such words at face value.

Especially when the focus is *Ramona*, Jackson remains a troubling figure situated between competing geographical, cultural, and political frameworks because she seeks redress for those living in the borderlands of the American Southwest by specifically addressing those in the halls of power in Washington, D.C. Southern and postcolonial American studies scholars have dislodged literatures of the American Southwest from New England and Puritan frameworks, especially with the rise of transnational American studies.[50] Jackson's mode of address and redress in her direct governmental appeal—if not in her novel—follow neither a model of hybridity still popular in much postcolonial theory and border studies, nor the moralism in the sentimental novel. In her recent biography, Kate Phillips places Jackson's long-standing debates about American regionalism, and scholars like Amy Kaplan have charged Jackson with complicity in American imperial expansionism.[51] In response to accusations that Jackson helped usher in dreadful federal assimilationist programs at the turn of the twentieth century, Phillips suggests that in her fiction, "Jackson was inclined to sympathize with the people she wrote about, rather than to stand apart from them, a condescending observer, because she always thought of herself as a rural person."[52] But Jackson does not claim insider status with her Indian subjects in the essay, which asks us to recognize Jackson's strategic use of her New Englandness. As a sentimental novel, *Ramona* might be particularly vulnerable to charges that it served its readers' interests more than its subjects'. But Jackson's direct governmental appeal for justice in the essay necessarily draws readers' (congressmen's) attention to the *difference* between the writer and her subjects. That is, Jackson cashes in her formal citizenship (albeit a parcel of full citizenship) on behalf of those who may lack legal standing to make claims on the state.

For writers like Jackson who speak on behalf of a group to which they do not belong, they are subject to rigorous suspicion from all segments of their racially, nationally, and culturally divided audience. Whiteness studies scholars rekindle debates about pluralism, imperialism, and multiculturalism to charge Jackson with participating in the history of forced assimilation by constructing and projecting her own whiteness onto the nonwhite bodies she represents.[53] From another direction, Shirley Samuels addresses the complex negotiations of writers like Jackson who bring disenfranchised groups into the national corpus, which depends on dividing lines to define its identity.[54] But Jackson's direct governmental appeal remains conflicted about nation building, expansionist projects of citizenship,[55] and the viability of multiculturalism. Robert McKee Irwin argues from a postnational agenda that Jackson's novel falls prey to long-standing obsessions with American exceptionalism and the U.S. nation-state.[56] According to Irwin, Jackson's critics, like her contemporary readers, are limited by an exclusive focus on literatures in English and

Ramona's narrow access to the tremendously conflicted, multilingual, and ethnically diverse region of the Mexican borderlands. Irwin looks at Cuban revolutionary José Martí's translation and championship of the novel as an anti-imperialism strategy, even though it risks endorsing annexation by embracing a Yankee depiction of racial harmony in a romance story and its obligatory mixed-blood protagonists.[57]

In *Century*, unlike in the novel, Jackson's claims to her whiteness are calculated, deliberate political moves. Jackson capitalizes on her relatively privileged access to the stage managers of political theater in Washington, D.C. By focusing on Jackson's strategic use of her partial citizenship and how she underscores her whiteness and New Englandness, we see an alternative to Jackson's assimilationist ventriloquism in her novel.[58] It is important to note that the American protest essay allows Jackson to speak from her own position as a (partial) citizen shocked at her government's duplicity, whereas the sentimental novel tradition requires Jackson to inhabit the problematic character of a moral woman of "unfortunate birth"[59] with a "stain on the blood" (93) born to a fallen Scottish colonialist and an unnamed "Indian squaw" (26). Like her contemporary readers, future readers often arrive at Jackson's Indian reform efforts through her novel rather than through her essay. Jackson's literary representation of borderlands, race relations, and state-sponsored violence through interracial romance have earned more attention than Jackson's equally complex, conflicted, and earnest portrayal of a citizen-speaker addressing a divided national audience and demanding honor.

I am not arguing that we should stop reading *Ramona* because it lacks the political mooring points anchoring the sentimental novel to its protest essay cousin. Rather, it is important to question why we rarely read the essay on its own. I suggest that we see protest essays as potentially more direct and fully realized manifestations of the political advocacy of literary figures. Rather than the notorious one-drop racial rules central to national identity in *Ramona*, Jackson's concerns in her governmental appeal are with the *state* and its attendant moral authority. If we overlook, downplay, or translate her use of authoritative state claims, we may miss the possibilities opened up by American protest essays that take national myths at face value. When we see how Jackson uses the essay to make direct claims on the state, we can shift our attention to the divided publics she addresses, and how she embraces national promises in order to make them real.

Chapter Four

THE ART OF POLITICAL ADVOCACY: JAMES BALDWIN, AMERICAN PROTEST ESSAYIST

> But this is the mountain standing in the way of any true Negro art in America—this urge within the race toward whiteness, the desire to pour racial individuality into the mold of American standardization, and to be as little Negro and as much American as possible.
>
> —Langston Hughes, "The Negro Artist and the Racial Mountain," 1926

> What it means to be a Negro is a good deal more than this essay can discover; what it means to be a Negro in America can perhaps be suggested by an examination of the myths we perpetuate about him.
>
> —James Baldwin, "Many Thousands Gone," 1955

> Pity spokesmen; their lot is hard.
>
> —Benjamin DeMott, "James Baldwin on the Sixties," 1972

This book sketches the American protest essay, and James Baldwin deserves a central place in that tradition. The fierce elegance of his essays, and the major cultural status they earned him, tell us a lot about the high-wire act protest essayists hazard when cashing in literary celebrity for political advocacy. Like Helen Hunt Jackson, Baldwin moves between artist and citizen in his essays and he was praised, vilified, or condemned for doing so. Baldwin's essays earned him a spot on center stage during the Civil Rights and Black Power movements. In 1969, a *New York Times* forum asked, "Can Black and White Artists Still Work Together?" Baldwin—long having served as artist-spokesman—assailed the question as "rendered nearly trivial by the terms in which the question is expressed."[1] He explains, "The question is not whether black and white artists can work together—artists need each other. . . . The question is whether or not black and white citizens can work together."[2] Many black artists were turning exclusively to black audiences as a self-determination act, and Baldwin reflects, "What they are rejecting is not a people, but a doctrine, and their seeming separation may prove to be one of the few hopes of genuine union that we have ever had in this so dangerously divided house."[3] So, the famed spokesman for black America questioned the viability of addressing America at all anymore.

As for many African American authors, the question of Baldwin's spokesman role dogged him from the outset with his widely successful first collection of essays, *Notes of a Native Son* (1955).[4] And Baldwin's detractors grew as his fame grew, especially following the blockbuster essay *The Fire Next Time* (1963) in which he calls on America to reject racial self-delusions in favor of truthful self-reflection. *Fire* catapulted Baldwin to the highest levels of political celebrity and immediately elevated the stakes of questions about the role of artist-advocates. *The Negro Digest* proclaimed that *Fire* "has entrenched [Baldwin] firmly as 'the angry young voice of the new Negro.'"[5] It explained, "Whether one agrees completely with Baldwin's statements or not, one cannot deny that his written and spoken words are searing and penetrating. If he is not the voice of this 'people's revolution,' then he is at least a disquieting echo."[6] The perennial question posed about Baldwin's work, starting with his national debut in *Notes*, remains, as literary luminary Robert Penn Warren bluntly asked, "Who speaks for the Negro?"[7] Other questions follow: To whom does Baldwin speak? Does he speak for others? And what is the effect on his art? As Langston Hughes's famous essay "The Negro Artist and the Racial Mountain" (1926) attests, literary figures from disenfranchised groups, especially African Americans, must address the relationship between art, group identity, and politics. For Baldwin, he answers with his oft-repeated claim that the future of the United States is as bright or as dim as that of African Americans. By framing the debate in this way, Baldwin attempts to resolve the long-standing dilemma of the black writer—and protest writer— by paving the way to the universal by insisting on the particular in the essay form; or, as Baldwin describes his position as essayist: "a Black citizen . . . captive in the promised land" (*Notes* xiii–xv).

Baldwin is arguably the most famous literary figure-cum-political advocate in the twentieth century. More so than his fiction, Baldwin's essays influenced nearly all major social movements and writers interested in political relevance. With Baldwin, we witness the full flowering of the American protest essay, especially in the way Baldwin crafts art out of political advocacy in his commitment to "genuine union." This chapter looks at representative passages from Baldwin's essays (1948–1985) in order to further map the terrain of the American protest essay, but it also examines Baldwin's changing reception to see how he antici-

FIGURE 4
During the Civil Rights movement, Baldwin achieved celebrity status. The photograph shows James Baldwin and actor Marlon Brando at the 1963 Civil Rights March on Washington, D.C. U.S. Information Agency, Press and Publications Service, August 28, 1963.
Still Picture Records LICON, National Archives at College Park, College Park, MD.

pates the artistic demands of political spokespersons. I attend mostly to his better known earlier essays, but I also question pronouncements of Baldwin's post-sixties artistic decline. Instead, I argue that the political climate changed, not necessarily Baldwin's essays. In the epigraph, Baldwin moves among subject positions as representative Negro, someone able to study the Negro, and the nation that created the Negro. In occupying these positions, Baldwin provides multiple access points into a national project of solving its racial nightmare. That is why readers from so many backgrounds found themselves invited into Baldwin's project: they can map their own identities and experiences onto the terrain of his essays. The key to Baldwin's rise and his subsequent perceived demise is the changing sense of who Baldwin did, could, or sought to represent, especially in Baldwin's own awareness of his role as spokesman. In the pan-African journal *Transition*, Baldwin explains, "My talent does not belong to me, you know; it belongs to you; it belongs to everybody. It's important insofar as it can work toward the liberation of other people, because I didn't invent it."[8] This could signal Baldwin's despair in a changed marketplace and political climate that found him increasingly irrelevant. But it is better to say that Baldwin recognizes that artist-advocates serve as representatives to and for an audience, and they serve that role at their audience's discretion.

Baldwin is among the major figures of the twentieth century; his career is the best example of the demands placed on literary artists who accept the role of political advocate. Maurice Wallace and Joe Wood follow Baldwin's lead and describe him as a witness for the persecuted,[9] while others consider him an "outsider citizen"[10] or a "divided soul."[11] Though he is nearly universally praised as an eloquent spokesman, critics and readers attend largely to Baldwin's *ideas* and have not yet fully accounted for the eloquence itself. Baldwin's enduring presence is due largely to his essays, yet both general and academic audiences tend to see Baldwin's art and political advocacy as separate, and often in conflict. In the bright light of his fame, we can survey Baldwin's changing reception across the various factions he sought, or was taken, to represent: African Americans, the literary establishment, Civil Rights workers, black militants, white liberals, among others. Many have noted Baldwin's sophisticated ability to vacillate between mutually exclusive positions within the essay. Marianne DeKoven tracks the shifting pronouns in *Fire* and notes that Baldwin's mastery is evident in his "multiple, contradictory fluidity of the subject positions Baldwin uses [the essay] to construct."[12] Further, she argues, "the essay, even when it has clear and ascendant political agendas, is a literary genre."[13] As chapter 1 argues, the essay is an ideal literary venue for Baldwin's shifting pronouns because it is an open-ended process of discovery—for both the speaker and the addressed readership.

In the essay, Baldwin is best able to bring together national ideals and the experiences and perspectives of those for whom inclusive pronouncements do not ring true. In more artistic terms, Baldwin explains, "What the writer is always trying to do is utilize the particular in order to reveal something much larger and heavier than any particular can be."[14] Famously, Baldwin catapulted himself into literary renown in his essay "Everybody's Protest Novel," which critiques the protest novel and its practitioners—namely, Harriet Beecher Stowe and Richard Wright. That essay is Baldwin's response to the quagmire of the protest novel tradition; the essay form best allows Baldwin to speak simultaneously to immediate social categories and enduring human complexities that allow us to imagine alternatives. Baldwin argued on the front page of the *New York Times Book Review* that a writer's job is to "speak out about the world" because "the effort to become a great novelist simply involves attempting to tell as much of the truth as one can bear, and then a little more."[15] To do this, Baldwin asks his readers to imagine America from the vantage of others: "And one must be willing to ask one's self what the Indian thinks of this [American] morality, what the Cuban or the Chinese thinks of it, what the Negro thinks of it."[16] Baldwin articulates unbearable truths about race, American promises of equality, and a clear vision of a new society attempting to live up to its promises. The American protest essay, not its more famous cousin the protest novel, provides Baldwin the best literary venue to address a nation on behalf of the disenfranchised, for as long as the nation let him.

BALDWIN AS CRAFTSMAN

"And what are you now?" Elijah asked . . . "I'm a writer."

—James Baldwin on his racial allegiance
in *The Fire Next Time*, 1963

In his essays, however, he was more and more explicitly a spokesman for the Negro people, and it seemed clear that he could not indefinitely keep out of his novels the problems he discussed in his nonfiction.

—Granville Hicks reviews *Blues for Mister Charlie* in *Saturday Review*, 1964

His [first] three books of essays . . . had cemented Baldwin's reputation as America's foremost literary spokesman for civil rights. In language unparalleled in its eloquence, insight, passion, and moral force, [they] bore witness to the corrosive effects of American society on the emotional and intellectual development of a young black man.

—Randal Kenan, *James Baldwin*, 1994

Protest historically carries an overt or implicit dismissal that such literature misses the mark of purer artistic concerns, as evidenced in Hicks's epigraph. But Baldwin's success with the protest essay allows us to see the artistry of political advocacy. Randall Kenan succinctly claims, "Though critics would charge that Baldwin's political engagement came at the expense of his literary art, his resounding fiery oratory was soon being heard at innumerable rallies, fundraisers, and demonstrations, in which was combined his keen intellect, precise yet poetic language, and the rhetorical skills and moral conviction of his past as a child minister in New York City."[17] In one of the more famous reviews of *Notes*, Hughes writes, "Few American writers handle words more effectively in the essay form than James Baldwin. To my way of thinking, he is much better at provoking thought in the essay than he is in arousing emotion in fiction."[18] Though Hughes may paint Baldwin as a racial spokesman unable to surmount the racial mountain in his fiction, Hughes's description of Baldwin as essayist is welcome praise. Many critics quickly recognized Baldwin's awesome talent as essayist. Esteemed literary critic Irving Howe noted in 1963 that Baldwin is "one of the two or three greatest essayists this country has ever produced"[19] even while defending Wright from Baldwin's attack. And in 1969, John Henrik Clarke argues, "Baldwin, more than any other writer of our times, has succeeded in restoring the personal essay to its place as a form of creative literature."[20]

After two influential essay collections, *Fire* gained Baldwin full recognition for his formidable talents as an essayist. In *Fire*, like all his essays, Baldwin carefully crafts a self speaking from personal experience who reflects on representative anecdotes that bring clarity to abstract and pressing national debates about race, American identity, and justice. To an American audience fiercely divided along racial and ideological lines during the Civil Rights and Black Nationalist movements, Baldwin offers *Fire*, a simultaneously personal and national reflection on the racial nightmare that gives legitimacy to Black Muslim calls for racial separatism. Those calls are based in superiority myths equally erroneous—if not as historically powerful—as American fantasies of white supremacy. The eloquence with which Baldwin interweaves personal and philosophical reflections is evident in the famous culminating passage in which he delivers an open-ended challenge to each reader: "If we—and now I mean the relatively conscious whites and the relatively conscious blacks, who must, like lovers, insist on, or create, the consciousness of the others—do not falter in our duty now, we may be able, handful that we are, to end the racial nightmare, and achieve our country, and change the history of the world" (119). This passage is famous for its message of hope amid despair and threats of a racial apocalypse. Many have debated the integration message in the purposefully loose collective pronouns, especially given Baldwin's affiliation with Civil Rights. But in the American protest essay tradition, we can also fully appreciate the art of Baldwin's political eloquence.

The intricate and dense culminating passage employs the stances sketched in chapter 1: Baldwin enters an inclusive national project by generating a collective "we" that is accessed through personal, almost private experiences. He further connects the personal to the political in the image of lovers, which dramatizes Baldwin's position that in our individual experiences lie keys to comprehending the national fantasies that define us and the attendant diminishment of human potential. Earlier in the essay Baldwin invites the reader to the dining table of the honorable prophet Elijah Mohammad and to the storefront churches of his youth. These are Baldwin's own access points to a collective project; the reader may bring other access points. He then draws on the discourse of civic duty to particularize his collective "we" with the modifier "relatively conscious" and with specific racial categories; but the particular is not overly proscriptive so that readers may join the potentially salvific collective. He lends urgency to his despairingly hopeful project through insistence on the immediate in a religious jeremiad—delivered in the conditional tense—warning the nation of imminent danger. In doing so, Baldwin draws on authoritative civic and religious discourses as seen through the vantage of a partial citizen speaking. Baldwin's speaking voice represents specific, but shifting, constituencies and figures in national history, especially the slave. He moves between particular and collective positions, since this will be required of his readers. Baldwin incites action beyond the essay so that his exploration of the Negro's place in the national imaginary is only a first step. The reader then must transform America and save it from the fate it has created for itself, a fate that Baldwin prophesies during the preceding hundred pages of personal experience and reflection.

Fire was an instant bestseller and delivered Baldwin as the poet-prophet able to save the American people. Before the book, *Fire*'s opening essay was published as "My Dungeon Shook" in *The Progressive*, and the longer essay as "Down at the Cross" over the course of two issues of *The New Yorker*. The initial publication not only fostered the blockbuster reception of *Fire*, it also elevated the personal and the political to the realm of the literary. Readers involved in black freedom struggles accepted Baldwin's spokesman role, but some insisted that Baldwin was an artist, not a political advocate. In *Freedomways*, a Civil Rights mouthpiece, Augusta Strong asked: "If we can determine that Baldwin is first of all an artist, no matter how many white audiences solicit his interpretation of the Negro problems, and if we will look at him as a writer and not as our self-appointed spokesman, then it becomes more easy to assess what he is and where he succeeds or fails."[21] Baldwin himself is wary of serving as an unelected spokesman, so he insists on his writerly role in giving voice to voiceless Africans Americans who have served as "fixed stars" in a "white man's world" (*Fire* 23). Baldwin's role is necessary because "For the horrors of the American Negro's life there has been almost no language" (*Fire* 83). Wolfgang Kärrer argues that Baldwin's essays are more than sermons rendered in print form[22] and James Cunningham tracks Baldwin's rhetorical "I" to explain how the personal essay becomes a wildly successful political forum for examining American racial delusions. For Cunningham, Baldwin recounts personal anecdotes so that his readers can also connect the private to the public, the personal to the political, in order to fashion what Lauren Rusk calls a "collective self."[23] For Cunningham, "the real subject matter" of a Baldwinian essay "turns out to be the business of acquiring a personal perspective on both the self and the world."[24] While readers come with a different set of personal experiences—which Baldwin teaches them to insist on and analyze—the reader follows Baldwin's blueprint to analyze individual experiences with the nation. Otherwise, as Baldwin warns in "A Question of Identity," without reflection on private experience, even when assumed to be common, there arises the "disturbing possibility that experience may perfectly well be meaningless" (*Notes* 124).

Baldwin's later essays were less influential in the political realm, but they evidence Baldwin's continued willingness to work across and experiment within literary forms. They also retain the eloquence of his early work, especially regarding Baldwin's signature sentences. A Baldwinian sentence is a loping, comma-filled, pronoun-laden, digressive, and insistent reflection on America's present inability to face the past in order to create a more hopeful future. These sentences connect seemingly disparate events, experiences, ideas, and people through a series of commas, clauses, and meandering examinations of national problems. From his first book-length essay *No Name in the Street* (1972), to his examination of Hollywood culture in *The Devil Finds Work* (1976), to his final book-length essay on the Atlanta child murders in *The Evidence Not Seen* (1985), Baldwin maintained his command of the protest essay form, even if his readership no longer accorded his essays the meteoric cultural status of *Fire*. For example, in *No Name* Baldwin reflects on the sea change in black politics from integration to self-determination and his own contested role as spokesman. Arguing that American race relations represent a holocaust (especially after the assassinations of many Civil Rights leaders), Baldwin describes his trip to Little Rock during school integration struggles in a classically dense sentence that compares the scene to Jewish children in Hitler's Germany:

> Here they were, nevertheless, scrubbed and shining, in their never-to-be-forgotten stiff little dresses, in their never-to-be-forgotten little blue suits, facing an army, facing a citizenry, facing white fathers, facing white mothers, facing the progeny of these co-citizens, facing the white past, to say nothing of the white present: small soldiers, armed with stiff, white dresses, and long or short dark blue pants, entering a leper colony, and young enough to believe that the colony could be healed, and saved.[25]

This sentence covers an incredible amount of terrain because it demands the reader to view the scene from two seemingly opposing, but actually reflective, standpoints: the child and the soldier, co-citizens. Baldwin insists on particular subject positions, but also leaves enough ambiguity to allow the comparison between Jim Crow and the Third Reich. The reader is not sure which location Baldwin describes. The past crowds into the present, and disallows its erasure because it remains unaddressed. Against the young soldier's naïve dreams of salvation, Baldwin's jammed sentence requires that we face the past and present in order to surpass the persistent and stiff divide between our children and our soldiers. Just reading the sentence requires an agility proportional to the effort to break apart cemented division so as to achieve a country. Baldwin increasingly entwined his essay craftsmanship with his political analysis. In an interview for *Black Scholar*, Baldwin responds to a question on black militancy with a language of craftsmanship: "It's a series of parentheses and it cannot be answered, you know. It can only be faced. I don't have any answers."[26] Baldwin offers a theory of his essayistic sentences as a way to truthfully face the complex past–present–future of race in America.

Sustained formal attention to Baldwin's essay is somewhat rare, but some critics prefigure more current work by DeKoven, Karrer, and Cunningham. In 1972, Eugenia Collier examined the use of irony and juxtaposition in Baldwin's overriding theme of the chaos of American racial paradoxes and the "self-imposed blindness" with which "men erect an elaborate façade of myth, tradition, and ritual."[27] Nick Aaron Ford placed Baldwin at the top of his surveys of black literature in *Phylon* in the early 1960s. Though Ford declared Baldwin just shy of greatness as a novelist for his negativity,[28] he declares, "[*Notes*] and [*Nobody*] are among the best examples of objective, philosophical analyses of the American mind, especially in its conscious and unconscious attitudes toward race and kindred matters."[29] Ford traces how Baldwin joins Emerson, "his nineteenth-century counterpart,"[30] in "provok[ing] humane thought," and adding to that essay tradition "his tendency to tie in his personal life and experiences with whatever commentary he offers on social and philosophical questions. . . . He, therefore, speaks with an authority that most essayists reject as not sufficiently objective."[31] These studies get at how Baldwin conveys certain ideas in individual essays, but not yet how Baldwin achieves the art of political advocacy itself.

In "Everybody's Protest Novel," Baldwin famously and damningly denounces Stowe and Wright for participating in the same myths about race and inferiority that their novels protest. The young Baldwin hangs his assessment of *Uncle Tom's Cabin* as "a very bad novel" (*Notes* 14) on a problem of genre: "This [argument that slavery is wrong] makes material for a pamphlet but it is hardly enough for a novel" (*Notes* 14–15). His essay incited furious debates about protest fiction, Wright, black male writers, and American literature. In one of the more influential responses, Morris Dickstein defended Wright's legacy and painted Baldwin as just another "angry young black of the sixties" who had "rehashed and flattened what was once a complicated, ironic view of the race problem in America."[32] Dickstein warned, "We ought not to underestimate the boldness and healthy egotism of Baldwin's thrusting his private case forward as significant public example."[33] So, rebuttals to Baldwin also expressed discomfort with the tendency of essays to address public problems through private experience. Further, Baldwin was subject to his own condemnations as others dismissed him as the latest in a line of protest novelists.[34] But this focus on novels misses the point: Baldwin successfully makes artful protest in another form—the essay.

In that essay, Baldwin presents an early version of his lifelong political and literary project: "But our humanity is our burden, our life; we need not battle for it; we need only to do what is infinitely more difficult—that is, accept it" (*Notes* 23). If Baldwin finds the protest novel wanting in its ability to address the reality of racial and other social divisions, then Baldwin turns to the protest essay to perform that task.

Most reviews at least nod to Baldwin's mastery of the essay form, but stop short of placing him at the center of an essay tradition. An early example from *The Massachusetts Review* notes "autobiographical and polemical techniques" that place Baldwin in the esteemed tradition of Benjamin Franklin, Ralph Waldo Emerson, and Henry David Thoreau, but then bristles at Baldwin's spokesman status: "Baldwin has come to represent for 'white' Americans the eloquent, indignant voice of an oppressed people, a voice speaking in print, on television, and from the public platform in an all but desperate, final effort to bring us out of what he calls our innocence before it is (if it is not already) too late."[35] This review moves quickly past aesthetic critique so that the essay genre becomes nearly invisible. When critics attend to the literariness of Baldwin's essays, they usually place them in Euro-American traditions of transcendental meditation, or chronicle national themes covered by Baldwin as racial spokesman.[36] Such moves universalize Baldwin's writing without attending enough to particular African American experiences and traditions. Some have nodded to Henry James's influence, but those appraisals tend to look at Baldwin's fiction for Jamesian techniques of complex, interior meditations.[37] Baldwin deserves a central place in an essay tradition, not as adjunct to others' traditions.

One reason that Baldwin's protest essays are not yet fully appreciated in an artistic tradition is that literary criticism tends to assume a split between art and political advocacy and often pits them against each other. For example, in a 1976 article, Louis Pratt argues that Baldwin is consigned to a black literary ghetto by white liberal critics who use the protest label to segregate Baldwin from other American literature. Pratt cites "the widespread and almost unanimous assumption that James Baldwin speaks for the black man."[38] In response, Pratt argues, "At the heart of the matter is the necessity for the separation of 'Spokesman' from 'Artist' in order to evaluate more effectively Baldwin's literary contribution"[39] In this same vein, Fred L. Standley rejects the "specious . . . dichotomy of [Baldwin's] life and literature" since Baldwin himself rejects this division.[40] Instead, Standley defends Baldwin and his "passionate devotion to his vocation"[41] and suggests that *everything* is protest literature. Standley concludes, "Consequently, for Baldwin the novel must be more than a sociological treatise or a political tract or a black power polemic."[42] Finally, for Sol Stein, Baldwin's early editor and friend, the dichotomy is obvious: "In both his fiction and his nonfiction, as time went on Baldwin allowed the preacher in him to overtake the writer."[43] Stein continues, "The fact that Baldwin's writings during his public career lack some of the power of his earliest work does not diminish his accomplishment."[44]

Critics tend to separate the literary from the political in order to praise Baldwin's artistry, or condemn it. For instance, Granville Hicks favorably reviewed *Nobody* in the *Saturday Review* by "emphasiz[ing] these two essays on literary themes, but this does not mean that I am left unmoved by the pieces in which Baldwin speaks out as an American Negro."[45] Tacitly dismissing other essays as simple "reportage,"[46] Hicks concludes, "Meanwhile, Baldwin speaks boldly as a Negro—that is to say, as a human being—while recognizing his responsibility to the craft he practises."[47] In an interesting reversal, Saul Maloff reviewed Baldwin for *The Nation* in 1962 by separating the novelist from the essayist, and he lauds the latter: "Baldwin appears in his essays as a witness, a prophet; but his testimony and prophecy are given their terrible force and urgency by his qualities as a writer. These qualities, most notably, are his poise and clarity and reverberant feeling; and as they are moral as well as literary qualities, they serve beautifully to criticize the life they are poised *against*, simply by existing, by being what they are."[48] If his novels fail, Maloff concludes, "For the time being, then, we shall have to look to the essays for Baldwin's exemplary moral—and literary, imaginative—achievement."[49]

The tension between art and politics permeates the American protest essay tradition, and Baldwin crafts his essay style out of this dichotomy. Reviews of Baldwin's early work, though celebratory, were at pains to understand how to read the protest essay genre. *Phylon* praises Baldwin outright: "Make no mistake about it, this is one of the most important works yet written on the Negro in America and abroad."[50] But that review struggles with how to approach such a form: "[*Notes*] is a collection of ten essays, in three groupings, dealing with the Negro as writer and actor, race relations in America, and the Negro abroad, as viewed primarily through the experiences and observations of the author. Most of the essays anatomize the hatred and confusion that separate races. All emphasize the Negro's search for identity. . . . Here, indeed, is fine writing. Here, also, is penetrating realism."[51] A review in *Crisis* is even barer in its formal understanding of the protest essay: "This book . . . is made up of an autobiographical note and ten essays. The latter are of uneven merit but the best ones are outstanding."[52]

Baldwin's initial acceptance into literary circles sloughed off his politicking from his art. *Critical Quarterly* noted with muted praise the personal turn in the poetry of Sylvia Plath and Baldwin's novels, though it largely portrays them as "adolescent" and mere analogues to his "passionat[e] involve[ment] with the conflict over negro rights."[53] In 1961 *The New Yorker* also lamented the intrusion into contemporary literature of "the problem of identity" because "often these literary explorations of the personal abyss have a gratuitous air about them, as if the explorer were not so much driven to discover his identity as eager to demonstrate it."[54] *Partisan Review* and the *New York Times Book Review* echoed this concern,[55] while sociological theorists praised the development.[56] Literary critics sought to salvage the literary in a post-Baldwin world. In a telling sky-is-falling example, *The American Scholar* decried the fate of the novel now that Baldwin had helped to usher in "A Literature of Fact."[57] In a counterpoint, *Mainstream* accused Baldwin of emptying politics from the democratic tradition of Whitman and Twain in favor of an apolitical tradition following James.[58] Finally, *Daedalus* traced the emergence of an activist literature in which Baldwin joins Walker Percy, Saul Bellow, and Bernard Malamud, among others. But it, too, remained skeptical of the personal in the new sociological novels: "The new activist hero remains to the end an intrepid opportunist of the self. He is an eager, insatiable explorer of his own private self."[59] These warning sirens about a new literature of self—be it activist, propagandistic, or psychological—signal an unidentified literary tradition. Baldwin's protest essays connect private experience to political reality more so than the protest novel or the Montaignean personal essay.

Despite critics' distrust of personal protest, Baldwin coaches his readers on how to read essays that position their speaker within a factionalized nation. In his second essay collection, *Nobody Knows My Name* (1961), Baldwin fashions a representative speaker able to address a starkly divided audience, especially in his visits to the Jim Crow South in the early 1960s. In "A Fly in Buttermilk,"[60] Baldwin employs a complex visual metaphor of darkness and lightness to dramatize the bravery and difficulty of school integration, as well as to bring clarity to the moral challenge of Civil Rights. Baldwin, born in Harlem and now expatriate in Paris, describes the eerie process of returning to a land in which he had never lived, but that had created him. As an outside-insider, Baldwin's own entrance allows each audience member to enter in their own fashion. Upon meeting a native son of the South who reminds Baldwin of the images of lynching so prevalent in the national imaginary, Baldwin reflects, "These had been books and headlines and music for me but it now developed that they were also a part of my identity" (*Nobody* 84). By creating a very personal space ("my identity") in which each reader must claim the South and its history of racial segregation and terrorism, Baldwin requires us to map ourselves onto the racial topography of the essay. When Baldwin declares, "For segregation has worked brilliantly in the South, and, in fact, in the nation, to this extent: it has allowed white people, with scarcely any pangs of conscience whatever, to *create*, in every generation, only the Negro they wished to see" (*Nobody* 96), the reader must reimagine "my identity" to break the racial cycle.

For Baldwin and the essay tradition, personal experience illuminates self-delusions about race and identity. Baldwin states plainly in the opening essay to *Fire*, "Color is not a human reality or a personal reality, it is a political reality" (118). Reflection on personal experiences—his own and others'—is the only way to puncture "political realities." Kenan explains, "As would be true of virtually all of his essays, Baldwin invariably uses the ostensible subject matter of the piece—his prison stay in Paris, a review of a movie opera—as a springboard to an examination of the subject that really interests him: the effects of the poisonous racial climate of the United States on the black American individual."[61] The essay form welcomes Baldwin's masterful ability to move between the particular and the universal, the personal and the political, the racial and the national. Whether as a black stranger in an all-white village or an intellectually curious child in a black Pentecostal household, Baldwin portrays his personal experiences within a racial system ensnaring his readers, too. In the title essay to *Notes*, for example, Baldwin confronts his father's death as well as race riots in America by recounting his experience with racial segregation in New Jersey. He explains, "I learned in New Jersey that to be a Negro meant, precisely, that one was never looked at but was simply at the mercy of the reflexes of the color of one's skin caused in other people" (*Notes* 93). The essay analyzes the effects of American self-delusions, but it also presents the way forward: look directly at the speaker's experience, not the racial myths that prematurely explain it. In Baldwin's movement between the personal and social, we see an essay technique that deduces patterns through illustrative personal experiences, which leads to political epiphanies. In an early study, Antony Wills argues, "The task of the non-fiction writer is to transmit truth, whereas that of the novelist or short story writer is to create the illusion of truth."[62] For Wills, Baldwin compresses events to make meaning out of coincidence. A *New York Times* review attributes the essays' power to "the fact that the point of view is a Negro's, an outsider's."[63] But Baldwin is not a stationary outsider; he moves among mutually exclusive positions in segregated America.

Autobiographical accounts are central to how protest essays work: they privilege experience over received wisdom. Baldwin explicitly directs his readers to trust the experiential over the assumed in "Notes of a Native Son." When recounting his first trip down South and how he came to inherit his father's bitterness, Baldwin explains, "I was part of that generation which had never seen the landscape of what Negroes sometimes call the Old County" (*Notes* 87). As a result, he is surprised by his reception because "I did not know what I had done, and I shortly began to wonder what *anyone* could possibly do, to bring about such unanimous, active, and unbearably vocal hostility. I knew about jim-crow but I have never experienced it" (*Notes* 92). In order to escape "the same story" (*Notes* 93) of racial segregation repeated everywhere without thought, the essayist experiences and analyzes that racial system in order to change the familiar story of race in America. Further, Baldwin asks his readers to understand others' experiences because, "whatever white people do not know about Negroes reveals, precisely and inexorably, what they do not know about themselves" (*Fire* 58). Some early criticism attributes literary merit to Baldwin's experiential mode, and the best criticism understands his anecdotes as highly crafted examinations of social issues in a personal mode. For instance, Daryl Dance argues that Baldwin's essays are about a search for home, which he finds in the South, not Africa, even if momentary peace cannot solve the "lack of a sense of positive self-identity" and "that having found his home, he has also found that one can't go home again."[64]

The central thread of conversations about Baldwin across political and literary spectra not only opposes art and advocacy, or the private/personal and social/political, but also integration and racial self-determination. For one critic, "If the two roles are not mutually exclusive, they are really not compatible either, and they have forced him to become a dual personality: both a fiery prophet of the racial apocalypse and a sensitive explorer of man's inmost nature."[65] In the opening letter to his nephew in *Fire*, Baldwin makes the case for connecting personal experience, racial pride, and the project of integration: "They do not know Harlem, and I do. So do you. . . . There is no reason for you to try to become like white people and there is no basis whatever for their impertinent assumption that *they* must accept *you*. The really terrible thing, old buddy, is that *you* must accept *them*" (*Fire* 22). Baldwin recognizes that he creates a political minefield by traversing doctrines of white supremacy, integration, and racial self-determination in the terrain of his essays. Baldwin moves among personal experience, reflection, and political reality so that he finds an acceptable means by which *you* and *they* can come together. In 1972, *Transition* asked Baldwin to update his earlier statement that spokesmen must "simplify the facts of his political case, in order to communicate directly, and broadly, as opposed to the novelist's need to remain faithful to the complexities of life. . . . Is this your dilemma?"[66] Baldwin responded, "It is difficult, and would be more difficult if I thought the particular political issues with which I am concerned were capable of being simplified. . . . So the dichotomy of my being a spokesman for civil rights and my being a novelist is not as it might appear."[67] Though political speechifying and the novel remain in opposition, the protest essay is able to bring together the immediate and the enduring, the experiential and the ideological, the particular and the universal, the factional and the national. It can do this because it addresses a divided audience through the prism of personal experience as social analysis.

BALDWIN AND HIS DIVIDED AUDIENCE

> We cannot be free until they are free.
> —James Baldwin, "My Dungeon Shook," 1962

> Mr. Baldwin is no racial specialist. He swims with equally sturdy, confident strokes in every bay of the great sea of letters, and is as likely to dip into a Gide or a James as into a Richard Wright.
> —Donald Malcolm in his review of *Nobody Knows My Name*, 1961

> The subject of his sermons is almost always the life that black Americans live, but his real audience—his congregation, if you will—is white America. . . . Baldwin was a startling voice from a land called black America that white America scarcely knew, but he was a voice that sought to reason with us even as he exposed our hypocrisies and cruelties.
> —Jonathan Yardley in *Washington Post Book World*, 1985

Throughout his career, but especially in *Fire*, Baldwin persistently addresses a deeply divided audience, and incorporates them into his essays. With his nephew and the one hundredth anniversary of emancipation as a conceit to open *Fire*, Baldwin avers, "We cannot be free until they are free" (24). By tethering the futures and the identities of seemingly intractable poles of *us* and *them*, Baldwin addresses division in order to achieve genuine, collective emancipation—cultural and psychological, as well as legal. Baldwin continues, "What it comes to is that if we, who can scarcely be considered a white nation, persist in thinking of ourselves as one, we condemn ourselves, with the truly white nations, to sterility and decay, whereas if we could accept ourselves *as we are*, we might bring new life to the Western achievements, and transform them" (*Fire* 107–08). Baldwin poses a conditional proclamation that requires his divided readers to sign onto a collective contract, and the flexible speaking position of the essayist brokers the agreement. With his readers, Baldwin nurtures a genuine union—a "we"—that can deliver the future only if readers are committed to the reality of their experiences, not sterile ideas about an already achieved free nation. For the experiment to succeed, his black and white audience must accept the contractual obligation to fulfill the promises of the nation-state.

The question of who or which faction(s) Baldwin addresses are symptomatic of debates about African American and protest writing.[68] Highly aware of the "problem of identity,"[69] Baldwin anticipates and solicits perennial questions of affiliation among multiple constituencies. Debates about Baldwin gauge his relative success or inability to walk what Stan West describes as a tightrope between black and white audiences.[70] In fact, in his review of *Blues*, Melvin Watkins detects two Baldwins: black polemicist and white romantic.

For Watkins, "This dual approach, the ability to assume the voice of black as well as white Americans, accounts, in great part, for [Baldwin's] popularity and acceptance among Americans on both sides of the racial issue."[71] With supreme craftsmanship, Baldwin's essays exhibit an acrobatic ability to move among a deeply, almost hopelessly, divided national audience. He can do this because, as DeKoven explains, his "slippage in subjectivity" binds his audience: "With the audience/reader now joined with him in a common project, occupying, at least for a moment, a common subject position, Baldwin defamiliarizes the conventional American meaning of the term 'majority,' which equates numerical majority in the population with racial whiteness."[72]

Many whites felt specifically—and exclusively—indicted. Heated denouncements ensued because if one segment of the simultaneously addressed divided audience feels exclusively indicted, then Baldwin's contractual experiment looks like a one-sided attack. An article in the *Catholic World* worries, "This lashing of the white subconscious stings many a cautious citizen and makes one wonder whether Baldwin may fall in step with the lunatic fringe."[73] Others explicitly detected "Baldwin's Message for White America."[74] A review of *Fire* suggested that "Mr. Baldwin knows how to prove the liberal conscience at its tenderest spots, how to stir up in the white reader a panicky feeling that, whatever his fine sentiments, he has perhaps never really looked a coloured man full in the face before."[75] Theodore Gross admonished Baldwin's political advocacy because he "created the Negro for his white audience just as Hawthorne, a century earlier, created and defined the Puritan world for his audience."[76] In response, many whites, including liberals, went so far as to join a chorus denouncing Baldwin as succumbing to racial hate. For instance, literary luminary Stephen Spender consigned Baldwin to the position of mere "race hatred" because "[Baldwin] has, as a Negro, a right, of course, to despise liberals, but he exploits his moral advantage too much."[77] Articles in sectarian papers were even surer in their dismissals. For instance, *The Christian Century* denounced Baldwin's sexual politics by attacking his artistry: "Baldwin seems bent on heading up an 'Overflowing Garbage Can School of writing.'"[78] In the end, many conservative commentators treated Baldwin as yet another pundit for the gristmill of ideological warfare, such as Robert Dwyer's scathing review of *Nobody*: "Since I am white, I cannot write of the colored problem from the inside" but he still submits that "most poor people in America today are poor because they want to be. They make themselves the way they are by being lazy, uneducated, sick, undependable."[79] These responses reject totally Baldwin's request that his divided audience see themselves in each other.

On the other hand, black readers sometimes felt under-addressed in Baldwin's essays. In the *New Left Review*, Orlando Patterson praised Baldwin's "brilliant craftsmanship,"[80] but disparaged his choice not to address primarily a black audience under the banner of racial solidarity. Patterson notes Baldwin's vacillation between mutually exclusive viewpoints (outsider looking in, outsider looking out, insider looking in, insider looking out), and concludes, "I have grave doubts about Baldwin's intellectual honesty, and as a Negro reader (pure and simple) I can't help feeling, paradoxically, that he has, somehow, betrayed me."[81] Ultimately, Patterson decides Baldwin's complex subject positioning fails: "The public he addresses is that of the White American liberal and the image which his art reflects is not that of the Negro but of the American protestant ethic with all its ambiguities."[82] The conflict Baldwin navigates in his essays, the contest that pits integration against racial self-determination, permeates the criticism: Was Baldwin addressing primarily a black audience or a white audience? Some black reviewers wondered about Baldwin's publication in mainstream, white liberal, or literary venues. *Crisis* openly distrusted Baldwin's decision to publish *Fire*'s opening essay in *The New Yorker* because it is "often merely an organ for self-congratulations among the nouveau riche and the snobs who populate the cleaner, more hygienic, and lifeless areas of twentieth-century America."[83] Hilton Als goes one further: "With the publication of [*Fire*] in book form . . . Baldwin became something of an intellectual carpetbagger."[84]

Given Baldwin's ultimate rejection by a younger, more militant generation,[85] it is surprising that early reviews in black nationalist publications were rather favorable. *Muhammad Speaks*, the mouthpiece of the Nation of Islam, praised *Fire* because "The old fashioned view that artists live in a hybrid world removed from reality is being shattered forever. In all the civil rights demonstrations we are noting increasing participation by performers, artists, writers, and musicians. . . . Artists are beginning to accept their moral responsibility with great seriousness."[86] The increasingly militant *Liberator* echoed this initially favorable reception when a young Lawrence Neal used Baldwin to "arrive at . . . some kind of synthesis of the writer's function as an oppressed individual and a creative artist."[87] Neal appreciates that "Baldwin acting as the *conscience* of the civil rights movement comes closer than any writer before him to an essential aspect of the problem. And that is the commitment to some kind of social dynamic."[88]

Reviews of Baldwin from the 1960s until his death in 1987 engage clashes between integration, militancy, and black nationalism, which garnered his hero status with *Fire* but also cost him that status when later generations no longer found his integration vision compelling. Although Baldwin's cultural status changed, the craftsmanship of his political advocacy did not. In 1951's "Many Thousands Gone" Baldwin avers, "One may say that the Negro in America does not really exist except in the darkness of our minds" (*Notes* 25). In 1963's *Fire* Baldwin writes, "And if the word *integration* means anything, this is what it means: that we, with love, shall force our brothers to see themselves as they are, to cease fleeing from reality and begin to change it" (10). And in his despairing 1980 essay "Notes on the House of Bondage," Baldwin writes, "One can speak, then, of an empire at the moment when, though all of the paraphernalia of power remain intact and visible and seem to function, neither the citizen-subject within the gates nor the indescribable hordes outside it believe in the morality of the kingdom anymore—when no one, any longer, aspires to the empire's standards."[89] These essays remain constant in their approach to race and national identity by moving among seemingly opposed subject positions: black and white, slave and free, citizen and imperial subject, us and them.

If the contact between these factions seems to lead to hate, not Baldwin's vision of love, it is more a failure of readership than craftsmanship. For instance, *The Christian Century* despairs, "[Baldwin's] writings may someday be ranked a landmark in race relations," but "Baldwin's angry trumpet sounds with an uncertain note.... His is a jeremiad of despair, a chronicle of outrage, but not much of a guide for those seeking a way to higher ground."[90] A 1963 *New York Times Book Review* essay is more reserved in accusations that Baldwin panders to hate: "As a writer of polemical essays on the Negro question James Baldwin has no equals," but with *Fire* Baldwin has "exchanged prophecy for criticism, exhortation for analysis."[91] A 1961 review in *Commentary* concludes much the same: "We hear too often in these essays the voice of his will rather than the voice of his sensibility; there are too many examples of rhetoric, of exhortation, of uplift, of reproach, in the book, and they undoubtedly weaken the impact it makes."[92] In these reviews, we see that Baldwin risks accusations of hate and irrationality when he addresses experiences of division, even within an integration vision. Further, it is important to see that any protest essayist hazards such rejection in the role of artist-spokesperson.

BALDWIN AS SPOKESPERSON

> Leaving aside the considerable question of what relationship precisely the artist bears to the revolutionary, the reality of man as a social being is not his only reality and that artist is strangled who is forced to deal with human beings solely in social terms; and who has ... the necessity thrust on him of being representative of some thirteen million people.
>
> —James Baldwin, "Many Thousands Gone" (*Notes* 33), 1955

> He can't be satisfied simply with relating a critical time in his early manhood to the tragedies of our country. He is impelled to expand his feelings, make them into the feelings of all Negroes, make his struggle theirs, his conclusions their demands, his frustrations their accusation, his anger their treat.
>
> —Robert Coles on Baldwin and other "'literary' social scientists,"1964

> Q: Who is in your audience now?
> A: I have no idea. I'd think it would be the young, white and black. I know that my books are reaching the Black communities, logically in paperback editions. I'm surely a problematical figure for many in the Afro-American world. On balance they trust me—I think. I know what my position is in any case. I know I love them. I don't know about them loving me."
>
> —James Baldwin interviewed by
Herbert Lottman in Black Times, 1972

During the 1960s and early 1970s, Baldwin was featured in virtually every mainstream and black periodical and in numerous television and radio interviews. Baldwin's meteoric rise to fame intensifies debates about tensions between art and advocacy, and about Baldwin's ability to speak on behalf of his diverse constituents. In 1964, *Esquire* announced, "No Negro writer or spokesman has had so great an impact on the entire white liberal world as James Baldwin."[93] *Ebony* declared Baldwin "preeminently an angry man of color, who addresses himself to both his fellow Negroes and white oppressors with passion and insight."[94] *Time* placed Baldwin on the cover of its 1963 examination of the Civil Rights movement. Though Baldwin deemed the price of fame "terrifying" in an interview with Nat Hentoff,[95] Baldwin's prominence represents the full flowering of the American protest essayist. In one of Baldwin's more famous interviews, Kenneth B. Clark questioned Baldwin after a famously frustrating meeting between Baldwin, Attorney General Robert Kennedy, and a small group of other black spokespersons.[96] To Clark's question if he is "essentially optimistic or pessimistic," Baldwin responds nearly verbatim from "Letter from a Region in My Mind," which was soon to appear in *Fire*:

> The future of the Negro in this country is precisely as bright or as dark as the future of the country.... What white people have to do is try to find out in their own hearts why it was necessary to have a nigger in the first place. Because I am not a nigger, but if you think I'm a nigger, it means you need it. The question you got to ask yourself—the white population has got to ask itself, North and South, because it's one country and for a Negro there's no difference between the North and the South; there's just a difference in the way they castrate you, but the fact of the castration is the American fact. If I'm not the nigger here and if you invented him—you, the white people, invented him, then you've got to find out why.[97]

In this response, Baldwin exhibits traits associated with his brilliant essay craftsmanship: he shifts among factional identities through pronoun play, delivers a religiously inflected extemporaneous speech, poses his self as representative of the voiceless, creates urgency by joining now and later, and insists on a collective national project to move beyond private selves. But what happens when Baldwin is no longer a literary writer and just a political advocate? The linkage between advocacy and/as art frays when Baldwin's urgent, personal, and nation-shaking pronouncements appear outside the essay venue and when interviewers ask Baldwin for political philosophies outside literary considerations. Outside the essay, Baldwin's connections between private and public, personal and political, and particular and universal—essayistic stances that allow a speaker to become a political advocate in the first place—may not translate to other venues in the machinery of culture and opinion-making.

Baldwin masterfully adopts the stance of representative speaker to a divided audience, and his shifting cultural status tells us a lot about the risks of spokespersonship: audiences have the power to bestow, or retract, the privilege of political representation. In chapter 1, I argue that the American protest essay is more concerned with the audience it addresses than creating a speaking self more aligned with the personal essay tradition. But this is not to suggest that the speaker is secondary, incidental, or irrelevant. Instead, protest essayists must consciously position themselves among the factions they address, and the best protest essayists are able to move among these factions. In his lead essay to *Nobody*, Baldwin recounts his travels to Europe as "A Discovery of What it Means to Be an American" in the tradition of the European tour so entwined with James and other white novelists. Baldwin reflects on his dilemma: "I left America because I doubted my ability to survive the fury of the color problem here. (Sometimes I still do.) I wanted to prevent myself from becoming *merely* a Negro; or, even, merely a Negro writer. I wanted to find out in what way the *specialness* of my experience could be made to connect me with other people instead of dividing me from them" (*Nobody* 4). This opening gesture posits leaving the physical nation as a means of entering the national imaginary, which risks pandering to American exceptionalism at the beginning of the Cold War and black writers' perennial worry that success requires embracing whiteness. But, in this opening passage, Baldwin maintains a cautious distance between the speaker and the object of his pursuit: genuine union with the complicated American populace. This way, the trajectory of the essay, and the collection, illustrates Baldwin's reconnection with his deeply divided audience.

By the end of the essay, Baldwin's speaker stands as a sort of cultural politician because "it is the writer, not the statesman, who is our strongest arm" (*Nobody* 12). At the end of the collection, in "The Black Boy Looks at the White Boy," Baldwin cautiously reassesses his reservations about Norman Mailer's notorious fascination with black masculinity. Their personal exchanges serve as a canvas on which Baldwin projects race relations in America, and generational anxieties when "serious citizens" who "may not respect Norman, but young people do, and do not respect the serious citizens"

(*Nobody* 238). Baldwin criticizes Mailer's desire to run for mayor because "I do not feel that a writer's responsibility can be discharged in this way" (238). Instead, the protest essayist is the responsible examiner of culture by "dealing as truthfully as we know how with our present fortunes, these present days" (239). It may be that the white boy ultimately fails to see the black boy as he is, rather than as he imagines him to be, but Baldwin begins the collective project of facing reality: "For, though it clearly needs to be brought into focus, [Mailer] has a real vision of ourselves as we are, and it cannot be too often repeated in this country now, that, where there is no vision, the people perish" (241). Baldwin presents the writer-statesman as central to the survival of the people, all the people.

When *Time* declared Baldwin the voice of the Civil Rights movement, it implicitly sided with those who assumed Baldwin addressed foremost a white audience. For *Time*, Baldwin is a voice for integration standing between the extremes of Malcolm X and the "unyielding southerner," and Baldwin "illuminated this grey gulf with bolts of intellectual lightning."[98] *Time* recognized that Baldwin is "not, by any stretch of the imagination, a Negro leader" and even "effeminate in manner," but "in the U.S. today there is not another writer—white or black—who expresses with such poignancy and abrasiveness the dark realities of the racial ferment in the North and South."[99] *Time* is not alone in these grandiose coronations (and unease with Baldwin's sexuality). *Catholic World* declared Baldwin, "The radical poet laureate of the Freedom March" but worried that he had become too "arrogant" who "points accusing fingers" because "The young man who never wanted to do anything but write has seemingly been tossed into the hate war on the side of Malcolm X."[100] These publications—one mainstream, one sectarian, both predominantly white—openly wonder if Baldwin "speaks for the average Negro?"[101] Baldwin's ability to move among potentially incommensurate locations—personal and social, us and them, then and now, black and white, collective and separatist—invites very different readings about whom or of what he speaks on behalf, which is a perennial question endemic to the protest essay.

While producing *Blues*, his play on the murder of Emmett Till, Baldwin reflected on his complicated artist-advocate role. In "Words of a Native Son," Baldwin explains why "that dead boy is my subject and my responsibility. And yours" (*Price* 401). Baldwin declares,

> It's a terrible delusion to think that any part of this republic can be safe as long as 20,0000,000 members of it are as menaced as they are. . . . I know you didn't do it, and I didn't do it either, but I am responsible for it because I am a man and a citizen of this country and you are responsible for it, too, for the very same reason: As long as my children face the future that they face, and come to the ruin that they come to, your children are gravely in danger, too. (400)

While accounting for his particular experiences and those of each reader, Baldwin presents his voice as a product of the American republic (a father of the next generation) and he asks—demands—that each reader also assess the nation that created the present racial nightmare, and their place in it. Otherwise, no one can wake from racial delusions until each citizen signs onto the collective project of assuring their children's futures. The discourse of civic obligation that permeates *Fire* becomes even more urgent in this essay amid legislative gains from Civil Rights without the more profound project of confronting history.

In all his essays, Baldwin maintains a taught awareness of the need to adopt a spokesperson stance, and he increasingly recognized how to invite the audience to actively participate. For instance, Baldwin's penultimate book-length essay, *The Devil Finds Work*, begins similar to *Fire* when he meditates on childhood contact with racial fantasies—his father's and Hollywood's.[102] Baldwin examines films because they project the racial fantasies he spent his life puncturing through lived experience; that is, "The language of the camera is the language of our dreams."[103] As audience member, Baldwin becomes increasingly aware of the power of the essay, which, like film, risks placing his readers in a passive posture. Enamored with the power of the theater, Baldwin recounts, "But I was aware of the audience now. Everyone seemed to be waiting, as I was waiting" (31). Baldwin stands as reader/spectator so that his personal anecdotes and political meditations occupy the same seats as those for whom he speaks. In this way, Baldwin's responses to films are representative so that, for instance, his response to *Dead End* tells us as much about American race relations as his father's death did in *Fire*. Baldwin writes, "The happy resolution of *Dead End* could mean nothing to me, since, even with some money, black people could move only into black neighborhoods: which is not to be interpreted as meaning that we wished to move into white neighborhoods. We wished, merely, to be free to move" (28). Baldwin moves dexterously between personal responses and statements of collective aspirations, all while rendering his integration vision complex enough to account for postures of racial separatism and skepticism of grand words like "freedom." Like Baldwin, audience members, too, are free to move among their experiences and the events in a Hollywood film, or a protest essay.

Though Baldwin's ability to craft a spokesperson stance remained constant in his essays, his audience's willingness to accept that role shifted with the political tides, especially as Black Power gained currency over integration visions. For instance, Orde Coombs dismisses *Devil* as rife with "tortured speculations" and "unfocused anger" in essays filled with "ideas that jump around and contradict one another."[104] Coombs concludes, "[Baldwin's] possible force, then, is scattered willy-nilly, to the winds, and all that vision and moral weight that fortified a generation, becomes as disturbing as the memory of a hurricane on a placid summer's afternoon."[105] Robert A. Lee also compares *Devil* to earlier essays: "But where these first *Notes* brought home a point of view, perceptions about life and race held tautly to a design, the latter pieces have tended to meander."[106] Whereas the meandering of Baldwin's earlier essays were largely praised for their ability to bring complex moral clarity to American race relations, the digressive nature of the essay appears as "unfocused anger" when the readership no longer deems Baldwin's voice relevant to their own experiences and perspectives.

Built into the American protest essay's contractual obligation and representative stance is the risk that the addressed audience—either particular factions or en masse—will reject the offer. This explains in part Baldwin's quick decline after ascending the throne of literary politician. At first, much of the mainstream black press accepted at face value Baldwin's coronation as racial spokesman. A 1961 celebratory portrait in *Ebony* succinctly states: "Explosive fury over racial injustice catapults James Baldwin to literary fame."[107] But the *Ebony* spread sees literary fame as a contradiction in terms: "Success has created for him pressures, both private and professional, so compelling as to threaten that sacred privacy and sense of anonymity which he profoundly feels a creative writer needs to have."[108] Baldwin is not only a prophet, but a sacrificial figure willing to put himself on the line. But the role of spokesperson is susceptible to partisan politics. This begins to explain why *Freedomways*, which hesitantly praised Baldwin a year earlier, became very skeptical, even hostile, to the idea of an unelected spokesperson because "One does not feel Mr. Baldwin's love for his people."[109] Instead, "In his essays there is always an excruciating, significant detachment from his subject matter; he writes of his people surfacely, slapping the powers-that-be on the wrist with 'perfumed phrases' that reek with a stop-it-you-naughty-boy sentiment, but never taking a definitive stand. One highly suspects that it is this, above all else, that has made him the fair-haired boy in high places: As a first-rate black writer with a first-rate mind, he has let his pen become a pin instead of a sword."[110]

The homophobic posture of *Freedomway*'s representative dismissal notwithstanding,[111] Baldwin purposefully cultivates literary positions of detachment—as well as connection—and moves among them to get at the possibility of genuine union. When reflecting on his experience reporting on the Jim Crow South, Baldwin explicitly poses his voice as pliable enough to move from stranger to insider, and back: "I have written elsewhere about those early days in the South, but from a distance more or less impersonal" (*No Name* 481). Baldwin's initial outsiderhood lends credibility to his reflections: "The racial dividing lines of Southern towns are baffling and treacherous for a stranger, for they are not as clearly marked as in the North—or not as clearly marked for *him*" (486). If Baldwin's experience-based positions become implausible, this is because his readers were no longer willing to follow the essays' journeys from collective self-delusions to real interaction across lines of difference. Instead, Baldwin's purposeful detachment en route to facing co-citizens becomes an opportunity for his readership to disengage.

Baldwin's co-status as literary star and political advocate unravels the moment his readership deems him nonrepresentative. A posthumous review in the *New York Times Book Review* goads, "For a certain generation, the writings of James Baldwin are like the date to the senior prom: a memory so luminous that it is never re-examined."[112] Though the Civil Rights movement "found eloquent expression in his novels and essays," the review attributes Baldwin's success to serendipity, not to his writing: "Famously a confessional writer, Baldwin compulsively wrote of self-hatred and salvation, identity and community, tears and tenderness; his themes were overdetermined from a childhood his emotions never escaped."[113] The tendency to expunge Baldwin prevailed by the 1970s. In a review of *If Beale Street Could Talk* (1974), John McClusky argues: "Admittedly, the rejection of Baldwin's logic as a spokesman reflected growing disenchantment with specific strategies of the Civil Rights Movement."[114] Though "we scurried to libraries and bookstores to study Baldwin's essays and novels," McClusky explains, as Baldwin's readership grew tired of his integration project, the contractual obligations seemed too nebulous: "We who had so diligently prepared ourselves for dialogue were left to endless integration-or-not discussions among ourselves or, possibly, involvement somewhere, somehow, to slow the dizzying whirl of our rhetoric."[115]

Debates about Baldwin's fitness as racial spokesman are often proxy debates about literary merit, especially his novels'. The literary establishment and black political commentators were abuzz in the 1960s about Baldwin's cultural status. Many literary critics dismissed the famed novelist of *Go Tell It on the Mountain* (1953) and *Giovanni's Room* (1956), accusing Baldwin of writing mere propaganda or best-selling agitprop. Mario Puzo negatively reviewed *Tell Me How Long the Train's Been Gone* (1968) by declaring, "Yet it would seem that such gifts [of lingual dexterity], enough for critics and moralists and other saintly figures, are not enough to insure the writing of good fiction."[116] Irving Howe described Baldwin's novels as "junk" (104) and *Tell Me* in particular as a "remarkably bad novel" that simply illustrates the problems of advocacy inherent in Negro writing in America.[117] Though some would come to Baldwin's artistic defense, most notably Houston Baker,[118] dismissals of Baldwin were the rule, not the exception by the 1970s. But even more so than the beautifully crafted open letters and speeches of Martin Luther King Jr., Baldwin's essays introduced the American reading public to philosophical debates about Black Nationalism and Civil Rights, and the vocabulary with which to talk about America's "racial nightmare" (*Fire* 119). In his review of a 1962 interview with Studs Terkel, Robert Shayon describes the transcript as "an extraordinary aural document, a very moving experience" because "out of [Baldwin's] intense, often reluctant responses come 300 years of the African's pain and wisdom gained in his American wilderness of the spirit."[119]

The essay, not the novel, play, or interview, best allows Baldwin to represent a factional public in an earnest collective project to achieve the nation's inclusive aspirations. The American protest essay tradition best allows us to fully account for Baldwin's legacy.

BALDWIN'S LEGACY

> Reading James Baldwin's early essays in the fifties had stirred me with a sense that apparently "given" situations like racism could be analyzed and described and that this could lead to action, to change.
>
> —Adrienne Rich, "Split at the Root," 1982

> The puzzle was—as anyone who read him should have recognized—that his arguments, richly nuanced and self-consciously ambivalent, were far too complex to serve straightforwardly political ends. . . . By the late sixties, Baldwin-bashing was almost a rite of initiation. . . . In the end, the shift of political climate forced Baldwin to simplify his rhetoric or else risk internal exile. . . . Desperate to be "one of us," Baldwin allowed himself to mouth a script that was not his own.
>
> —Henry Louis Gates Jr., "The Welcome Table," 1993

> But in the end Baldwin could not distinguish between writing sermons and making art.
>
> —Hilton Als in *The New Yorker*, 1998

> The poet or the revolutionary is there to articulate the necessity, but until the people themselves apprehend it, nothing can happen. . . . The poet and the people get on generally very badly, and yet they need each other. The poet knows it sooner than the people do. The people usually know it after the poet is dead; but, that's all right.
>
> —Baldwin in *The Black Scholar*, 1972

Critics are often lukewarm about Baldwin's fiction and drama, but celebrate his essays largely without question. For instance, in an otherwise tepid review of *Another Country*, James Finn ventures, "What seems to be the case is that Baldwin has yet to find the artistic form that will reveal the mystery, that will uncover the truth he knows is there."[120] In response, Finn returns to the essays: "It is difficult to grasp the moral effort that must have been required to bring to the surface, to place under the harsh light of critical examination, things that both black and white have for so long kept buried deep."[121] Baldwin's prime legacy is his work as an American protest essayist.

The American protest essay offers a narrative of national belonging that addresses inequities amid grand pronouncements of equality, and Baldwin is a central figure that solidifies the form into a formidable tradition. Baldwin is a preeminent essayist, one of its most prolific practitioners, and among the most widely read African American writers in the twentieth century. In his essays, art and political advocacy are inseparable. In fact, the crucible that creates our memory of Baldwin is heated by the vigor with which diverse critics debate Baldwin's perceived artistic decline following his ascendance to best-selling essayist. If we view the essay as a transparent platform for ideological writing, we can only see Baldwin's popularity as a simple analogue to the political winds. For instance, in an otherwise excellent study of subversive anti-Stalinism in Baldwin's early essays, Geraldine Murphy argues, "The value of James Baldwin's stock in the literary critical market, like Ralph Ellison's, rose with the political fortunes of racial integration in the postwar period."[122] And a 1998 *New York Times Book Review* essay declares, "Baldwin's private demons were astoundingly congruent with ghosts haunting American history. He projected his terrors onto his country, which, for a time, found a fearsome mirror in his torment."[123] Understanding the essay as simple political mirror has a long history. A 1963 review in the *New Statesman* also attributes Baldwin's success to timing: "The appearance of 'Letter from a Region in My Mind,' coinciding as it did with a critical turn in relations between white and coloured in the US, has transformed Baldwin into a spokesman and a culture-hero. . . . Mr. Baldwin has reverted to a pulpit style. The 'Letter' is an intensely personal document, but it was also perfectly timed as a manifesto for the new mood of militancy among American Negroes."[124] Mel Watkins adds, "His influence and popularity depended upon the extent to which his psyche corresponded to the mass American psyche."[125] And *Commonweal* paints *Fire* "as a convenient lightning rod for much of [our present racial confusion]."[126]

Increasingly, Baldwin's audiences ceased accepting his experience and voice as reflective of the political moment. Baldwin's signature moral clarity also requires the cooperation of his readership. Otherwise, in his later essays, Baldwin is accused of wandering self-absorption and simplification. Many critics look for a change in Baldwin's craftsmanship to explain his demise. In addition to Gates's epigraph to this section, Watkins finds *No Name* less important than Baldwin's earlier work because his "essay style, in fact, set a literary precedent that would later develop into the 'New Journalism'" but while *No Name* remains a "consummate literary adaptation of the stylistic features of black preaching" he explains that "only if an eloquent appeal for morality is irrelevant in the seventies, is James Baldwin anachronistic."[127] In this vein, Derek Wright detects a "mellower"[128] Baldwin in essays out of step with the separatist politics of the 1970s. Indeed, Baldwin's later interviews evidence a simplified rhetoric. In 1972, Baldwin rehashed his argument from *Fire* with brevity and simplicity: "Color is a great American myth. Babies and corpses have no color. It's part of the great American masturbation."[129] For an exasperated Baldwin, his complex examination of identity and division becomes a few tired glosses of previous arguments—at least in the interview format.

To avoid losing Baldwin's craftsmanship amid debates about changing political climates, we must recognize the American protest essay tradition and accord Baldwin a central place in it. Some critics begin this project when they reverse traditional generic hierarchies and read Baldwin's fiction secondary to his essays. A 1965 review of *Going to Meet the Man*, for instance, praises Baldwin's indictment of America's race problem and sees the short stories as "dimly recognize[able]"[130] manifestations of his essays. Whitney Balliet calls *Another Country* (1962) simply a "turbid melodrama" that he only kept reading because "Baldwin the polemicist-moralist-essayist is, no matter how obscurely, always close at hand, and it is this passionate being who keeps us reading, reminding us of the tough, humming essays for which he has become celebrated."[131] Though these critics may perpetuate a zero-sum competition between art and advocacy, many critics celebrate the essays as literary achievements beyond politicking. For those who praise the essays in their own right, Baldwin's novelistic and dramatic endeavors might be "the wrong pulpit."[132] David Anderson begins to realign Baldwin's essay legacy by showing that his essays "remain historically grounded and politically engaged,"[133] even if some deemed him irrelevant in a post-integration age.

In mid-twentieth-century America, the simultaneous emergence of the Civil Rights movement and the Cold War brought matters of domestic exclusion and national identity into the fore. Not since Reconstruction failed and westward imperial expansion closed America's policed borders had the United States engaged on such a popular scale discussions of making national promises apply to all its people. By the 1960s, social movements seized on excluded, oppressed, or otherwise disenfranchised identities—from African Americans to women to Chicanos to American Indians—in order to simultaneously claim and critique declarations of American democracy as rightfully belonging to them.[134] In this tradition stands Baldwin's consistent demand, laid out in the essay "Many Thousands Gone," that "Negroes are Americans and their destiny is the country's destiny" (*Notes* 42). Baldwin provides an answer for how to engage a nation in debates over identity, founding documents, and the daily evidence of oppression, racism, and broken promises in the lives of so many Americans.

On his path to earning posthumous full respect as a literary craftsman who excels in the art of advocacy, Baldwin has weathered political squabbles about identity and representation that preoccupy social movements and contemporary literary studies. In a 2004 letter to the *New York Times*, William H. Banks Jr. of the Harlem Writers Guild unequivocally claims Baldwin as a literary and political forebear: "Far from being a 'counterpoint' to the rage some blacks felt in the 1960's, Baldwin was very much in harmony with it, if not with all those who expressed it. . . . Baldwin chose to live in France and he crossed over to the promised land of white acceptance, but he never became a stranger on the shore of the African American experience."[135] Banks's unqualified endorsement contrasts with reviews immediately following Baldwin's death, such as Bruce Bawer's contention that Baldwin's work "seems to have been designed to please both the black radicals and white liberals but succeeded in pleasing neither—for his language was too fancy and his politics too tame for one party and his sentences too sloppy and his rhetoric too hostile for the other."[136]

The trend across political and literary spectra is now to claim Baldwin as a central figure in American literary and political traditions. Dwight McBride's 1999 collection of a new generation of scholar's responses to Baldwin ushered in renewed interest in Baldwin's legacy,[137] but this important collection is still dominated by evaluations of Baldwin's politics largely divorced from more literary concerns. Black, feminist, and queer studies scholars continue to explore Baldwin's relationship to Black Power and the black nationalist project of racial separatism. Most focus on Eldridge Cleaver's famous devastating attack in which he unseats Baldwin from the throne of racial spokesperson by playing to the rampant homophobia in the nation and in Black Power,[138] and some critics now place Baldwin at the center of the emergent field of Black queer studies.[139] In addition to Baldwin's current status as a black gay icon, feminists reclaim Baldwin, too, by noting his important early, messy depictions of the experience of race, gender, and sexuality in America.[140] Baldwin is also recognized for his role in generating a political philosophy of inclusion.[141]

In these reclamations of Baldwin's legacy, critics and readers celebrate his role as a *witness* in an era when literary figures no longer carry the cultural capital necessary to serve as political advocates on the national stage. Baldwin's essays lie at the center of his literary and political legacy. The *New York Times* said as much in his obituary: Baldwin's "passionate, intensely personal essays in the 1950's and 60's on racial discrimination in America made him an eloquent voice of the civil-rights movement."[142] Baldwin's tremendous importance in the political and literary scenes was felt as soon as he departed. The *New York Times* printed excerpts from elegies by Toni Morrison, Maya Angelou, and Amiri Baraka at Baldwin's funeral celebration at the Cathedral of St. John the Divine to pay homage to "Baldwin's insistent, passionate voice—as an essayist, novelist and playwright—[that] helped to inform and transform the debate on civil rights for Afro-Americans."[143]

Not long after Baldwin's death, many praised Baldwin's ability to recount personal-as-collective experience, even those who had sparred with or denounced him. Baldwin's essays cross indentitarian lines within a divided audience, and so, too, his influence also crosses diverse political and literary interests. Baldwin is now a key player in feminism, Civil Rights, racial self-determination, multiculturalism, anti-colonialism, and black gay studies, as well as literary studies. Baldwin invites this reclamation by diverse groups because he recognized that universality and collectivity are only accessible by attending to the particular and the divided. Hilton Als's 1998 essay on Baldwin is a good bridge between laments of Baldwin's demise and later celebrations of his artistry. Subtitled "The making and unmaking of James Baldwin," Als begins with his first encounter with Baldwin's essays. Als remembers projecting himself onto Baldwin on the dust-jacket cover and reflects, "I had never seen an image of a black boy like me—Baldwin looked as if he could have been posing in my old neighborhood, in East New York—gracing anything as impressive as a collection of essays."[144] Als then recounts his personal odyssey with Baldwin's writings—mainly his essays. He argues, "It was in Baldwin's essays, unencumbered by the requirements of narrative form, character, and incident, that his voice was most fully realized."[145] Many other personal essays follow this formula of projecting the reading self onto Baldwin.[146] Baldwin's readers are ready to renegotiate the two-way contract between protest essayist and audience. The protest essay, more so than politically engaged work in other genres, allows Baldwin the universalist-integrationist to be claimed by the identitarian social movements and literary camps that comprise the latter part of the twentieth century, and beyond.

Chapter Five

Identity Politics, Collective Futures, and the Cross-Essay Conversations of Audre Lorde, Adrienne Rich, and Alice Walker

Protest essays are vulnerable to charges that their focus on urgency, immediacy, and specific experiences of exclusion threatens their literary sensibilities on one hand, and their commitment to national ideals on another. When protest essays originate as speeches and incorporate that scene into the essay itself, as explored in chapter 1, this makes them further vulnerable to charges that they are too specific within collective visions. This tension strains almost to the breaking point when the utopian aspirations of many sixties movements shifted away from universalist ideals in the New Left and Civil Rights and into more location- and identity-specific concerns with the rise of Black Power, women's liberation, chicana/o, gay liberation, and other identitarian movements. Identity politics brought a renewed emphasis on self-determination, cross-identity solidarity, and what Marianne DeKoven aptly calls, "utopia limited." James Baldwin's tenuous status as racial spokesman indicates an ever-present pitfall for protest essayists, and the identitarian turn amplifies suspicions about the relationship between speaker and spoken for. Protest essays draw on the genre's insistence on experience over abstract truth, but they also underscore the difficulty of moving beyond that experience. Protest essayists tether experiences of exclusion to aspirational visions of national belonging, but this move may jeopardize visions of full equality for all if they reside in the particulars of identity.

To explore the fate of the protest essay in this identitarian moment, we can turn to the essays of Audre Lorde, Adrienne Rich, and Alice Walker, all celebrated feminist writers known as much for their politics as their artistry. Like Baldwin, these writers turn to the essay for political advocacy, but they add another dimension: they address each other and fellow writers and thinkers, both from their time and generations past. This cross-essay conversation illustrates a key way that protest essayists create inclusive visions amid the challenge of identity politics. The essays illustrate an important moment in the American protest essay tradition when writers respond to heightened suspicions about collectivity.

In the late 1970s, women's liberation was widely criticized for deemphasizing or even erasing experiences of race, class, nation, and black women in particular in its focus on sisterhood. Lorde writes in 1979, "The history of white women who are unable to hear Black women's words, or to maintain dialogue with us, is long and discouraging."[1] Lorde's charge echoed longstanding concerns of black feminists, and it would be amplified greatly in the ensuing decade, especially in influential anthologies like *This Bridge Called My Back* (1981), *All the Women Are White, All the Blacks Are Men, But Some of Us Are Brave* (1982), and *Home Girls* (1983). In response, Rich writes, "A few years ago I would have spoken of the common oppression of women,"[2] but instead she asks, "Once again: Who is *we*?" (231). The protest essay generally asks this question, and feminist essayists respond with pained conversations about how to access collectivity while attending to difference. Chapter 2 trace a tradition of re-vising founding documents, and this chapter examines a moment of intertextuality among essayists themselves, similar to re-visions of Whitman by Vidal or Thoreau by Jordan discussed in chapter 1. Lorde, Rich, and Walker draw on their specific experiences, and the conversations among them, to stake out a vision of national belonging that attends to group difference. Their dialogic model enacts that collective vision. Ruth-Ellen Boetcher Joeres traces how radical feminist essayists draw from and critique a privileged tradition of the personal essay by moving beyond a unified speaker and normative "we" and into the promise of communication between fellow sisters. This chapter further explores how an inclusive, experiential "we" arises *across* these essays. These protest essayists strive toward a collective "we" that addresses difference, even if that collective "we" must now emerge across essays.

Feminist historians and social activists widely point to the late 1970s and early 1980s as a turning point in U.S. social movements' increasing attention to the diversity within their fold, and an attendant politics of identity. The big social movements of the mid-twentieth century are marked by universalist tendencies, from Civil Rights integration to the New Left project of participatory democracy, and they turned to the protest essay to unveil hypocrisy between universalist state declarations of equality and practices of exclusion. But many movements, including Students for a Democratic Society (SDS) explored in chapter 1, understood these exclusions as *aberrations* of an ideal, not as constitutive of the ideal itself. When feminist activists insisted on the primacy of their experiences of gendered exclusion, the New Left, SNCC, and Marxist organizations often failed to address feminist concerns on the grounds that they were too particular, secondary, or distracting.[3]

In their essays, Lorde, Rich, and Walker respond to an important moment when feminists intensified their criticism of the erasures practiced under some of the universalist impulses of social movements, including women's liberation.[4] For many, identitarian concerns usher in an era of embraced difference. In her study of the sixties and the emergence of the postmodern, DeKoven turns to the Second Wave to characterize what she terms "subject politics." For DeKoven, subject politics—speaking from and grounding a political vision in one's own experience and contingent identity—represents the best of the bitter and energizing insights from the women's movement, anti-war movement, and Civil Rights as they addressed internal contradictions that sometimes replicated the very hierarchies they critiqued.[5] For DeKoven, this turn to subject politics marks a point when emancipatory social movements remained steeped within universalist revolutionary goals, but began to attend to the particularity of identity by envisioning—and often enacting—smaller, more grounded, possibly inconsistent, or "limited," utopias.[6] Since American protest essays cleave particular experiences to inclusive visions, the feminist cross-essay conversation demonstrates how a focus on particular identities may be an avenue toward universalist impulses—not its antithesis.

AUDRE LORDE'S CHALLENGE TO FEMINIST COLLECTIVITY

Lorde is a prolific poet whose work in the essay, especially in *Sister Outsider* (1984) and the autobiographical collection of essays, diary entries, and research in *The Cancer Journals* (1980), established her as a key voice in American feminism during the rise of identity politics, black feminism, third-world solidarity, and multiculturalism. Lorde is a key figure in African American letters, contemporary feminist writing, and political poetry, though recent scholarship is also beginning to draw connections between Lorde and canonical American literature.[7] In general, critics celebrate Lorde's dexterity in navigating complex identities,[8] her commitment to black women's and lesbian empowerment,[9] and her emphasis on the black female body.[10] In this last area, the relationship between Lorde's rhetoric of empowerment and her use of the essay for what Atkins describes as "embodied truth" most come together.

In one of her most famous essays, "Poetry Is Not a Luxury" (1977), Lorde meditates on the power—both aesthetic and political—of poetry and declares, "For each of us as women, there is a dark place within, where hidden and growing our true spirit rises."[11] Though Lorde praises the ability of poetry to access the intimate and the experiential, like W. E. B. DuBois she comes to this revelation in an essay. Lorde explicitly claims the province of poetry for the disenfranchised, the silenced, the oppressed, and the political. She does this by positioning her voice primarily as a woman in this early essay, but also as a black woman, a lesbian, and a voice for the variously oppressed as she becomes a spokeswoman in the time between the essay's initial appearance in *Chrysalis: A Magazine of Female Culture* in 1977 and *Sister Outsider* in 1984. So, Lorde invokes a "we" that moves among more universalist aspirations and identity-specific locations within and outside the essay. Her "embodied truth" can only be partially inhabited by her essay's speaker; it must also be inhabited by those she addresses.

While Lorde contends that "poetry is not a luxury" and that poetry is the medium best able to think the heretofore unthinkable, the *essay* form allows her to address a divided, differently embodied audience so that intimate truths come into conversation. Further, in her essays Lorde speaks from a collective space between the poles of abstraction and experience, male and female, white and black: "The white fathers told us: I think, therefore I am. The Black mother within each of us—the poet—whispers in our dreams: I feel, therefore I can be free. Poetry coins the language to express and charter this revolutionary demand, the implementation of that freedom" (38). As a woman-identified woman, African American, and lesbian, Lorde attends to the particularity of each individual and the relevance of identitarian groupings. Joeres notes the clunky grammar, but ultimate necessity, of Lorde's movement between first-person singular and collective voice because of "the obvious importance for Lorde of the subjective inclusiveness for the group to whom she is talking and to which she claims to belong."[12] For Joeres, these deliberate moves between Lorde and her readers, or perhaps between the particular and the universal, incite the idea of communication.

But can feminism—or the American protest essay—respond adequately? Lorde challenges her feminist community to deliver a collective voice able to attend to difference without privileging one group over another. Like Baldwin's slippery pronouns, Joeres argues that Lorde moves among pronouns in a "clear effort to create connections, dialogic and otherwise, between the essayist and her readers/listeners. From the outset, there is a presence of what could be viewed as a collective 'we': no single individual, instead a group despite the single authorship."[13] I go one step further: multiple essays and their cross-essay conversations deliver a model for that collective "we" beyond the individually authored essay.

Many of the most influential anthologies of writings by women of color in the 1980s included dialogues between representative feminists. In this way, a purposefully heterogeneous collective "we" emerges across multiple speakers anchored in personal experience and identity. In an instructive study, Norma Alarcón looks to readers of *This Bridge* for whom the "we" speaks because, "Women of color often recognize themselves in the pages of *Bridge*."[14] Rather than embodying "difference," as most Anglo-feminist readers felt, the speakers in *This Bridge* occupy a privileged space (access to speaking, writing, publishing) under which future readers can claim representation. For Alarcón, the subject(s) of *This Bridge* offer a "plurality of self" whose speaking voice is much more viable than politics of oppositionality, unity, or even solidarity. Individual essays followed suit, such as Gloria Anzaldúa's widely influential "Speaking in Tongues: A Letter to Third World Women Writers" (1981) in which she quotes, responds to, and moves among fellow feminists of color in a search for a collective vision of justice. In this way, Anzaldúa builds on a transnational and transidentitarian essay tradition that responds to desires for collectivity amid the demands of identity politics.

ADRIENNE RICH'S RESPONSE

Lorde delivers her challenge to white feminists in the form of an open letter to radical feminist Mary Daly, but only after receiving no reply to the personal copy she sent directly. By distributing an open letter publicly to a feminist community in an essay collection, Lorde draws on the conversational convention of essays and infuses it with the epistolary tradition. As a result, the ensuing conversation makes literal the intimate, face-to-face interaction for which Lorde calls. Rich accepts the challenge. She responds with essays that refer by name to key feminist writers of the present and past, which creates a conversation among diverse women who, like Anna Julia Cooper's voice from the South, stand in for diverse readers gathering in sisterhood, or at least coalitional dialogue. Rich is as prolific an essayist as poet, delivering highly regarded essay collections including *On Lies, Secrets, and Silence* (1979), *Blood, Bread, and Poetry* (1986), and *What Is Found There: Notebooks on Poetry and Politics* (1993). Like her poetry, many remark on Rich's ability to make the personal both political and poetic in her essays, and her essays have greatly influenced American feminist thought. Though some scholars focus on Rich's essays in a tradition following Virginia Woolf or other Anglo-American feminists,[15] this chapter concerns her role in creating a collective "we" in cross-essay and cross-identity conversations with her contemporaries.

In *Blood, Bread, and Poetry*, Rich enters conversations with contemporary feminists—including Lorde specifically—to respond to challenges of exclusion in the women's liberation project of sisterhood. A prime example is her reflective essay "Notes Toward a Politics of Location" (1984) in which she draws on the provisional, tentative, and experiential conventions of the essay in a humble and heartfelt re-vision of past thinking about women's oppression—without jettisoning her collective aspirations. Rich admits that a few years prior, "I would have spoken these words as a feminist who 'happened' to be a white United States citizen, conscious of my government's proven capacity for violence and arrogance of power, but as separated from that government" (210). Rich narrates her evolution in thinking so that she now fully accepts the salience of the experiences and identities she "happens" to inhabit. In doing so, Rich embraces experience-based ideas about collectivity, or what G. Douglass Atkins calls "embodied truth" in the essay. True to the essay form's open-endedness, Rich "comes here with notes but not absolute conclusions. This is not a sign of loss of faith or hope. These notes are the marks of a struggle to keep moving, a struggle for accountability" (211). Rich creates a space for genuine dialogue, both within the provisional essay and as a model for ongoing conversation among herself and her divided audience.

Many essays—especially protest essays—originate as lectures or speeches, and they purposefully create an embodied audience, as well as speaker. Joeres argues that radical feminist essayists build on the conversational aspect of essays but move toward actual communication. She argues, "The essay must at least signify dialogue although it is itself a monologue."[16] In a tradition of "passionate essays" of radical feminists, Joeres suggests that Rich uses speeches and lectures to imbue her essays with "a sense of initiated dialogue, of communication, that also removes it from the interiorized self-examination practice of many traditional essays and connects it with the material conditions present in the production of her essay."[17] Indeed, most scholars of the essay account for a dialogic aspect of the form, especially in its propensity for interpellation of others' words, which brings the essayist into conversation with ideas and people who came before. For instance, Thomas Recchio draws on Thoreau's *Walden* and Mikhail Bakhtin's concept of heteroglossia to identify a "dialogic" aspect of essays, both literary and analytical, in which "a writer struggles to locate himself and to find his own voice within a discourse, to enter a dialogue that discourse itself preconditions and that he tries to control."[18] The dialogue enacted by these feminist essayists, however, is welcoming and embodied; it is not just a struggle with abstract discourse. Further, these essayists draw not only from the dialogic quality of the traditional essay but also from the immediate addresses to divided publics in American political oratory. In this way, the protest essay is particularly well-suited to those cultural moments when literary figures occupy real platforms of national dialogue—be it at academic conferences, protest rallies, or a senator's apartment.

While many essays originate as lectures (Emerson's writings are good examples), Rich purposefully incorporates the scene of oral delivery: an academic conference on semiotics in Utrecht, Holland, then at Cornell University and Pacific Oaks College in the United States. She writes, "I will speak these words in Europe, but I am having to search for them in the United States of North America" (211). This move enacts not only Atkins's "embodied truth," but also the "politics of location" necessary to any viable collective. Her scene of address may be removed from the United States, but her provisional conclusion about "struggling for accountability" requires her to return to her home location, at least in the terrain of the essay. In doing so, Rich rises to Lorde's challenge and rejects Woolf's uprooted abstraction of women without a country. She declares, "As a woman I have a country; as a woman I cannot divest myself of that country merely by condemning its government or by saying three times, 'As a woman my country is the whole world'" (212). In response to suspicions about sisterhood and even solidarity, Rich does not reject collective aspirations. Instead she uses the essay to document her own place in that collective enterprise, and make room for others.

Rich offers her readers a model for how they might also enter this collective enterprise. The looseness of Rich's subject locations—her "I" and her "woman"—provide the right amount of slippage between the particular and the universal, similar to the dexterous pronouns of Baldwin or Lorde. In this way, Rich avoids the problem of endlessly chronicling one's specific location, in which she would drift hopelessly further from the possibility of collectivity across identitarian lines. One of the key ways that Rich connects her located, accountable self to her feminist contemporaries is by folding them into the essay itself and documenting her process of learning from a text-based dialogue with them. Rich recounts how she came to recognize and move beyond white-centered feminism through the writings of black feminism. She goes so far as to list by name some of the key writers and texts, including Lorde, alongside people like June Jordan and Barbara Smith and key texts like *This Bridge*. Beyond offering a reading list, Rich maps out a direction for her audience to pursue, but in the form of a question:

> And if we read Audre Lorde or Gloria Joseph or Barbara Smith, do we understand that the intellectual roots of this feminist theory are not white liberalism or Euro-American feminism, but the analyses of Afro-American experience articulated by Sojourner Truth, W.E.B. DuBois, Ida B. Wells-Barnett, C.L.R. James, Malcolm X, Lorraine Hansberry, Fannie Lou Hamer, among others? (231)

Rich charts the different sources from which she learns in order that she—and her audience—can help create a collective future that addresses difference and recognizes division, both historically and in the present. The assignment is delivered in the form of a question to reflect not only the provisionality and humility of Rich as a speaker, but also the desire for her audience to carry the assignment forward. For, as Rich contends, "This is the end of these notes, but this is not an end" (231). Rich makes space for those from other locations to enter into and lead this conversation. At least in this dialogic essay, the provisionality of Rich's stance and her emphasis on the intractability of her own location require her to stop short of offering a collective vision. For that, I turn briefly to Alice Walker.

ALICE WALKER'S COLLECTIVE VISION

In one of her essays collected in the influential *In Search of Our Mothers' Gardens* (1983), Walker meditates on the persistent question of the relationship between the writer and her subject, a question particularly heightened both in the American protest essay and African American literary traditions. She writes, "And when I write about the people [from her Georgia childhood], in the strangest way it is as if I am not writing about them at all, but about myself. The artist then is the voice of the people, but she is also The People."[19] Walker is acutely aware of the dangers—but also the necessity—of tethering her voice, personal experience, and vision to those of others. In that essay, humorously titled "The Unglamorous but Worthwhile Duties of the Black Revolutionary Artist, or of the Black Writer Who Simply Works and Writes," Walker delivers a speech to the Black Students' Association at Sarah Lawrence College. She explains, "When I was here there were six of us and none of us was entirely black. Much has clearly changed, here as in the rest of the country. But when I look about and see what work still remains I can only be mildly, though sincerely, impressed" (133). Using the dialogic conventions of the essay, and the protest convention of incorporating an immediate audience, Walker invites the students into her present vision for future progress. Walker's "us" moves among specific referents: the six black students from her days at Sarah Lawrence College, current black students at the college, African Americans generally, and the collective nation that must improve.

As Walker moves among "The People," herself, the nation, and specific audiences, she sets out a collective vision that requires the participation of those before her, and those beside her. As I noted in chapter 1, Cheryl Wall suggests that Walker does some of her best work in the essay. For Wall, one of the reasons is that "the form of the essay which strives to produce the effect of the spontaneous, the tentative, and the open-ended lends itself to exploring the complex and contentious issues which Walker addresses. She invites readers to puzzle the issues out with her and welcomes them to share those epiphanies she achieves."[20] In this way, Walker uses the essay not only to craft a literary lineage and meditate on current events, but also to bring her fellow readers and citizens into her texts. A brief look at her evolving stances in her essays on Civil Rights between 1967 and 1987 chronicles Walker's increasing comfort with a universalist vision for justice amid identitarian concerns.

Many have written about, and been inspired by, Walker's persistent desire to construct a wide-ranging literary lineage, one that connects Zora Neale Hurston to Phyllis Wheatley to Woolf to Flannery O'Connor to Richard Wright. Like the concern with literary and historical predecessors in Lorde's and Rich's essays, *In Search of Our Mothers' Gardens* is rife with intergenerational intertextuality. One of Walker's most famous—and moving—

essays, "Looking for Zora" (1975), recounts her journey to locate Hurston's unmarked grave, which has become an influential case study of literary recovery projects. In that essay, Walker goes so far as to pass as Hurston's niece, which is why she is such a ripe subject for Wall's study of black women writers' long-standing concern with lineage. Walker responds, "Besides, as far as I'm concerned, she *is* my aunt—and that of all black people as well" (*Gardens* 102). For Walker, the embodied truth of the essay extends well beyond the individual essayist and into an intimate, genealogical, but nevertheless heterogeneous literary tradition.

Walker's cross-generational and cross-identitarian vision of literary history undergirds her focus on a similar dialogue in the present. In that dialogue, Walker strives for collectivity somewhat counterintuitively by emphasizing personal experience and identitarian difference. For instance, Walker discusses reading fellow black feminists Barbara Smith and Gloria Hull in "Breaking Chains and Encouraging Life" (1980), or in an open letter to *Ms.* (1982) she quotes from radical feminist Andrea Dworkin as a way of thinking about Jewish women and the Middle East. The intimate, personal, yet still pained dialogue embodies not just the essayist's own journey, but the text-based conversation she enters.

Walker's essays also lament fellow writers, students, neighbors, and friends who stop short of crossing identitarian lines. In my favorite example, "A Child of One's Own: A Meaningful Digression within the Work(s)" (1979), Walker meditates on black women's lineage, Woolf and women's writing, her own pregnancy, and a historical record that excludes women. In a key scene, Walker explores the emerging emphasis on identity politics in academic feminism by discussing Patricia Meyer Spacks's decision to discuss only white women's literature at an academic conference. Walker quotes Spacks: "'As a white woman, I'm reluctant and unable to construct theories about experiences I haven't had'" (*Gardens* 382). Walker recoils at this take on black women's self-determination, especially since, as Walker points out parenthetically, "Yet Spacks never lived in the nineteenth-century Yorkshire, so why theorize about the Brontës?" (382). In response, Walker searches—through essayistic digression into films, dinner parties, staged dialogues, academics, Sojourner Truth, and folk music—for a theory of imagination that allows women to connect across identitarian lines. For Walker, we must imagine beyond ourselves and into the experiences of others, as risky as that collective project may be. Further, in "Looking to the Side, Looking Back" (1979), Walker meditates on the problem of collectivity through anecdotes about her childhood, lesbian separatism, her education, her writing, ordinary Civil Rights activists who desegregated institutions, and most specifically her experience at a Radcliffe symposium on black women with her friend, Jordan. At the symposium, Walker becomes upset when she is told she is wrong to carry the burden of her mother, and by extension all black women who came before. Walker responds, "June, who was sitting beside me, and who was angry but not embarrassed by my tears, put her arms around me and said: 'But why shouldn't you carry your mother; she carried *you*, didn't she?'" (319).

Walker embodies inter- and intra-generation intertextuality so that her collective project stands a chance of becoming real. Throughout her essays, Walker embarks on a quest to build an inclusive, cross-generational tradition of women writers. Tuzyline Jita Allan explores how Walker "(re)writes/rights"[21] Woolf, especially *A Room of One's Own*, through signifying strategies. Allan focuses on the formal difference between Woolf and Walker in their common project of creating a space for women writers and "a voice of one's own." She argues, "The omnipresent first-person pronoun 'I' is the most salient feature of Walker's narrative repertoire and a marker of her radically different rhetorical style."[22] In this way, Walker rejects Woolf's overemphasis on the general and the universal, a move that places Walker more in line with the protest essay than the familiar essay. Further, Allan traces how Walker uses the anecdote as a narrative device, which fits well within the essay tradition, but also risks overemphasizing personal or identitarian experience within a feminist collective vision. Nevertheless, by insisting on her own perspective and experience *in dialogue* with those who came before and those beside her, Walker "exemplif[ies] a discursive technique that accommodates other voices but leaves sufficient room for her own."[23]

Walker's ultimate response to the challenges of self-determination and universalist aspiration come to fruition in her later, less widely celebrated essays. In her collection *Living by the Word* (1988), Walker first commemorates Martin Luther King Jr.'s birthday with the speech-cum-essay "Everything Is a Human Being" (1983) and then a meditation on that piece in "The Universe Responds" (1987). These essays reflect on and update earlier essays on Civil Rights in *In Search of Our Mothers' Gardens*. In those essays, Walker uses the essay to witness—and Wall points out that she also invites other witnesses to present evidence[24]—the truth of black people's experience in Civil Rights, which often contradicted white media portrayals of the movement as finished. The Civil Rights movement—or, more intimately, "The Movement"—is a central preoccupation for Walker perhaps because, as Wall suggests, it is life-giving and "as a writer as well as a citizen, she is indebted to the cause."[25] Wall traces how Walker, like Baldwin, loses some cultural capital in the ascendancy of Black Power ideology; but I want to illustrate briefly how Walker *gains* status in a collective-minded American protest essay tradition through her evolving engagement with The Movement.

In her early Civil Rights essays, Walker maintains a semidetached witness stance akin to the familiar essay. She holds King at arm's length by describing her experience with the televised movement in "The Civil Rights Movement: What Good Was It?" (1967). She recounts, "Like a good omen for the future, the face of Dr. Martin Luther King, Jr., was the first black face

I saw on our new television screen" (*Gardens* 124). Further, in an essay ten years after the March on Washington, Walker stands semidistanced from the crowd in that famous freedom march. In fact, she sits in a tree. Even though her relatives claimed to see her on television, she writes, "I was not anywhere near [King]. The crowds would not allow it. I was, instead, perched on the limb of a tree far from the Lincoln Memorial, and although I managed to see very little, I could hear everything" (*Gardens* 158–59). Walker concentrates on the words emanating from the platform, rather than the sheer emotion of inclusion and historical import. These moves to maintain the integrity of her personal voice guard her from abstract narratives of equality promised not only by the nation, but also by The Movement. Walker writes, "I think Medgar Evars and Martin Luther King, Jr., would be dismayed by the lack of radicalism in the new black middle class, and discouraged to know that a majority of the black people helped most by the movement of the Sixties has abandoned itself to the pursuit of cars, expensive furniture, large houses, and the highest scotch" (*Gardens* 168). In these somewhat rare moments of unhumorous pessimism, Walker cements a division between speaker and spoken about, admonishing those who should be in her collective vision but aren't. Here, the collective, heterogeneous "we" so central to the protest essay threatens to recede.

Walker's later essays in *Living by the Word*, however, attempt to envision and possibly bring about the full range of collectivity that The Movement promised. For a 1983 keynote on King's birth, Walker does not attend a rally and find a tree perch. Instead, evocative of Thoreau's retreat to Walden to address the nation, Walker begins, "Some years ago, a friend and I walked into the countryside to listen to what the Earth was saying, and to better hear our own thoughts" (*Living* 140). In this deeply intimate posture of listening, Walker enters American history and hears the words of Black Elk, early American Indians, slave owners and Indian killers, early anthropologists, and the voice of the Earth, who "has become the nigger of the world" (147). Whereas Hurston turns to nature to compare Janie to the mule of the world in *Their Eyes Were Watching God* (1937), Walker inverts the metonymic connection and sees the universe through sociological constructs. In this way, Walker is able to address—and protest—suffering, injustice, and division while at the same time lay the groundwork for an earthbound collective vision that can analyze and refuse sociological, historical, and political divisions. Though she risks rejection on grounds that her vision is overly metaphysical, New Age, or romanticizes American Indians, it is the essay—not a mythical Earth or stereotyped American Indian—that conjures this collective vision. She locates her vision in everyday practice as she ends with the words of Black Elk, a Pacific News Service excerpt, and a demand that we attend to our actions, not aspirations, because "only our behavior can we re-create, or create anew" (151).

In response to criticisms of her turn to humanist and naturalist visions, Walker reflects on that essay four years later in "The Universe Responds" so that she may further anchor her vision in experience. To justify her ability to speak to and for the universe, Walker writes, "Ironically, Black Elk and nuclear scientists can be viewed in much the same way: as men who prayed to the Universe for what they believed they needed and who received from it a sign reflective of their own hearts" (192). She finds models for her vision in unlikely places, then anchors it in personal experience: "Believing this, which I learned from my experience with the animals and the wild flowers, I have found that my fear of nuclear destruction has been to a degree lessened" (192). Only through a stubborn move outward from personal experience through collectivity to universality—literally encompassing the universe—can Walker deliver a "we" that does not exclude unnecessarily. Finally, risking derision from cynics about bland platitudes, she writes, "We are *indeed* the world" (193).

FEMINIST ESSAYS AND THE CHOICE OF COLLECTIVITY AND INDIVIDUAL DISSENT

The cross-essay dialogue between Lorde's challenge and Rich's and Walker's responses points to a larger concern in the American protest essay tradition: the call for collectivity is both the hallmark and gnawing anxiety of a tradition that demands inclusion by addressing division. Further, suspicions about inclusion and exclusion are particularly heightened in essays that speak collectively during the rise of identity politics. If national utterances like "we the people" ring hollow for those outside the echo chambers of power, the "we" of protest essays embody a collective voice speaking from both vision and experience. The collective "we" that emerges across the essays of Lorde, Rich, and Walker is wanting: it must seek out future, past, and present participation from those not yet fully included. This model may go a long way toward solving the paradox of the one and/in the many (*e pluribus unum*) and the persistent American tendency to prematurely announce the end of inequity.

Protest essays are vulnerable to allegations that their collective utterances were, are, and will always be much more specific than the seemingly comprehensive pronoun "we." In her study of the manifesto, a close sister genre of the protest essay, Janet Lyon traces how the manifesto embodies the paradoxes of the modern subject in which "we the people" is a fantasy that signifies inclusion as it enacts exclusion. For Lyon, the manifesto's "we" always turns out to be premature, exclusionary, and destined to fall under the weight of its demand for utopia now. She argues that the manifesto is central to a modernity marked by "the first emergence of the idea of the universal subject and its ever-deferred completion." In Lyon's study, the Second Wave's oppositions—essentialism and social construction, equality and difference, universality and particularity—cohere: the manifesto requires already constituted collective speakers ("women") arguing for immediate radical change in a vision for the future. Lyon notes, for instance, the problematic irony of the "we" in Valerie Solanas's singularly written S.C.U.M. Manifesto (1968) built on a "society" totally defined and inhabited by the author. Lyon argues that manifestos are unstable because the "we" of, for instance, the Redstockings Manifesto is an "impossible pronoun, signifying both an imagined group of 'brutally exploited' women *and* a group of women testifying to their mutual differences."[26]

So, too, Lorde's, Rich's, and Walker's collective-minded vision is vulnerable to charges that it promises a "we" much larger than it initially enacts. Even amid a movement that prizes models of participatory democracy and looks with great skepticism on abstraction, most Second Wave documents have more modest authorships than the wide net cast by their collective pronouns and universalist aspirations. In addition to Solanas's one woman society, a good example is Alix Kates Shulman's influential "A Marriage Agreement" (1970). Shulman offers the principles of her marriage in the form of collective declarative statements: "We reject the notion . . . ," "We believe that . . . ," "As parents we believe we must. . . ."[27] Ostensibly, the "we" is Shulman and her husband speaking in concert. However, in a 1998 memoir essay, Shulman divulges that she was the sole author, while her husband "obligingly acquiesced" to the agreement in lieu of an acceptable divorce decree at a time when New York lacked joint custody laws.[28] The fact of individual authorship of a collective document, along with the biographical scene of a dissolving union, might render the "we" partial or one-sided at best and hopelessly flawed or hypocritical at worst. But that misses the point—and the promise—of texts that imagine a collective that has not yet been (and perhaps never will be) achieved. In fact, Shulman's collective statement of principles *is* accepted—by the agreement's readership. Her agreement appeared in mimeographed copies, new feminist magazines like *Up from Under*, popular women's magazines like *Redbook*, and on the cover of *Life*.[29] We should not feel duped by Shulman's "Marriage Agreement." Though her husband may not have participated in its writing, when the agreement circulates, the "we" lends service to women's liberation, even if he personally does not.[30]

True to the protest essay, Lorde, Rich, and Walker demand speaking positions anchored in personal experience, but also invest in a collective that includes historically disenfranchised groups. In doing so, they join a protest tradition that values the perspectives and experiences of black women, and excluded groups generally. These essayists, of course, were not the first to politicize black women's invisibility. They join a long history, such as Anna Julia Cooper's insistence in 1892 that "only the Black Woman can say 'when and where I enter.'"[31] Or, in 1959, Lorraine Hansberry ironically diagnosed U.S. popular culture where "Women are idiots. People are white. Negroes do not exist."[32] Or, as the title of a famous 1983 anthology declares, "All the Women Are White, All the Blacks Are Men, But Some of Us Are Brave." Beyond their roots in twentieth-century social movements, the "we" of this cross-essay conversation dates back to the founding of a republic that announces independence and inclusion amid practices of exclusion and oppression. Further, like Garnet's admonition to "Remember that you are THREE MILLIONS," Lorde, Rich, and Walker insist upon identitarian experience and cross-group dialogue to show that the "we" of collective protest is a means as well as an end.

The Offer of the New York Radical Feminists

The protest essay tradition is well-suited to the universalist orientation of women's liberation, which sought women's collectivity—sisterhood—as a revolutionary model in opposition to the isolation of patriarchy, capitalism, modernity, and consumer culture. Early women's liberation attacked the scattering of women into domestic units under patriarchy. For many, including especially Rich in her early essays, the answer was to (re-)form women's unity, a project often read as averse to a politics of difference. This initial project set the terms for future feminist debates in America about the promises, limits, and general appeal of collective concepts like sisterhood. It also provides a window on how protest essayists access universalist aspirations by attending to the particular, the experiential, and the excluded.

In 1969, the New York Radical Feminists (NYRF) presented "The Politics of the Ego" to a new women's movement at pains to offer a political theory in which sex was not secondary to other forms of oppression. In the statement, NYRF argue that women's subordination is a result of the institutionalization of the male "ego" that imagines women as its appendage. The NYRF critique purely individual subjectivity in a footnote explaining the term ego: "We are using the classical definition rather than the Freudian: that is, the sense of individual self as distinct from others."[33] Like other critiques of marriage as a system that isolates women, the NYRF reject the stultification of women citizens in which full human potential depends on the distinction from and against others, where "he necessarily must destroy her ego and make it subservient to his" (443). The NYRF find individualism itself a key aspect of patriarchy. NYRF explain, "a group of individuals (men) have organized together for power over women, and . . . they have set up institutions throughout society to maintain this power" (442). The cross-identitarian essays of Lorde, Rich, and Walker join a women's liberation project of collectivity as an antidote to the "group of individuals" who set up patriarchal systems of exclusion and hierarchy.

The NYRF purposefully distinguish patriarchy's tenuous connection between distinct egos from genuine union. In a self-determination stance, the NYRF "assert ourselves as primary to ourselves" (443) and construct "alternative selves that are healthy, independent and self-assertive" (445). But the alternative is not a simple replication of the existing politics of the ego with women occupying the center. While maintaining distance from the "she" and "he" of enforced sex roles, the NYRF speak in a "we" that will "organize politically to destroy this sex class system" (442). The collective "we" of their manifesto is not fixed. Instead, at various moments, "we" speaks as radical feminists, as women and, ultimately, from a collective subject position in a future when the sex class system has been destroyed. This "we" can even include those formerly known as "men." The NYRF explain, "For while we realize that the liberation of women will ultimately mean the liberation of men from their destructive role as oppressor, we have no illusion that men will welcome this liberation without a struggle" (442). Like Rich's speaker, "we" is specific to the moment but also provisional and temporary. Since the NYRF simultaneously inhabit and protest available classes of people ("women" and "men"), they risk replicating de facto segregation of given social units, but the NYRF manifesto desires to move beyond, and even destroy, existing social units. "We" is a space to act before, after, and within the revolution, which will destroy the sex class system where "we are cut off from human relationships" (443).

Feminists often place the advent of identity politics at a breaking point when the Second Wave goals of unity or sisterhood are perceived as impossible because they exclude those who do not inhabit the current centers of feminism (historically, white, middle-class, heterosexual women). Veteran activists and feminist historians are recognizing more fully the presence and impact of black women in the Second Wave. They are rewriting feminist history by collecting documentary and narrative histories of women's liberation in order to better capture the spirit, internal debates, and importance of the women's liberation movement and its project of sisterhood.[34] If the "we" created by this feminist cross-essay conversation—and identity politics generally—addresses the particular at the same time that it reaches for larger collectives, then this cross-essay conversation is a crucial site for responding to familiar accusations that, to borrow Ti-Grace Atkinson's famous maxim, "Sisterhood is powerful: it kills sisters."[35]

The protest essay's "we" is both a rhetorical act and an ongoing project, or what Peggy Phelan describes as constative and performative events. Phelan argues that feminist criticism is utopian in that, unlike merely descriptive scholarship, "it *promises and, in the act of promising, brings a feminist future closer.*"[36] Upon circulation, a specific "we" or "I" in this cross-essay conversation encounters a diverse readership. At multiple sites the "we" becomes flexible and future-oriented, thereby enacting in part the collective vision desired by Lorde, Rich, and Walker. Further, the American protest essay anticipates and addresses discrepancies between substance and performance. The future the essays imagine—and make possible—necessarily speaks in a "we" that will outlive its present particularity.

Dworkin's Refusal

The universalist impulse of sisterhood arises from—not despite—addressing particular identities and divisions within women, including especially a critique of the violent erasure of women of color under some manifestations of women's liberation. Cross-essay conversations like those of Lorde, Rich, and Walker aspire to the meaningful equality promised in the project of sisterhood, but other feminist writers purposefully work outside collectivity—or reject it outright. A good example is the final collection of essays by Andrea Dworkin, whose writings from the 1980s were the eye of the storm in furious feminist debates about sex and sexuality.[37] In *Heartbreak*, Dworkin chronicles moments of disillusionment incited by her teachers, role models, and influences who often turn out to be pedophiles, molesters, abusers, or some other permutation of violent misogyny. Dworkin frames her reflective essays with a polemical stance: "I have been asked, politely and not so politely, why I am myself."[38] Indeed, Dworkin's long career was defined by an adversarial relationship to both a culture-at-large that often accused her of being not woman enough and to feminist academics who accused her of being anti-sex. Yet in "accounting for herself" Dworkin continues to question many of the sacred tenets of the last thirty years of feminism. With a long history of Dworkin-bashing in feminism, she maintains a taut awareness of the rhetorical place of her published self as a hotspot for feminist debates. The series of memoir essays, then, is not an autobiographical analog to her already well-known stances against sex abuse, male power, prostitution, and pornography. Instead, Dworkin continues to delight in lambasting people and their ideologies—both past and current—and thus offers a feminism based in an oppositional or contrarian stance, not collectivity.

In an essay that begins "Becoming a feminist" (157), Dworkin provides a model of feminist development that is specifically anti-collective: "One weekend someone took me to a benefit for one of the pacifist groups. I was so offended by the anti-woman lyrics to a song that I got up and walked out. Someone else did too. . . . That man was John Stoltenberg and I've lived with him for nearly twenty-seven years" (159). The scene is noteworthy because it locates righteous protest in breaks *away* from collective politics. In her "political memoir," Dworkin becomes an individualist, especially in this scene of heterosexual coupling opposed to sisterhood. Dworkin delivers anecdotes in which she breaks away from social movements, such as the pacifist New Left, anti-racist organizations, and NOW. Dworkin's oppositional stances work against a feminist conversation that seeks ideological and identitarian diversity. Instead, Dworkin persistently casts herself in the position of outsider—not being a "good girl" for anyone, including feminists. Dworkin proclaims, "You write the rule in your secret and silent script, and I will find it and break it" (4). Dworkin's raw, irreverent tone echoes many manifestos and essays of the 1960s and 1970s, and the targeted "you" cuts across all political spectrums, including especially feminism and other social movements.

Hansberry's "Nothingism"

As Dworkin illustrates, the collective "we" is neither the only nor the inevitable outcome of demands for justice in American protest essays. There is another option: individual dissent, following the example of Thoreau through Dworkin. What is at stake, finally, is the value of collectivity itself in American protest traditions. It is important to remember from chapter 1 that state hypocrisy in announcing inclusion and performing exclusion has given rise to individual dissent as another model of protest. Even more so than the Port Huron Statement's collective horror at U.S. hypocrisy in the face of "the facts of Negro life in the South" and U.S. international aggression under the banner of "peace," Thoreau's model of social retraction and individual non-participation looms large over many versions of civil disobedience and dissent. Thoreau's essay has inspired collective efforts from the Civil Rights movement to Mohatma Ghandi in the Indian independence movement, and his model of individual divestment characterizes a key strand of counterculture in the 1950s through 1970s.

The collective impulse in many American social movements and protest essays is in tension with writers who cast the individual as the antidote to social conformity, especially in the Beat and some counterculture movements. For instance, while contemplating state-sponsored crimes against humanity like the genocides of World War II, Norman Mailer's 1957 response in "The White Negro" is indicative: "one is a rebel or one conforms."[39] Mailer's protest essay is notorious as both a signal text of the counterculture's impact on mainstream America and as a document of white liberal inability to fully appreciate African American history and struggles. For Mailer, whose antagonism to women's liberation is well known, the social itself is a problem inextricably linked to mass conformity and fascism. He locates protest in an individual writer swashbuckling through state hypocrisies. His anti-statism is accompanied by a terror of the masses, be they conforming Americans or "committee-ish" liberals. In direct opposition to the NYRF's rejection of the ego, Mailer argues for "the liberation of the self from the Super-Ego of society" (354). For Mailer, protest is social divestment, the opposite of collectivity.

The Port Huron Statement, Thoreau, and Mailer all cite the second-class, non, or partial citizenship of others as central to their postures of divestment. As detailed in chapter 1, Thoreau cites, "the fugitive slave, and the Mexican prisoner on parole, and the Indian come to plead the wrongs of his race" (235) in order to stand outside American society in Concord jail. Likewise, for Mailer, the "Negro" is an idea antithetical to American conformity.

Mailer keenly reads the space occupied by African Americans excluded from social systems—but he projects a social fantasy that negates any struggles to claim, as well as critique, the ideal of full citizenship or social participation. The White Negro he proposes is a basic contradiction because it requires the already-had-and-given-up state security constitutive of whiteness, as defined against not-whiteness. The White Negro can only exist alongside Negro second-class citizenship. The partial citizenship of the "Negro" unveils inconsistencies between the promises and the actions of the state, but the "Negro" is not central to Mailer's ensuing collective future vision.

Many black women writers signaled the ultimate ineffectiveness of the individual rebel model. Hansberry succinctly dismissed the paradox of Beat blanket rejection of society:

> [The Beats] have broken away to form their own vague, non-inspirational rebellion of rejection and nothingism. . . . They are a failure. They disturb no one because they attack everything and nothing. They are a source of amusement and confused misunderstanding to the very people who should feel most indicted by their emergence. They serve no significant purpose, neither to art nor society.[40]

Hansberry scornfully dismisses Beat "nothingism" because it is a dead end. Effective indictment is neither unthinking rebellion nor a retreat into individualist nonconformity. Hansberry rejects politics of social divestment out of her commitment to a black protest history, and to the future. A dominant counterculture model equates protest with retraction from social systems and mass participation; but the collective voice in American protest essays joins a tradition that might live up to Hansberry's desire to move past "nothingism" to inspire a just future.

Combahee River Collective's Insistence

Following Lorde and Hansberry's calls, we can turn to a key document of identity politics and black self-determination to understand how insistence on particular experiences and identities aspires to collective futures in the Combahee River Collective's (CRC) *A Black Feminist Statement* (1977). Named for an 1863 anti-slavery guerilla campaign led by Harriet Tubman, the CRC begin their widely influential *Statement*, "We are a collective of Black feminists who have been meeting together since 1974."[41] Like the feminist cross-essay conversation, the *Statement* articulates a "we" that is simultaneously particular and inclusive, both historically specific and future oriented. The *Statement*'s "we" firmly roots itself in its own location and history of black liberation struggles, but it also generates a collective space that cannot foresee the manifold groupings that would claim it. The full potential of the collective utterance "we" comes to fruition in the *Statement*'s subsequently diverse reprintings and the various groups that were inspired by the *Statement*. I have written elsewhere about the *Statement*'s robust publishing history in identitarian movements—especially feminism—that learned to distrust universalist impulses.[42] For this section, I look briefly at the *Statement* to show how it is close kin to the American protest essay in their shared desire to carve out a space for collective protest. If Baldwin's representative voice accesses collectivity through personal experience and Lorde, Rich, and Walker access it through a conversational essay model, the CRC and the manifesto address division from an already constituted collective "we."

The CRC's brief six-year history of political action, planning retreats, and organizing in Boston and throughout the northeastern United States holds a significant place in debates about race-consciousness, representation, and visibility with vast implications not only for black feminism, but for all U.S. feminist movements. The CRC began in 1974 as the Boston chapter of the National Black Feminist Organization (NBFO, 1973–1975), and its most well-known members are Barbara Smith and Demita Frazier. The CRC became an influential organization as it brought issues of sexism to national debates about race that might have been otherwise ignored or downplayed in Civil Rights and black liberation organizations like the Black Panther Party, the Student Non-Violent Coordinating Committee (SNCC), and the Congress of Racial Equality (CORE). In line with Lorde's project, the CRC was crucial in demanding that the diverse concerns of black women occupy the center of political analysis, national debates, and community organizing. The CRC vocally rejected any manifestation of sisterhood that did not adequately address race, sexuality, and class differences. The CRC's insistence on lesbian visibility and socialist politics challenged existing homophobia in African American social movements, and it shaped the direction of feminist thought toward identity politics, critiques of capitalism, and inclusive understandings of sexuality. The CRC organized women to create a community of likeminded black feminists who met in small groups and staged protests, educated each other, and published tracts, such as *Eleven Black Women: Why Did They Die?* (1980).

Like Lorde's challenge to her feminist sisters, the impetus for writing the *Statement* was the failure—and possibly the inability—of other movements to adequately speak to or for black women. The CRC explain, "Above all else, our politics initially sprang from the shared belief that Black women are inherently valuable, that our liberation is a necessity not as an adjunct to somebody else's but because of our need as human persons for autonomy" (11). The rise of identity politics suggests that the project of sisterhood overemphasized the universal; the "shared belief" announced in the CRC's collective "we," however, is not usually subject to charges of unacknowledged specificity. The *Statement* remains understood as anathema to the perceived naïve unity imagined by an earlier moment in women's liberation.

The *Statement* sharply critiques the present and simultaneously demands a reimagined future. The CRC explain, "This focusing upon our own oppression is embodied in the concept of identity politics" (12), but this does not mean personal experience or balkanized identity is an endpoint. In fact, the *Statement* rejects separatism: "Although we are feminists and Lesbians, we feel solidarity with progressive Black men and do not advocate the fractionalization that white women who are separatists demand" (12). By capitalizing key identities (i.e., Black Lesbian), the *Statement* uses its immediate "we" to imagine a future that is inclusive even if the demand for a rigid equation of speakers and subjects ("no one can speak for me but me") in the now is necessary to achieve an inclusive, transformed future.

The CRC demand identity-based speaking positions anchored in personal experience. Like Cooper, they name and embody a heretofore invisible subjectivity; the *Statement* creates the "we" it describes. In a section on the genesis of black feminism, the *Statement* offers a temporal model of coming into subjectivity that Susan Stanford Friedman characterizes as a Second Wave model of "becoming" feminist.[43] The CRC explain, "Black feminists often talk about their feelings of craziness before becoming conscious of the concepts of sexual politics, patriarchal rule, and most importantly, feminism, the political analysis and practice that we women use to struggle against our oppression" (11). The *Statement* performs rhetorical acrobatics that connect specific speakers (black women, black feminists, women, the CRC, and so on) to an inclusive, provisional subjectivity because the "we," the subject "black feminists," and the CRC are not perfectly synonymous. Rather than rigid balkanization, these identity politics allow readers to construct multiple feminisms with black women's concerns at the center.

Many anthologies and disparate political groups claim the *Statement*, even potentially incongruent orientations and identities: black feminists, lesbian feminists, womanists, theorists, rhetoricians, cultural feminists, women's historians, CR groups, socialists, and so on. The Appendix chronicles the many reprintings of the *Statement* over the past thirty years, and its popularity shows no sign of abating. The robust pluralism suggested by its publishing history belies any easy dismissals of utopian universalism in the manifesto or pragmatic balkanization in identity politics. Instead, like the protest essay, the *Statement* resides in the immediate as a way of accessing the enduring. In its circulation, the *Statement* played in some of the CRC events that brought together now famous thinkers such as Lorde and Cheryl Clarke, it called out to proximate feminist groups in the pages of *Off Our Backs* in 1979 and to a future generation of feminists in the pages of *Ms.* in 1991, and it introduces feminism itself in many student-oriented anthologies. Indeed, because they convene without necessarily enforcing sameness,[44] anthologies are able to reflect the diversity of women's experiences and politics as well as identitarian concerns. Contemporary feminism, defined as much by its variety as by shared concerns, is unified in the way it has learned from the insistence on the local, the particular, and internal division we see in the *Statement* and the cross-essay feminist conversation.

I underscore its diverse publishing history because the *Statement* gains meaning beyond its initial location, especially when future readers are not in perfect consonance with the letter, or even the spirit, of the original. Barbara Smith expresses such hope in her 1986 introduction: "*The Combahee River Collective Statement* is just as useful today as it was when it was first conceived. Perhaps its wider circulation will play a role in alerting women of color that the time to organize is now."[45] The *Statement* imagines identity as both product and process. Rather than fix identity, it imagines a collective toward which we must work. Therein lies the importance of traveling across identity, time, and place in subsequent distribution so that the *Statement* sparks collectivity beyond the original group members speaking in a dynamic "we." The *Statement* retains its self-determination stance while its diverse circulation speaks to the resilient capacity of the shifting umbra of its "we." Smith writes, "The fact that some non-Lesbian Black persons are now able to value and respect the work of Black Lesbians is a 'miracle' that our integrity made possible."[46] Identity politics demand that black lesbian experiences and concerns inform political analyses so that future readers extend the project of the collective "we" who, at the end of the *Statement*, "are ready for the lifetime of work and struggle before us" (18).

HOW TO GO BACK TO THE FUTURE

Writers who advocate for historically disenfranchised groups must construct a lineage that includes them, and those like them. This is why writers affiliated with identitarian social movements often embark on recovery projects in their essays and engage history in their fiction, as has been studied at length and in recent work by Wall and Keith Byerman. The essays of Lorde, Rich, and Walker join others that specifically address the exclusion or erasure of women of color in all aspects of modern life. Identity politics have evolved into current feminist ideas about the relation between the global and local, especially in the concept of "intersectionality."[47] In her contribution to the aptly titled collection *Feminist Locations: Global and Local, Theory and Practice*, Friedman describes a "locational feminism" based in "glocational politics" where the particular (identity, culture, ideology, geography) is central to feminist global literacies that refuse balkanization but also refuse accusations of a naïve unity.[48] The protest essay is especially well-suited to this contingent universalism given its insistence on the experiential as a means of accessing broader truths. Friedman argues for a "re-singularization of feminism" that is not inimical to the debates that pluralized feminism in the first place and largely in response to ideas in the *Statement* and identitarian essays of the 1970s and 1980s.

Feminist scholars now move between global and local without jettisoning the gains and insights of identity politics. This poses an opportunity to reclaim the evolving relevance of the essays of Lorde, Rich, and Walker, and manifestos like the *Statement*. To that end, Elaine Chang reconsiders the efficacy of earlier feminist coalition-building models by capitalizing on the incomplete futurity of poststructuralists and postcolonialists. Chang latches onto the "post" signifier as a means of bringing futurity into the present: "Perhaps arrested development and prematurity can suggest for feminists modes of anticipating and mobilizing toward a future over which we can nevertheless claim no prior understanding or sovereign control."[49]

As we saw in chapter 4, Baldwin proclaims, "We cannot be free until they are free." Baldwin's integration project shows that self-determination cannot succeed if it reinscribes the very social divisions it protests. Lorde, Rich, Walker, and the CRC accept Baldwin's fiercely difficult charge to tether one's freedom and one's subjectivity to those who occupy positions across seemingly intractable chasms between "we" and "they." The collective "we" that emerges from their essays shows us that the supposedly limiting sovereignty of identity politics and the supposedly hopeless utopia of collective protest are not opposites, but necessary co-constituents. Their simultaneously specific and universalist "we" can help us revalue the collective in general, as well as the possibilities of the goal of sisterhood. In response to Lorde's challenge to a collective "we" that might erase those for whom it wishes to speak, Rich asks, "Who is we?" When we accept the challenge of reading their essays, we must simultaneously attend to specific locations and collective-minded aspirations. In this way, we are able in the present to accept the unfinished projects of past invocations of future utopias: We are a collective of Black feminists; We cannot be free until they are free; We the people.

Chapter Six

June Jordan and Transnational American Protest

So far I have concentrated specifically on an *American* tradition because many writers are concerned with living up to the nation's as yet unrealized aspirations of liberty and equality for all. But many protest essayists harbor concerns well beyond U.S. borders, from the transnational visions of Emma Goldman and Bread and Roses to Helen Hunt Jackson's shaming of her government on behalf of American Indian nations to James Baldwin's transnational turn in his later essays. Further, the previous chapter chronicled feminist suspicions about collectivity itself, and so my national focus may not fully capture desires for cross-national women's solidarity or other transnational concerns. The essays of June Jordan provide a good case study for how American protest essayists navigate the twin pulls of national promises and transnational visions.

In the introduction, I proposed the concept of the partial citizen speaking: a figure with some claim to national citizenship who uses that toehold to speak on behalf of others denied full citizenship and in the process claims full citizenship for herself. Jordan is a prime example of such a figure in essays that masterfully understand the power, possibilities, and quicksand of national promises. While Jordan works within a national context, she also maintains a resolutely transnational vision of global justice. For Jordan, the transnational can be housed within the frame of the U.S. nation-state, and thereby protest essayists can claim the best aspects of narratives of national belonging while rejecting unacceptable practices of domestic exclusion and international imperialism. In the first five chapters, I showed that many writers specifically draw on, cite, or embody state promises of universal equality, national ideals of democracy, and often founding documents. In doing so, writers claim and critique the authoritative words of the U.S. nation-state. Yet the national focus of my project and of many American protest essayists seems to run counter—at least on initial glance—to transnational aims. Therefore, in this chapter I push against a core tenet of this book: the nation remains a meaningful way to group a literary tradition, at least regarding the protest essay. If the American protest essay primarily concerns struggles over national belonging between official utterances of equality and the experiences of groups excluded from such promises, then what happens when an American protest essayist explicitly enters the terrain of the transnational?

Jordan's ability to occupy national and transnational spaces without jettisoning either is a key contribution to the work of activists and scholars in the U.S. context who have sought, trumpeted, or decried the rise of transnational, postnational, or global politics.[1] In a recent issue of *Tulsa Studies in Women's Literature*, Shirley Geok-Lin Lim asks, "Where in the World is Transnational Feminism?" The question continues a heated feminist debate about the paradox of how to *locate* abstract, universal human rights and/as women's rights. The question dates back at least to Hannah Arendt's observation that Jewish people during World War II had all the rights in the world except one: the right to have rights. In modernity, rights—even under universalist doctrines of natural rights—are conferred primarily through the nation-state.[2] Susan Gillman contends that we are "answering a disciplinary call to arms . . . to rectify the absence of empire in the study of U.S. culture."[3] So, for its 2006 meeting, the American Studies Association decided that "the time has come for us to address, even more directly than we have thus far, such issues as American imperialism, militarism, and unilateralism, as well as domestic intimidation and limits to free speech."[4] In this transnational context, Jordan's essays move within and across borders of national promises so that she uses state apparatus to rewrite a story of national belonging that brings justice to oppressed peoples in the nation and across the globe.

JORDAN'S 1992 STATE OF THE UNION ADDRESS

Jordan is a celebrated black feminist writer and activist whose work persistently calls our attention to the lines that divide us, whether from racial segregation, political ideology, gender oppression, sexual bigotry, rigorously policed national borders, and so on. In poetry, essays, novels, political appearances, teaching, and even a libretto over three-plus decades, Jordan sought to connect literature to social movements and the everyday experiences of oppressed peoples, such as in her Poetry for the People project. In doing so, like the cross-feminist essays in chapter 5, Jordan seeks an inclusive vision by attending to identity politics and particular experiences of exclusion. In her autobiography, she describes being one of the first African Americans to enroll (on scholarship) at a previously all-white elite private school: "I was the 'only' one. . . . I felt outnumbered. I was surrounded by 'them.' And there was no 'we.' There was only 'me.' I didn't like it."[5] In her subsequent career, Jordan attempts to build real collectivity amid diverse constituents by drawing on her own and other's experiences crossing social borders into potentially hostile terrain.

When Jordan became the first black woman to publish a book-length collection of her own essays from a national press with *Civil Wars* (1980), she found her best genre. In *Technical Difficulties*, her third book of essays, Jordan espouses the confidence and clout to speak to and for the nation in the form of what she calls "African-American notes on the State of the Union." By posing her collection as a series of "notes," Jordan taps into the essay's provisional nature and attention to contingent experience; by posing her collection on the platform of a presidential address, Jordan draws on the protest essay's ability to re-vise national scripts from a minoritarian vantage. Whereas Helen Hunt Jackson addresses the state directly, Jordan herself occupies the platform of the state. In her take on the State of the Union, Jordan proposes a true democracy that can achieve equity for Americans who find themselves under siege by nativist and ethnocentric ideas about national belonging, and sometimes by the state itself. Individual essays might concern the unfinished work of Civil Rights or neo-imperialism in Latin America, but the essays are joined in that they claim the best aspects of U.S. declarations of equality and then apply them throughout the globe. By inhabiting an authoritative platform, Jordan risks lending further legitimacy to national institutions that exclude or oppress her and numerous groups. But her move is more than strategic pandering to patriotism because she finds inclusive state declarations compatible with her aim to ensure full social participation for all groups.

Jordan's collection responds in part to George H. W. Bush's celebration of U.S. global hegemony in his 1992 State of the Union Address. "A world once divided into two armed camps," he professed, "now recognizes one sole and preeminent power, the United States of America. And they regard this with no dread. For the world trusts us with power, and the world is right. They trust us to be fair and restrained. They trust us to be on the side of decency. They trust us to do what's right."[6] The State of the Union evidences an intractable divide between "us" and "them," a certainty in speaking for "them," and a fundamental inability to imagine others as full participants in a global vision of justice. It also represents a particularly odorous version of American exceptionalism, which Jordan risks endorsing by mounting the presidential platform. Yet for Jordan, it is important not only to protest U.S. violence throughout the globe, but also to claim the authority to speak on behalf of a nation from a location outside the halls of power.

By presenting her essays under the banner of a response to a State of the Union Address, Jordan claims the language of democracy and the rhetorical forms of the state. At the same time that she sets herself as the rightful heir to democratic promises, however, she attends to locations of partial citizenship: first-generation West Indian immigrants, African Americans living under the residue of second-class citizenship, political refugees, or anyone who has been constructed by official state discourse as "fringe or freak components of some theoretical nether land."[7] Jordan speaks on behalf of people who do not typically have access to platforms of power like the State of the Union address. Ruth Ellen-Boetcher Joeres argues that Jordan belongs in a tradition of essays from nondominant groups, especially radical feminist essayists who "*spend considerable time marking herself and her point of departure.*"[8] She explains, "If the essays of radical feminists wish to speak to a particular reading public, it behooves them to establish connections with that public."[9] Jordan demands that we account for our specific identities and experiences and that we use our partial access to national citizenship and state authority. In this way, she finds flexibility under the banner of a universalist "we" for an inclusive story of national belonging.

Throughout her work, Jordan is aware of her position as a black spokeswoman addressing fiercely divided audiences; scholars, too, remain divided about Jordan's national and transnational investments.[10] At the same time that she celebrates lofty goals of national democracy, Jordan rigorously seeks out voices of displaced and disempowered peoples across the globe. There is not enough scholarly attention paid to Jordan, but that criticism primarily concerns Jordan's political commitments. Philip Metress traces a movement into transnational interests in Jordan's poetry, which requires us to "reach outside of national bounds."[11] On the other hand, scholars recognize Jordan's fierce attention to national concerns: Ramona Coleman traces how Jordan primarily targets U.S. myths perpetuated by a compliant media where black women are largely absent, Nicky Marsh values Jordan's ability to create publics striving toward "the possibility of democracy" in her poetry,[12] and Christina Accomando examines Jordan's persistent critique of white bias in supposedly neutral national venues.[13] These two locations—global and national—get at how Jordan consistently uses the apparatus of the nation-state to address division and exclusion both intranationally and transnationally. As a partial citizen, her commitments are bound up with the nation, but not circumscribed by it.

Like Baldwin, Audre Lorde, Adrienne Rich, Alice Walker, and many other literary figures who serve as political advocates, Jordan is arguably at her best in the essay form. Yet her poetry and fiction receive considerably more public and scholarly attention. While Jordan's poetry and fiction deserve this attention, the tendency to sideline her essays as secondary to more literary projects causes us to overlook how Jordan turns to the essay as the best vehicle in which to stage her rights to full citizenship, and to claim those rights on behalf of disenfranchised groups across the globe. Marsh argues that Jordan follows a Second Wave feminist tradition to find in poetry the language of a renewed pluralism for heterogeneous publics, which comprises a "democratic model of feminist poetics."[14] In the essay, perhaps more so than in poetry, Jordan questions, claims, and extends the project of a substantive U.S. democracy, and global equality.

NATIONAL CONCERNS IN A NATIONAL APPARATUS

The essay connects the particular and the general, so Jordan uses the genre to connect the personal and the political, the local and the larger, the excluded and the universal, and possibly the national and the transnational. As we can expect in the American protest essay tradition, Jordan connects particular experiences of exclusion from general national promises of equality. To do this, she documents domestic inequality amid a national story of inclusion, and she often places transnational experiences and subjects at the center of domestic matters. For example, the opening essay of her notes on the State of the Union, "For My American Family," concerns Jordan's immigrant heritage and her family's starry-eyed belief in America's promises. Jordan invokes genealogical and political connotations of "family" in an essay on citizenship and national belonging. At the head of the essay, the Statue of Liberty overlooks her immigrant parents, who are black naturalized citizens. Jordan describes a picture of Lady Liberty taken by her father: "He couldn't very well ask that lady to 'hold that smile' or 'put on a little something with red to brighten it up.' He'd have to take her 'as is'" (4). Jordan's immigrant parents may be regarded as *alien citizens*, Mae Ngai's concept that explains why some groups with formal citizenship may still be perceived as not belonging to the nation. Nevertheless, Jordan counters, "hundreds and hundreds of thousands of Americans are hardworking, naturalized Black citizens whose trust in the democratic promise of the mainland has never been reckoned with, fully, or truly reciprocated" (5). By looking at a key national symbol from the vantage of naturalized black citizenry, Jordan offers an immigrant, transnational American democracy from its most revered images and political platforms.

Throughout the collection, Jordan seeks a culturally pluralist position to speak for the nation. She reverses dominant narratives of America's open arms and instead claims America's promise as the rightful heritage of her family, who stand for the dispossessed generally. Jordan writes, "And what I want is to uphold this America, this beckoning and this shelter provided by my parents and my aunt" (9). By inhabiting cornerstones of the nation-state, Jordan's "American family" has the formal status to cite inclusive promises of U.S. democracy and to divest those promises from the exclusive practices of Jim Crow, de facto segregation, and imperialism, for a few examples. That way, in another essay subtitled "An Essay on Black Folks and the Constitution," Jordan wrests ownership of state apparatus from what she calls the American king, in a clear reference to the American Revolution. She writes, "We were never the intended beneficiaries of the Founding Fathers of the Founding Documents of America" (57). With this authoritative but usefully nonspecific "we," Jordan writes herself and those for whom she speaks into the Constitution. Much like feminist re-visions of the Declaration of Independence, Jordan suggests that if the seemingly inclusive "we" of founding documents were adopted by exclusionary practices, then she is better able to live up to the original inclusive promises by being up front about her own identity, experiences, and political commitments.

Jordan fits well within an American protest essay tradition that speaks directly back to founding documents and dominant stories of belonging. In addition to re-vising the Constitution and ascending the platform of the State of the Union, Jordan also offers a "New Bill of Rights" in an essay called "Don't You Talk about My Momma!" Jordan shifts the frame of national power to place immigrants, diasporic subjects, and the forgotten urban poor at the center of national ideals. Jordan adopts the personal, anecdotal stance associated with the essay, and she directly counters dominant assumptions about African Americans. Specifically, she speaks back to a particularly odious report from Senator Daniel Patrick Moynihan. As the colloquial title suggests, Jordan draws on her experience-based knowledge of African American life—she speaks as a "ghetto culture product" (79)—to counter the dominant story about African American families in the infamous Moynihan report. But Jordan goes beyond protesting the official report by drafting a "New Bill of Rights" that can better attend to African American experience within a collective vision of justice and equality. She draws on the demands of twentieth-century social movements and drafts thirteen new rights, from guaranteed housing to equal pay for equal work to national health insurance. The "New Bill of Rights" is necessary because, she writes, "It is not the Black family in crisis but American democracy at risk when a majority of American citizens may no longer assume the preservation and/or development of social programs to let them stay alive and well" (75). By framing her demand for justice and enfranchisement of black citizens in a totally rewritten founding document, Jordan casts herself as the true spokeswoman of American democracy. Reminiscent of Baldwin's integration vision, Jackson's earnest belief in national justice, and W. E. B. DuBois's emphasis on experience-based examinations of race, Jordan refuses to cede official platforms to any story of national belonging that excludes her or those for whom she speaks.

As she draws upon state apparatus to address domestic exclusion and inequality, Jordan stretches the borders of state jurisdiction to enfranchise both domestic and transnational subjects. In her examination of "Problems of Language in a Democratic State," for instance, Jordan furthers the political effort to claim a democratic history of her own against "patriotic" calls to jail poor blacks and to disown those who do not speak the language of the state. The problem, Jordan contends, is not that blacks, immigrants, and other disenfranchised peoples do not speak the language of American democracy but that their histories have been covered over—and that we have participated in that cover-up. In another essay, she explicitly vies for ownership of the nation as she asks in the provocative title, "Where are we, and whose country is this, anyway?" That essay provisionally documents the work of disenfranchised groups at the center of American history, but Jordan calls for further documentation in a characteristic open-ended stance outlined in the first chapter. To start the project, Jordan reports one woman's presentation at a gathering of academics and activists:

> "We are here," she said, "because of the struggle of women like," and here her sentence broke down. She tried again. "We have come this far because of all the Black women who fought for us like, like . . ." and, here, only one name came to her mouth: "Sojourner Truth!" she exclaimed, clearly relieved to think of it, but, embarrassed because she couldn't keep going. . . . But here somebody in the audience spoke to her rescue, by calling aloud the name of Harriet Tubman. At this point I interrupted to observe that now we had *two* names for 482 years of Afro-American history. (35)

The sarcasm is meant to jar her readers to come to the speaker's rescue. In these characteristic moments of citing others' words and experiences, Jordan incites the conversational quality of the traditional essay for political ends. Joeres argues that Jordan works within and against Montaigne's model of address because, "if the essay has a specific political purpose, and the essays of radical feminists will by definition be of this variety, the communication will go beyond the one-sided offering of information and advice and at least imply the need for a response."[15] Without many more voices, Jordan's essay—and the history of African American women that it seeks—will remain inadequate. On one level, Jordan calls for us to recognize African American history more fully. But Jordan goes further and asks readers to place their own experiences, forgotten histories, and demands for justice in the middle of dominant stories of national belonging, including in state documents meant to enfranchise us all.

TRANSNATIONAL CONCERNS IN A NATIONAL APPARATUS

In her notes on the State of the Union, Jordan uses state apparatus not only to protest domestic exclusion, but also to build a platform of transnational justice. In this way, Jordan is able to do what some say the United Nations cannot: provide a rooted location for a transnational vision. In the provocatively titled essay, "Toward a Manifest New Destiny," Jordan invokes the violent history of

U.S. westward imperialism for her vision of transnational solidarity. For instance, Jordan connects the experiences of Asian Americans in the 1940s to the doomed inhabitants of Hiroshima who suffered unspeakably from U.S. actions. Beyond protesting expanding American borders that mow down those in their path, Jordan inhabits nationalist rhetoric of manifest destiny to stake out an alternative: "a destiny that will carry us . . . into an educated, collective vision of a really democratic, really humane, a really really good time" (211). Jordan repeats the word "really" like a drumbeat in a national story that may ring hollow for those who experience oppression and exclusion. Jordan uses her partial citizenship to make claims on a state in the name of human rights. She redefines national citizenship in the most inclusive way, which requires her to claim, rather than divest from, the imperial U.S. nation-state.

In a postcolonial era of increasing transnationalism and global calls for justice, Jordan considers the limits of national borders, as well as the identity politics infusing the feminist essays in chapter 5. But, finding no acceptable alternative, Jordan builds on national and identitarian platforms to aspire to a substantive global "we" of humanity. In an essay called "Waiting for a Taxi," for instance, Jordan follows a Montaignean model of seemingly ephemeral anecdote that says something grand. While waiting for a taxi on a rainy Parisian street, she looks for "an umbrella big enough to cover the tactical and moral implications of 'identity politics'—politics based on gender, class, or race" (162). Her quest for a meaningful collective position is material: she searches for an umbrella of "political unity and human community" (164) that can somehow cover U.S. domestic politics and transnational social justice networks. Jordan writes, "I was thinking that if we, all of us Black, all of us women, all of us deriving from connected varieties of peasant/immigrant/persecuted histories of struggle and significant triumph, if we could find and trust each other enough to travel together into a land where none of us belonged, nothing on earth was impossible anymore" (162).

Drawing on the provisional nature of the essay form that documents a thought process as well as a thought, Jordan tentatively offers an umbrella of collective hope. Jordan joins the tradition of Baldwin's move from personal "I" to collective "we" and the simultaneously specific and open "we" of the feminist cross-essay conversation. This enfolding, enveloping "we" imagines a geographical territory—a "land"—of human rights and genuine union. Jordan's imagined land of possibility does not erase national borders and histories, it uses them. The inclusive promises America delivers to the globe, especially in cherished images of immigrants and the Statue of Liberty, are more than hollow rhetoric because they are powerful platforms on which to build substantive inclusion and equality if a protest essayist takes them at face value.

Jordan is aware of risks in claiming official platforms and nationalist ideas like manifest destiny that have bolstered the practices of oppression and exclusion she protests. Invocations of national authority can ensnare those caught inside its borders and exclude those on the other side. But Jordan reclaims the language of democracy in an anti-imperialist stance. She refuses to concede the tools as belonging to the master, as Lorde so famously warned. For instance, in an essay called "On War and War and War and . . . ," Jordan recounts her proposal at an anti-war rally to exchange the billions spent on foreign war for domestic social programs. "One billion dollars a day for seven days for Oakland!" Jordan demands. "Can you imagine that? . . . This is our city! This is our money! These are our lives" (182). Jordan folds the polemical mode of speechifying into the wandering path of an essay that takes seriously this "modest proposal." Jordan is at pains to acknowledge the imperialist destruction waged by the United States, but also to build collectivity within and beyond the nation using preexisting state tools, such as the billion-dollar-a-day bill for war in February 1991. Jordan declares the memories of Martin Luther King Jr. and Malcolm X "desecrated" (184) by the leaders of America, and she claims their memories on behalf of transnational American protest because "they, in different ways, developed into global visionaries persisting against racism in Alabama, in Harlem, in South Africa, in Vietnam" (185). Within a resolutely transnational scope, Jordan retains a national frame. She warns, "And we are many, Mr. President. We are most of the people on this godforsaken planet" (186). In this collective stance, Jordan speaks on behalf of peoples across the planet, and directs their gaze to the United States in a posture of vigilance.

NATIONAL CONCERNS IN A TRANSNATIONAL APPARATUS

By making the nation-state and imperialism locations of transnational solidarity, Jordan draws connections between exclusion from full citizenship within the state and America's history of imperial violence and acts of injustice beyond its boundaries. In doing so, Jordan also looks at domestic politics through a transnational lens. In the essay "Wrong or White," and through her African American notes on the State of the Union generally, Jordan depicts a polarized world of racially divided landscapes. Further, divisions become explicitly moral, and thereby she questions the moral authority of the state. For instance, she responds to U.S. efforts to quash or hamper the emergent nonwhite leadership of South Africa, Latin America, and the Gaza Strip because, she insists, "These were matters of wrong or white" (142). In her polemical essays, justice, morality, and equity fall along stark color lines as much as along national borders. Yet, Jordan engages this polarization in a larger project committed to a fulfilled democracy inclusive across identitarian and national lines. Rather than reject outright the hypocrisy of an imperial nation-state, she carves out a space *within* the moralizing rhetoric that her immigrant parents sincerely cherish. At the end of the essay, Jordan asks, "If we are afraid to insist that we are right, then what?" (179). The question, like all of her questions, is not rhetorical. She cites national ideals so that inclusive pronouncements prove meaningful in practice. She makes universalist statements apply to particular cases within and beyond national jurisdiction.

Because the national and transnational sometimes come into conflict, especially in matters of imperialism, Jordan must seek a unifying language and location for her vision. Jordan turns to a discourse of home to connect national and transnational concerns, to bring the authoritative promises of the Constitution and the State of the Union to the everyday lives of people across the globe. For instance, in an essay on "Finding the Way Home," Jordan begins in the anecdotal, personal mode so central to the personal essay tradition. She starts with a meditation on her mobility and privilege to choose where she lives, but quickly moves outward to a discussion of homelessness in America and issues of Palestinian homelands in the Middle East. She dedicates the essay, and the year 1989, to twin domestic and transnational issues: the memory of a six-year-old homeless girl, Lisa Steinberg, who died neglected on the streets and a pledge by Yasir Arafat to peace and coexistence. The essay connects these two events because, like Lisa Steinberg, "The bottom line for six million Palestinian men, women, and children is that they are living and they are dying, homeless, in full view of the world" (137). Jordan places the experience of Lisa Steinberg and six million Palestinians—not her own experience—at the center of her vision of justice. Their particular experiences are put on full view for the world, and the world must respond with a vision that can bring justice to both locations. For Jordan, the two issues are "the same: the question is whether non-Europeans and whether children, everywhere, possess a human right to sanctuary on this planet" (137). Jordan distinguishes the two experiences, but insists on the sameness of the cause and response.

In connecting Lisa Steinberg to Palestinians, Jordan turns to a discourse of human rights, which almost exceeds the jurisdictional limits of the nation-state. But she does not leave the national frame behind because she asks her American audience to take their national concerns and systems to the transnational arena. She asks, "Who among us would accommodate to an absence of civil liberties or no control over the light switch in our house?" (137). By offering experiences of homelessness—both domestic and transnational—and mourning the absence of national rights, Jordan fully enters a transnational space, but worries about the lack of substantive rights in that space. Further, Jordan personalizes the story so that each reader must take her own frame of reference—the civil or human rights she takes for granted—and apply them to those unable to claim such rights. In this way, the American protest essay crosses national and identitarian lines not through shared experience but through a shared commitment to rights.

Jordan's call to connect Lisa Steinberg to Palestinians provides a blueprint for a transnational American protest that is able to invest the abstract universalism of human rights discourse with the formal power of the nation-state. Will Kymlicka, an influential champion of transnational rights, has reconsidered gains made by the nation-state to bring substantive rights to national subjects. He writes, "So globalization need not undermine the scope for meaningful democratic citizenship at the national level. I am rather more skeptical about the likelihood that we can produce any meaningful form of transnational citizenship."[16] Jordan, too, worries about the limits of transnational systems to deliver substantive rights, which may explain her reluctance to cede the language and power of the nation-state. That is, if Jordan doesn't have direct access to the floor of the United Nations—which fuels cosmopolitan scholars like Kymlicka to worry about the paradox of human rights aspirations in the absence of democratic structure—Jordan has the formal status to enlist the nation-state in service of truly universalist aspirations.

Jordan claims her membership in the U.S. nation-state and uses the American protest essay to document and give voice to those lacking meaningful political power anywhere. That is, Jordan uses the essay to document what she calls in one essay title "Unrecorded Agonies," so that these subjects have political voice. In response to a woman in Brooklyn who was violently raped and died "screaming but inaudible" (147), Jordan's essay connects this woman to an atrocious history of unrecorded agony. She writes, "Her unrecorded, unremembered murder joined her to the legions of Black women whose demise, whose violated bodies never lead to rallies/marching/vigilante/vendettas/legislation/loudspeaker-scale memorial services/determined prosecution and community revenge" (148). Jordan indicts both national democracy and American social movements to bring voice and healing to this woman. But she does not turn to transnational organizations as the alternative. To provide substantive rights and voice to the oppressed and excluded, she resides in the State of the Union.

JUNE JORDAN'S COSMOPOLITAN AMERICANISM

While it might seem more logical for Jordan to refer to transnational documents such as the United Nations Declaration of Human Rights (1945) on behalf of global citizens in a global age, her silence around such documents is noteworthy. Jordan's peristent use of national apparatus points to how she understands ethno-racial identity and the nation-state in a global era. To bring substantive rights to the oppressed, Jordan seeks a cosmopolitan Americanism. In recent years, postcolonial, feminist, and political theorists interrogated the nation-state, declared it dead, or perceived that it is eclipsed by transnational rights organizations, international solidarity movements, and diasporic identities and migration patterns.[17] Noted cosmopolitan philosopher Kwame Anthony Appiah argues for the importance of "contamination" to avoid paradoxes between the universal and particular, the authentic and performed, the pure and mixed. Appiah argues that individual groups are able to incorporate global cultures—including imperialist American cultures—into their own cultural practices. That is, if we see a member of a group (Appiah prefers to focus on the individual) borrowing from global capitalism, that does not automatically signal the dissolution of a self-determining culture or ideology. The past decade *also* witnessed champions of the transnational reconsidering the death certificate of the nation-state,[18] especially in an era of American empire. Many scholars notice the arrival of supranational forms, on the one hand, especially in Western Europe, while at the same time ethnic separatist movements fracture existing nation-states from within. For political theorists Sima Godfrey and Frank Unger, the former movements "want to overcome the nation-state by extending it" and the latter "want to overcome the nation-state by breaking it up." But they argue, "On closer inspection, however, these opposing challenges often reveal themselves as two sides of the same coin."[19] Political theorists and activists now return to the nation-state as a potentially viable form, even in a transnational era.[20] Further, as Jordan is keenly aware, the United States has a history of citing human rights for other countries, while also immunizing itself from those standards.[21]

Jordan's silence around transnational frames for justice and her deference to her parent's earnest belief in American promises means that her transnational vision cannot supersede the national. Cosmopolitics, a political theory informing progressive transnationalism,[22] is now critiqued as erasing the local, the rooted, and the particular. In this vein, cosmopolitans impose a universalism whose Western bias is not unlike earlier imperialism.[23] In response, feminists are working on a theory that can effectively tie the local and the global, whether in the form of glocational politics,[24] a multicultural feminism that roots human rights discourse in local cultures,[25] rooted cosmopolitanism,[26] Rogers Brubaker's "ethnicity without groups,"[27] or Chandra Mohanty's borderless feminism anchored in women's experiences and cultures.[28] As these debates continue, especially around the formation of the European Union,[29] we cannot discount the continued power of the nation-state.

Given the transnational turn—both celebrated and lamented—now is the time to consider Jordan's use of national apparatus in her essays on domestic and transnational justice. American literary studies remain reluctant to jettison the national in order to provide compelling and truly transnational narratives of equitable global citizenship. The January 2003 special issue of *PMLA* on "America: The Idea, the Literature" evidenced a fascination with and commitment to transnationalism, but the nation persists. In her contribution, Marietta Messmer proposes a "Declaration of Interdependence" and traces the "inward turn" of American literary studies in the second half of the twentieth century in response to the challenges of transnationalism and subnationalism. Messmer notes that the rise of multicultural literary studies diversifies the canon but in doing so deemphasizes transnational connections. She writes, "American literary historians have so far exclusively concentrated on a discussion of intra-American cultural pluralism and heterogeneity, emphasizing America's internal cultural and ethnic diversity and difference."[30] Notwithstanding transnational work like that on the *Black Atlantic*, Messmer shows how transnationalism worries the idea of a national literature, but does not supplanted it. In fact, Michael Bérubé notes that the nation-state is far from the supposed decline of the "hegemonic imaginary"[31] and he worries that a transnational turn in American literary studies fits all too neatly with the rise of American global capitalism.[32]

So why has the transnational turn not created a robust culture of transnationalism in American protest essays? The answer may lie in part in the differing cultural statuses of national and transnational stories of belonging. In an influential article, Martha Nussbaum worries that the appeal of world citizenship is failing. "It fails," Nussbaum instructs, "because patriotism is full of color and intensity and passion, whereas cosmopolitanism seems to have a hard time gripping the imagination."[33] Nussbaum seeks a cosmopolitanism where putting "right before country and universal reason before the symbols of national belonging, need not be boring, flat, or lacking love."[34] Jordan may help us solve this zero-sum competition between an aspirational but empty transnationalism and a rooted but problematic nation-state. Jordan responds to Nussbaum's call by using the powerful, historically thick narrative apparatus of the nation-state to offer a vibrant, compelling, and politically meaningful story of transnational American promises. American writers have yet to find inspiration in the stories of belonging offered by transnational organizations like the United Nations or NGOs. The United Nations Declaration of Human Rights, for instance, has not secured a space of prominence in American protest literature similar to the Declaration of Independence. The reluctance to champion such transnational documents concerns me because every death knell tolled loudly for the nation-state potentially diminishes the strategy of drawing on the authority of inclusive national pronouncements. If transnational promises of full equality for all do not replace those of the nation-state, the American protest essay possibly loses a cornerstone in the twenty-first century.

JORDAN'S PLACE IN A TRANSNATIONAL AMERICAN PROTEST ESSAY TRADITION

Transnational concerns, audiences, and speakers permeate the American protest essay tradition, which suggests that the nation is not the only frame for Jordan's essays, or many others. Jordan contributes to a long-standing interest in transnational topics by key American protest essayists. For example, Baldwin's early essays are set in the European context to tell us something about American identity. In fact, many essayists discussed in previous chapters could easily find a place in a transnational tradition, considering especially the international postures of Emma Goldman, Bread and Roses, and the Combahee River Collective in chapters 2 and 5. Or, works like Zitkala-Ša's essays in *American Indian Magazine* (1916–1919), Vine Deloria Jr.'s *Custer Died for Your Sins* (1969), and Leslie Silko's "Border Patrol" (1996) could constitute an American Indian protest essay tradition, especially in the way they address division among and within different tribal nations. Or, we could look at transnational ethnic groupings for many protest essays: we could place Gloria Anzaldúa's essays in a Latin American essay tradition following the work of Cristina Kirklighter, Martin Stabb, and Doris Meyer, or a Chicana/o essay tradition following the work of Chon A. Noriega and Wendy Belcher. Much the same can be said of feminist essayists following work by Joeres and Elizabeth Mittman who look at radical feminist writers from multiple national traditions in the twentieth century.

Nevertheless, it is important to appreciate how each of these essayists addresses the U.S. nation-state within transnational, cross identitarian, or inter-ethnic aims. For example, in her protest essay on borders and nations, Silko recounts, "On the Laguna Pueblo reservation, where I was raised, the people were patriotic despite the way the U.S. government had treated Native Americans. As proud citizens, we grew up believing the freedom to travel was our inalienable right, a right that some Native Americans had been denied in the early 20th century."[35] Silko moves between the United States and Laguna nations, proud citizenship and government protest, patriotism and racism. For her, these frames must be permeable, unlike the borders of the U.S. police state. Silko traverses and underscores these borders, so she fits well in an American protest essay tradition of simultaneously claiming and critiquing grand stories of national inclusion and unalienable rights, especially for those whose citizenship is in question.

Jordan also belongs in a vibrant subnational tradition of black feminist essays. This tradition builds on Sojourner Truth's influential oratory and Anna Julia Cooper's foundational essay *A Voice from the South* (1892), through the rise of black women writers working in the essay like Pauline Hopkins and Zora Neale Hurston, and into the renaissance of black feminist essayists in the latter twentieth century such as Walker, Lorde, and Toni Cade Bambara. Juanita Rogers Comfort studies the demands and rewards of the black feminist essay for its reader,[36] and Pamela Klass Mittlefehldt places Jordan in a black feminist essay tradition in which black women refuse silence and "resist the traditional voice of the essay by insisting on the signature of their own respective voices."[37] For Mittlefehldt, Jordan uses the essay because it allows her to construct a black feminist self where self-definition "is an act of self-preservation."[38] This approach is warranted by Jordan's early work, which was published alongside other African American women writers gain-ing recognition in the 1970s by emergent Black Arts and feminist movements. Jordan directed much of her early work toward black women, and she sustained a commitment to Black English. Jordan's rise to prominence is due in large part to feminists who valued creative work for its ability to bring women's experiences into the public sphere. We can further appreciate her acrobatic work to tether international concerns to national narratives of belonging if we discuss her in a transnational American tradition of the essay.

In the end, Jordan refuses to decide between national citizenship and global humanism. In her four essay collections and as a political essayist for journals such as *The Progressive*, Jordan stakes out a place for transnational feminist protest within the apparatus of the nation-state. National utterances of equality and full social participation serve as a rhetorical bank for Jordan to imagine rights for all displaced and disenfranchised peoples, within and beyond U.S. borders. Jordan's essays ask us to revisit the terrain of national citizenship. Toni Morrison insists that "we are forced to recognize the circumstances in which the human being and the citizen are not the same thing."[39] For Morrison, "It is precisely at the moment when a person loses or forfeits or is deemed to be without citizenship that she or he can be allowed to claim 'human' rights."[40] Yet Seyla Benhabib confronts the legal difficulties and historical failures to implement a human rights agenda outside the nation-state so that the aspirational ideals of universalist human rights are meaningful in actual people's lives. For Benhabib, citizenship inherently excludes others and marks them as foreign, alien, and undeserving of rights. However, because "sovereignty has been frayed"[41] amid unprecedented transnational migration, she suggests that new opportunities have emerged to implement a human rights agenda of international justice. Jordan, in turn, shows that the apparatus of the nation-state will continue to play a role alongside the United Nations, at least in the American protest essay tradition. While we come to terms with the challenges of transnationalism, we do well to recognize how American protest essayists have bridged the divide between human and citizen all the way back to the nation's founding. Following Jordan's example, the ability to connect particular citizens to universal human rights secures a place for the American protest essay in a transnational era.

Conclusion

Why the Essay?

Literary figures who serve as political advocates turn again and again to the essay. Why the essay? To answer this question, I return to where I began: *The Souls of Black Folk*. Throughout the series of fourteen essays, W. E. B. DuBois marks, then moves across, over, and around, lines of social division: the veil of race, the Black Belt, European and African American cultural texts, and so on. DuBois presents the essayist as uniquely able to inhabit the particular in order to access the universal. In the opening and most famous essay, DuBois presents his widely influential concept of double consciousness, which is both an obscuring veil and a gift of second sight for the Negro to view and experience

> this American world,—a world which yields him no true self-consciousness, but only lets him see himself through the revelation of the other world. It is a peculiar sensation, this double-consciousness, this sense of always looking at one's self through the eyes of others, of measuring one's soul by the tape of a world that looks on in amused contempt and pity.[1]

Many have read and remarked on this important, moving, and brilliant passage. In the essay form, DuBois finds the ability to value and move among the experiential and philosophical, the particular and general, the provisional and certain, the ephemeral and enduring. For DuBois, the "two-ness" of the American Negro also describes the best asset of the essay, a form uniquely able to bring experiences of exclusion and particular cultural practices into direct conversation with universalist beliefs and utterances of equality, especially on the national level.[2]

In the essay form, DuBois not only crosses over, under, and around the color line, he also sees each citizen and social group "through the revelation of the other world," which creates a contingent universalism. More specifically,

American protest essayists who cite specific national utterances or documents of equality use a very real and very powerful "tape" against which to measure, as well as record and value, experiences of exclusion from those promises. Because the essay is able to—indeed must—move between the particular and the universal, it is uniquely able to engage debates in American social movements that might pit integration against self-determination, sisterhood against separatism, lone dissent against collective politics, individual against group rights, race against nation, the local against the larger. If G. Douglass Atkins is right that the essay is a form uniquely able to offer "reflection upon experience,"[3] the distinct tradition of the American protest essay reflects on the juxtaposition of the inclusive ring of national stories and experiences of exclusion.

The inextricability of the personal and political, or the immediate and enduring, gets at the essence of the American protest essay. That is why it is important to see that this distinct strand of the essay in the American context draws equally from the personal essay genre with European roots and American political oratory arising from social movements. Audre Lorde's brilliant work in the essay provides a useful parting example. Like DuBois's immensely personal elegy for his departed firstborn son in the public venue of *Souls*, Lorde invited her readers into her intensely personal battle with cancer in order to analyze, protest, and improve women's—and everyone's—health care. In *The Cancer Journals*, Lorde draws on her formidable powers as essayist, activist, poet, philosopher, and speaker in a form that signifies privacy (the diary) on public display in her series of essays that constitute the slim volume. Lorde delivers personal meditations on her radical mastectomy, bombastic political oratory about the oppression of black lesbians and other disenfranchised peoples, snippets of her personal journal, occasional speeches rendered in print for posterity, and useful health care information. For Lorde, her personal struggle with social systems, experiences that she understands at the deepest bodily level, requires language and action. To combat the threat of silence, Lorde turns to the essay, which promises to provide meaning through the publics it creates. Lorde explains, "The fact that we are here and that I speak now these words is an attempt to break that silence and bridge some of those differences between us, for it is not difference which immobilizes us, but silence. And there are so many silences to be broken."[4] This passage, originally delivered as a speech, insists on the personal as a means of ushering in a future of true, loud, meaningful community. It is also worth noting that in addition to literary figures who address divided publics, nonliterary writers who become public intellectuals also turn to the essay. Perhaps the best example is Rachel Carson's beautiful, moving, and important *Silent Spring* (1963).[5] The American protest essay is available to a variety of literary figures and political activists of starkly different specialties, political orientations, and backgrounds.

Not since the eclipse of the 1960s and the dream of American integration have American writers harbored a political power near that of James

Baldwin. The protest essay tradition and the cultural capital afforded to literary figures in other national and global traditions appears strong, especially given the popularity and impact of writer-advocates like Arundhati Roy and Nadine Gordimer. These proximate and often overlapping traditions of politically engaged essayists deserve their own studies, too. But for this book it is important to note that the position of artist-advocate in the United States is dwindling at a time when the nation remains as divided as ever, if not as monochromatically so. From this vantage, it is important to understand how Baldwin achieved the universal through the particular via personal engagement with national aspirations. In a review in *Phylon*, Finley Campbell suggests that the essay is what allows Baldwin to be a spokesman: "The rise of Negro militancy is shaking America with her first social revolution since the industrial wars of the Thirties. Yet, no novels of power and value are documenting its tragedy and comedy. But of brilliant essays there are plenty."[6] Campbell finds a "Negro humanism" in, for instance, Baldwin's discussion of southern segregation as not limited to the South: "Their forms may be sectional, but their essence lies within the racist emotions permeating our national life. Baldwin implies that lying below the form of racism is a national betrayal of America's promise."[7] National declarations of equality provide the forum for Baldwin to access general equality through particular cases. Though Baldwin's acrobatic travels across lines of identity did not fare well in the rise of racial self-determination in politics and letters, it may have helped give rise to it.[8] It remains to be seen how the American protest essay will fare in the future, especially given Paul Gilroy's observation that modern times and "the century of the color line have now passed. Racial hierarchy is still with us."[9] For Gilroy, this may provoke "postcolonial melancholia," but the best-selling work in the journalistic protest essay by Barbara Ehrenreich and Eric Schlosser seems to offer at least a hope that the tradition will remain vibrant in the twenty-first century.

It is important to continue to track the resonance of the American protest essay across identitarian, period, political, and literary lines because it provides a story of struggles for meaningful national belonging amid a history of exclusion and oppression that could otherwise lead to despair. In doing so, we readers, citizens, and academics are answering in part June Jordan's call in her 1992 essay "Where Is the Rage?" Since this book is meant as an illustrative sketch of the American protest essay, especially in the twentieth century, many more studies are necessary. This book, then, is an opening foray to understand how and why politically engaged literary figures turn to the essay in order to challenge and, to borrow from Adrienne Rich, "re-vise"[10] stories of national belonging. Michael Moon and Cathy Davidson suggest in their influential collection *Subjects and Citizens* that the line between being under power and in power depends on the moral worth assigned to each body in the national script.[11] The American protest essay refuses to let lines of social division within a national "we" create hierarchical categories of moral worth—and it cites the nation-state itself for authority. The American protest essay underscores the urgency of the immediate moment and the meaningfulness of experience; then it tethers these pressing concerns to hopes for a just nation. In these essays, there is a tension between the ferocity of hope and the melancholy of loss embodied in the word *belonging*. Those on behalf of whom the essayist speaks understand well the difference between announcements of equality and the experience of exclusion, between *longing* for full citizenship and *being* partial citizens. The American protest essayist asks—insists—that we reconcile in the present the persistent American story of never-achieved but always-promised full equality for all. Baldwin should have the last words: "If we do not now dare everything, the fulfillment of that prophecy, recreated from the Bible in song by a slave, is upon us: *God gave Noah the rainbow sign, No more water, the fire next time!*"

Appendix

Pritings of the Combahee River Collective, *A Black Feminist Statement* (April 1977)

"Ain't I a Womon?" Special Spring Issue by and about Wimmin of Color. *Off Our Backs*. June 1979: 6–8.

Burrell, Barbara C. *Women and Political Participation: A Reference Handbook*. Santa Barbara, CA: ABL-CIO, 2004. 186–91.

Eisenstein, Zillah R., ed. *Capitalist Patriarchy and the Case for Socialist Feminism*. New York: Monthly Review Press, 1979. 362–72.

Freedom Socialist Organizing Series. *Combahee River Collective Statement: Black Feminist Organizing in the Seventies and Eighties*. Foreword by Barbara Smith. Latham, NY: Kitchen Table: Women of Color Press, 1986.

Guy-Sheftall, Beverly, ed. *Words of Fire: An Anthology of African-American Feminist Thought*. New York: New Press, 1995. 232–40.

Hermann, Ann, and Abigail J. Stewart, eds. *Theorizing Feminisms: Parallel Trends in the Humanities and Social Sciences*. Boulder, CO: Westview Press, 1994, 2001. 29–37.

Hull, Gloria T., Patricia Bell Scott, and Barbara Smith, eds. *All the Women Are White, All Blacks Are Men, But Some of Us Are Brave: Black Women's Studies*. New York: The Feminist Press, 1982. 13–22.

Jaggar, Alison, and Paula S. Rothenberg. *Feminist Frameworks: Alternative Theoretical Accounts of the Relations Between Men and Women*. 2nd ed. New York: McGraw-Hill, 1984. 202–09.

James, Joy, and T. Denean Sharpley-Whiting, eds. *The Black Feminist Reader*. Malden, MA: Blackwell, 2000. 261–70.

Manning, Marable, and Leith Mullings, eds. *Let Nobody Turn Us Around: Voices of Resistance, Reform and Renewal: An African American Anthology*. Lanham, MD: Rowman & Littlefield, 2000. 524–29.

McCann, Carole R., and Seung-Kyung Kim, eds. *Feminist Theory Reader: Local and Global Perspectives*. New York: Routledge, 2003. 164–71.

McCarthy, Timothy Patrick, and John Campbell McMillan, eds. *The Radical Reader: A Documentary History of the American Radical Tradition*. New York: New Press, 2003.

Moraga, Cherríe, and Gloria Anzaldúa, eds. *This Bridge Called My Back: Writings by Radical Women of Color*. Watertown, MA: Persephone Press, 1981. 210–18. 2nd ed. Brooklyn, NY: Kitchen Table: Women of Color Press, 1983. 210–18. 3rd ed. Berkeley: Third Woman Press, 2002. 234–44.

Ms. 2.1 (July/August 1991): 40–44.

Nicholson, Linda J., ed. *The Second Wave: A Reader in Feminist Theory*. New York: Routledge, 1997. 63–70.

Ritchie, Joy, and Kate Ronald, eds. *Available Means: An Anthology of Women's Rhetoric*. Pittsburgh: U of Pittsburgh P, 2001. 292–300.

Ryan, Barbara, ed. *Identity Politics in the Women's Movement*. New York: New York UP, 2001. 59–66.

Schneir, Miriam, ed. *Feminism in Our Time: The Essential Writings, WWII to the Present*. New York: Vintage, 1994. 176–87.

Sigerman, Harriet, ed. Printed as "Black Women Are Inherently Valuable." *The Columbia Documentary History of American Women Since 1941*. New York: Columbia UP, 2003. 316–21.

Smith, Barbara, ed. *Home Girls: A Black Feminist Anthology*. Latham, NY: Kitchen Table: Women of Color Press, 1983. 272–82. 2nd ed. New Brunswick, NJ: Rutgers UP, 2002. 266–74.

Ware, Susan, ed. *Modern American Women: A Documentary History*. Chicago: Dorsey Press, 1989. 297–305. 2nd ed. Boston: McGraw-Hill, 2002. 249–57.

NOTES

INTRODUCTION

1. Atkins, *Tracing the Essay*, 11. Atkins follows E. B. White's description of the form.

2. Williams, "One Patriot," 38.

3. Ibid., 38–39.

4. Honig, *Democracy and the Foreigner*, 108.

5. Parts of this section draw on my article, "Allegiance and Renunciation at the Border."

6. Govindarajan quotes Department of Homeland Security Director Tom Ridge, "'I am concerned that this construction diminishes and confuses the "true faith and allegiance" . . . necessary to foster a new citizen's ongoing attachment to this country.'" Govindarajan notes that some of the language dates back to 1790, but the wording was last changed fifty years ago—the beginning of the Cold War.

7. For a more thorough discussion of the revival of a masculinist politics of violent protectionism that creates a "subordinate citizenship" (women, the feminized) to protect, see Young, "Masculinist Protection." Young explores how the rise of the security state after fall 2001 "illuminates the meaning and effective appeal of a security state that wages war abroad and expects obedience and loyalty at home. . . . To the extent that citizens of a democratic state allow their leaders to adopt a stance of protectors toward them, these citizens come to occupy a subordinate status like that of women in the patriarchal household" (2).

8. Citizenship Day Proclamation, 2003. In an effort to advocate a doctrine of preventive war on foreign soil, the president used Citizenship Day 2002 to invoke a unified nation amid great public debate and dissent over plans to invade Iraq, but curiously the focus on internal unity *crossed* national borders in a bid to establish imperialism as a civic duty: "Citizenship not only involves a commitment to our Nation but also to our neighbors and those in need" (Citizenship Day Proclamation, 2002).

9. White House, "Citizenship Day Proclamation 2005."

10. For alternative examinations of African Americans as partial U.S. citizens with a primarily domestic focus, see Shklar and Weiner. Recent multicultural literary studies place migration at the center of American literature. See, for example, Brown and Ling, Schueller, and Sollors.

11. Nelson, "Patriots," 11.

12. In addition to the revised oath, long-serving Democratic senator Robert Byrd provided an alternative response: a requirement that all federally funded educational institutions observe "Constitution Day" in order to rescue remaining liberties before "'that much slips away from us.'" Quoted in Fischer, "Required." Byrd suggested such a curriculum would not "impose a particular view or interpretation of the Constitution." Quoted in Fischer, "Education Department."

13. Smith argues, "[Leaders] worry less about whether their various appeals are true, or whether they fit together logically, than about whether they work politically. They thus simultaneously appeal to lofty rational moralities and thinly veiled greed and lust for power. But most have found irreplaceable the engaging, reassuring, inspiring, often intoxicating charm provided by colorful civic myths" (*Civic Ideals* 33). In his more recent work, Smith's disparagement of "civic myths" has evolved to value the work of people-building fostered by "stories of peoplehood," stories that often arise from *within* actual political struggle and dialogue instead of being imposed upon people by those already in power. See Smith, *Stories of Peoplehood*, esp. 9–15, 21–24, 74–76.

14. Handy, *E Pluribus Unum*.

15. See Bosniak, "Citizenship."

16. A good example of relatively autonomous and sometimes contradictory versions of citizenship is what Mae Ngai calls an *alien citizen*: "persons who are American citizens by virtue of their birth in the United States but who are presumed to be foreign by the mainstream of American culture and, at times, by the state." Ngai, *Impossible Subjects*, 2. The inextricability of liberal notions of citizenship as rights and republican notions of citizenship as the willingness to participate in foreign wars are further evidenced each May 1: Loyalty Day. In his statement for Loyalty Day 2004, President Bush conflated citizenship and loyalty through foreign war: "Loyalty Day encourages citizens to demonstrate their commitment to our country by supporting our military, serving each other, and teaching our young people about our history and values. Being an American is a privilege, and our patriotism is a living faith in our country's founding ideals and the promise of the American Dream." See White House, "Loyalty Day Proclamation 2004."

17. Honig, 101.

18. See especially Bercovitch, *The American Jeremiad*; Davidson, *Revolution and the Word*; Tompkins, *Sensational Designs*; Wald, *Constituting Americans*; and Warner, *Letters of the Republic*. On American protest literature, see Trodd.

19. For key examples, see Edwards, *The Practice of Diaspora*; and Schueller and Watts, *Messy Beginnings*.

20. See Anderson, *Imagined Communities*; Cheah and Robbins, *Cosmopolitics*; and Kaplan and Pease, *Cultures of United States of Imperialism*.

21. See Atkins, *Estranging the Familiar* and *Tracing the Essay*; Butrym, *Essays on the Essay*; Joeres and Mittman, *The Politics of the Essay*; Kirklighter, *Traversing the Democratic Borders of the Essay*; and Obaldia, *The Essayistic Spirit*.

22. Atkins, *Tracing*, 126.

23. See, for example, O'Neill, *Essaying Montaigne*.

24. See, for example, Ketchum, *Transparent Designs*.

25. See, for example, Hamilton, *America's Sketchbook*.

26. Lyon, *Manifestoes*.

27. Howard-Pitney, *The Afro-American Jeremiad*; Newman, *Pamphlets of Protest*; and Porter, *Negro Protest Pamphlets*.

28. Hubbard, *The Sermon*.

29. See, for example, Bennett, Brickhouse, Crane, and Grasso. In a particularly good example, Warner's *Publics and Counter-Publics* crosses periods to draw from his interest in eighteenth-century prose and Habermas's theories of publics in modernity as he offers contemporary cultural criticism that employs rigorous literary analysis.

30. See Breines, Collier-Thomas, DuPlessis and Snitow, and Roth.

31. See, for example, Byerman; Griffin; and Wall, *Worrying the Line*.

32. See DeKoven, *Utopia Limited*; Docherty; T. V. Reed; and Trodd.

33. Ishmael Reed, xv, xiv.

34 Many echo Shklar's claim that "black chattel slavery stood at the opposite social pole from full citizenship and so defined it" (16). Toni Morrison's literary discussion of the "Africanist" presence of black characters in white American literature serves an analogous role: the free is defined by and against the unfree (*Playing in the Dark*). My response to these projects is to reclaim the language of citizenship, social participation and collectivity through the vantage point of partial citizens.

CHAPTER ONE

1. Carby, *Race Men*, 27.

2. Ibid., 29–30.

3. Early, *Speech & Power*.

4. Hardison, "Binding Proteus," 11. For more on formlessness, see Butrym, *Essays on the Essay*; Good, *The Observing Self*; O'Leary, *The Essay*; and Snyder, *Prospects of Power*.

5. Good, *Encyclopedia of the Essay*, xix.

6. Obaldia, *Essayistic Spirit*, 3.

7. For more on the personal essay tradition, see Atkins, Glenn Clark, Haefner, and Obaldia.

8. Atkins, *Tracing the Essay*, 6.

9. Ibid., 31.

10. Good, *Encyclopedia of the Essay*, xxi.

11. Obaldia, 4.

12. Butrym, *Essays on the Essay*, 2.

13. Ward, "Everybody's Protest Novel," 173–74.

14. Hughes, "Negro Artist," 88.

15. Wall, *Worrying the Line*, 211.

16. Atkins, *Tracing the Essay*, 29; and Lopate, *The Art of the Personal Essay*.

17. Kirklighter, *Traversing the Democratic Borders of the Essay*.

18. Jordan, *Technical Difficulties*, 24. Further citations given in text.

19. King, "Letter from Birmingham City Jail," 291. Further citations given in text.

20. Americanist critics trace how other oral forms (e.g., jeremiad, sermon) influence the American literary imagination. See especially Bercovitch, *The American Jeremiad*; Howard-Pitney, *The Afro-American Jeremiad*; and Dolan Hubbard, *The Sermon and the African American Literary Imagination*.

21. Jehlen and Warner, *The English Literatures of America*, 643.

22. Occom, "A Sermon Preached by Samson Occom," 650. Further citations given in text.

23. Hoffman, *Montaignes' Career*, 50–51. I thank Cristina Kirklighter for this point.

24. Kirklighter, esp. 25–26 and 41.

25. Hall, "The Emergence of the Essay," 73.

26. Ibid., 74.

27. Ibid., 74–75.

28. On Thoreau's and Emerson's debt to Montaigne, see Kirklighter, esp. 41–48, 62.

29. Warner, *Letters of the Republic*.

30. Warner, *Publics and Counter-Publics*.

31. *Letters*, xii.

32. Ibid., xiii.

33. Ibid., xiii.

34. Garnet, 94.

35. Anderson, *Imagined Communities*. Anderson's work is seminal to ideas about national belonging in postcolonial literature. For my study, I am interested in how protest essays engage a community through its social divisions, rather than as strangers sharing a national identity.

36. Mary Helen Washington, "Introduction," xxx.

37. Haefner, 259.

38. Mary Helen Washington, xxxi.

39. It is instructive to compare my reading of Cooper's public, representative "I" to Tuzyline Jita Allan's celebration of the personal in an essay tradition, following Virginia Woolf, that embraces impersonality in order to get at the universal, not the particular.

40. See Metress and Pollack for more on Till in literary and political life. See Metress, "No Justice," for a study of Till in literature. See Norman, "Baldwin's Unifying Polemic" on Till's role in Civil Rights literature.

41. Hughes, "Emmett Till," 250. Further citations given in text.

42. Lopate, *The Art of the Personal Essay*, xxiii.

43. Atkins, *Tracing the Essay*, 116.

44. Spellmeyer, "A Common Ground." See also Kauffman who describes the essay's "I" as the site of knowledge: a "vital standpoint, or weltanschauung." Kauffman, "The Skewed Path," 227. Kauffman contends, "Montaigne revels in the *quest* for knowledge, the pleasure of the chase, not its goal" (224). For Kauffman, Spellmeyer, and many more, the essayist is the center of the essay.

45. Hall, 83.

46. Douglass, "Fourth of July?" 116. Further citations given in text.

47. Cunningham, "Public and Private." Similarly, Virginia Jackson thinks of the lyric "I" as an empty space of subjectivity, despite the tendency of readers—especially of lyrics by women writers—to conflate the lyric and the autobiographical "I."

48. Atkins, *Tracing the Essay*, 108.

49. Kirklighter, 16.

50. Atkins, *Tracing the Essay*, 116.

51. Adorno, "Essay as Form," 159. See also Kauffman's reading of Adorno's "rejection" of Lukacs's instrumentalizing of the essay as form.

52. Toni Cade Bambara's posthumous novel about the Atlanta child murders, *Those Bones Are Not My Child* (1999) was largely panned on similar grounds. The controversy around Baldwin's last book is long and complex. In his elegy *"Jimmy!"* Amiri Baraka points to racism and Baldwin's legal battles with his publisher.

53. "Brief Description."

54. Kauffman, 238.

55. Granger, *American Essay Serials*, 6.

56. Granger distinguishes the periodical essay from mere journalism: "This book focuses on essay serials which are primarily elegant, instructive, and diverting—that is to say, literary—rather than on those of immediate purpose, like William Livingston's *Independent Reflector* (1752–53) which defended civil and religious liberty at New York" (vii–viii).

57. Ibid., 9–11.

58. Ellison, "Richard Wright's Blues," 144.

59. Ellison, "Change the Joke, 108–09.

60. Vidal, *Dreaming War*, 5. Further citations given in text.

61. Whitman, "Democratic Vistas," 362. Further citations given in text.

62. Rogers Smith, *Civic Ideals*, 33.

63. David Walker, "Walker's Appeal," 11. Further citations given in text.

64. Hinks, *To Awaken My Afflicted Brethren*, xvi–xvii.

65. Ibid., xvii.

66. Students for a Democratic Society, "Port Huron Statement," 1.

67. Deloria, "From the Archives," 295. Further citations given in text.

68. Deloria, "Missionary and the Religious Vacuum," 22. Further citations given in text.

69. Barry, "The Indian in a Cultural Trap," 284.

70. Adorno, 152.

71. Lukacs, "On the Nature and Form of the Essay," 13.

72. Joeres, "The Passionate Essay," 158.

73. Jordan, "Problems of Language in a Democratic State," *Technical Difficulties*, 37.

74. Joeres, 151.

75. Ibid., 154–55 (emphasis in original).

76. Wolfe, "The New Pamphleteers," 12.

CHAPTER TWO

I am grateful for the assistance and generosity of Candace Falk and Barry Pateman at the Emma Goldman Papers Project. Pateman's encyclopedic knowledge was crucial in tracking down many of this chapter's references. This research was partially supported by Grant No. FY2005-2 from the Humanities/Social Sciences Research Committee at Idaho State University, Pocatello, Idaho.

1. T. V. Reed, xiv.

2. Gates, *Signifying*, 131.

3. Rich, *Blood, Bread, and Poetry*, 35.

4. Drawing on trauma studies, Byerman argues, "If the African American story is one of extended Holocaust, then the national history cannot be understood as primarily the story of individual achievement and democratic progress." See his *Remembering the Past*, 3.

5. Foner, *We, the Other People*.

6. Lucas, "Justifying," 69; and "Rhetorical Ancestry," 144.

7. Howell, "Some Adventures with America's Political Masterpiece."

8. William Smith, "The Rhetoric of the Declaration of Independence."

9. Renker, "'Declaration-Men' and the Rhetoric of Self-Presentation."

10. Bacon, "'Do You Understand Your Own Language?,'" 57.

11. Huberman, *We, The People*. In his immigrant view approach to the Declaration, Huberman tends to deemphasize or skirt around the history of slavery or indigenous peoples' displacement.

12. Walzer, "Pluralism: A Political Perspective," esp. 57–61. See Handy for a study of nineteenth-century American literature and ideals of *e pluribus unum*.

13. Lucas, "Justifying," 79.

14. See, for example, Starr, "Separated at Birth."

15. Emerson, "From Equivalence to Equality," 78.

16. Ibid., 99.

17. Becker, *The Declaration of Independence*.

18. Gittleman, "Jefferson's 'Slave Narrative,'" 242.

19. Ibid., 252–53.

20. Ibid., 248–49.

21. Stanton et al., "A Declaration of Sentiments," 139. Further citations given in text.

22. Co-authorship is usually attributed to Matilda Gage, Mary Ann McClintock, Lucretia Coffin Mott, and Martha Coffin Wright. Stanton is widely seen as the lead author.

23. The relation between black abolitionists and women's suffragists is reciprocal. Douglass spoke in favor of the Declaration of Sentiments just before its ratification.

24. See, for example, Henry, Matterson, and Marth Solomon Watson.

25. Matterson, 86.

26. Martha Solomon Watson, 97

27. Ibid., 101.

28. Ibid., 104.

29. Ibid., 105.

30. Hariman, "Relocating the Art of Public Address," 178.

31. Carby, *Reconstructing Womanhood*.

32. Haraway, "Ecce Homo."

33. See Kelley, *Private Woman, Public Stage*; Kerber, "No Constitutional Right to Be Ladies"; Berlant, *The Queen of America Goes to Washington*; Tompkins, *Sensational Designs*; and Zaeske, *Signatures of Citizenship*.

34. See Huxman, "Perfecting the Rhetorical Vision of Women's Rights"; Loeffelholz, "Posing the Woman Citizen"; and Diane Miller, "From One Voice a Chorus."

35. Strange and Brown, "The Bicycle, Women's Rights, and Stanton," 616, 621.

36. Armitage, "The Declaration of Independence and International Law"; and Mishra, "'All the World Was *America*.'"

37. Holton, "'To Educate Women into Rebellion,'" 1112.

38. Ibid., 1113.

39. Goldman, "A New Declaration of Independence." Further citations given in text. *Mother Earth* ran from 1906 to 1917 for ten cents a copy. There are at least two versions of the leaflet. One is true to the original version, but it excises the footnote discussed below. Another removes the footnote and replaces the phrase "maintain special privilege" with "maintain social privilege" and replaces the phrase "arrogance of national, racial, religious, and sex superiority" with "arrogance of national, social, religious, and sex superiority." The changes point to either a softening of the argument for a wider audience or a change in Goldman's uneven understanding of race in America. My thanks to Barry Pateman for helping to sort out the different versions.

40. Goldman, "The Tragedy of Women's Emancipation," 10.

41. Quoted in Falk, *Volume 2*, 38.

42. Goldman, Introduction, 2.

43. Ibid., 3.

44. Falk, *Volume 2*, 427.

45. Ibid., 426, 427.

46. Ibid., 373.

47. Goldman, "Tragedy at Buffalo," 471, 472. Thank you to Barry Pateman for this reference.

48. Falk, *Volume 2*, 17. This marks the first time political orientation was used as grounds for exclusion. The first immigrant exclusion acts in the early 1880s centered on mental capacity, physical health, and national origins (Chinese). See also Erika Lee.

49. See, for example, Voltairine de Cleyre's essay, "Anarchism and American Traditions" printed in the December 1908 edition of *Mother Earth*. Pages of socialist and communist anarchist magazines like *The Rebel* and *Liberty* were often devoted to studying the Declaration of Independence and how American history failed to live up to its reputable ideals. See especially Joseph A. Labadie's paper in the February 1905 issue of *Liberty* and Lucy E. Parson's letter in the October 20, 1895, issue of *Rebel*. I thank Pateman for these references.

50. Falk, *Volume 2*, 51.

51. Falk, *Guide*, 15.

52. Falk, *Volume 2*, 66.

53. Ibid., 137.

54. Ibid., 341.

55. Ibid., 342.

56. Further, Goldman often used the language of enemies, such as in the short essay "Our Friends, the Enemy" (1909) in which she quotes the U.S. Constitution to argue that sneaky local police tactics that suppress her meetings are out of alignment with stated national ideals.

57. Goldman acquired citizenship via marriage to Jacob A. Kersner who had been naturalized in 1884, then again in 1907 in an effort to block deportation efforts.

58. Falk, *Volume 1*, 148.

59. For instance, long before her citizenship was revoked and she was deported, in November 1907 a field agent from the Bureau of Immigration reported on Goldman's activities and wondered, "I tried very hard to find out as to how Miss Goldman gained entrance to this country, but there was no one [in the crowd] who could throw any light upon it." Falk, *Volume 2*, 260.

60. Ibid., 328.

61. Ibid., 337.

62. Cowles, Letter to George W. Wickersham.

63. Falk, *Volume 2*, 42, 39.

64. Monk, "The Little Magazine Impulse," 114. He compares *Mother Earth* to other small literary magazines and finds that Goldman's production schedule "dwarfs the achievement of the twentieth century's most important literary publications" (116).

65. Ibid., 113, 118, 120.

66. Ibid., 119.

67. Solomon, *Emma*, 132.

68. Solomon, "Rhetorical Constraint," 184.

69. Solomon, *Emma*, 132.

70. Drinnon, *Nowhere at Home* and "Harking Back to the Future."

71. Wexler, *Emma Goldman in Exile* and *Emma Goldman, An Intimate Life*.

72. See especially Falk, *Emma Goldman: A Documentary History of the American Years, Volumes 1 and 2* and *Love, Anarchy, and Emma Goldman*.

73. Quoted in Drinnon, "Harking Back to the Future," x.

74. Shulman, "A Re-appraisal," 8.

75. This is a defining moment in Goldman's life, which might paint her as a Jewish immigrant woman without a country during her years in her adopted United States.

76. Goldman, *Anarchism and Other Essays*, 47.

77. Ibid., 48.

78. Goldman, "Tenth Anniversary," 402.

79. Goldman, *Social Significance of Modern Drama*, 4.

80. Ibid., 7. Though most of her literary criticism concerns European drama, Goldman includes Emerson and Whitman in her list of great artists in the foreword to *Social Significance*.

81. Goldman, "Joys of Touring," 36.

82. Ibid., 40.

83. Goldman's redefinition of the literary was not necessarily recognized on a large scale. This is evidenced by the Immigration and Naturalization Service's reluctant issue of a visa to Goldman to reenter the United States on a speaking tour—on subjects confined to literature and drama. The U.S. government's acceptance of the bargain illustrates their assumption that the literary is divorced from the political and is therefore safe. For an account of the petition process to get Goldman a visa, see Wexler, *Emma Goldman in Exile* 158–59.

84. Goldman, Letter, August 30, 1910.

85. The Emma Goldman Papers Project itself came under fire by the University of California Regents when a solicitation letter adorned by a quotation from Goldman's writings on war and the suppression of free speech. According to the *New York Times*, "The University deemed the topics too political as the country prepares for war." Murphy, "Old Words," A1. Though the university eventually relented after the publicity, the showdown illustrates how Goldman's potentially time- and location-bound writings remain urgent and relevant in reactionary political climates. When asked about why Goldman's potentially ephemeral concerns remain so vital and urgent to groups who reimagine her, Falk postulated, "Emma always felt she was speaking for the ages. She genuinely believed she was writing for a movement that might not happen for years, for five hundred years." For Falk, Goldman is constantly aware of the future she is describing and trying bring about, but "Emma didn't believe in a blueprint" (Falk, interview).

86. Falk, *Volume 2*, 65.

87. Shulman, "Goldman's Feminism," 8.

88. Solomon, *Emma* 149.

89. Drinnon, "Harking Back to the Future," xi, xii.

90. Bread and Roses, Outreach Leaflet, 35.

91. Ibid., 35.

92. Bread and Roses, "Declaration of Women's Independence," 45. Further citations given in text.

93. Morgan, *Sisterhood*, 602.

94. Baxandall and Gordon, *Dear Sisters*, 258

95. Breines, "What's Love Got to Do with It?," 1103.

96. Echols, *Daring to Be Bad*, 387.

97. Ibid., 158.

98. Flora Davis, *Moving the Mountain*, 86–87.

99. Morgan, *Sisterhood*, 583.

100. Baxandall and Gordon, *Dear Sisters*, 45.

101. Breines, "What's Love," 1108.

102. Ibid., 1108.

103. Ibid., 1108–09.

104. Mishra, 234, 235.

105. See also Armstrong (esp. 16) on ephemeral documents in women's liberation.

106. Baxandall and Gordon, ix.

107. Ibid., 2.

108. Ibid., 2.

109. Ibid., 15.

110. Echols, *Daring*, 204.

111. This is a famous phrase by Joreen, a.k.a. Jo Freeman.

112. Zinn, *Declarations of Independence*.

113. Pocock, "The Ideal of Citizenship Since Classical Times," 32.

114. Zinn, 12.

115. Spooner, "Treason No. II, The Constitution," 3.

116. Ibid., 3.

117. Lorde, "The Master's Tools," *Sister Outsider*, 110.

CHAPTER THREE

1. For a narrative of Jackson's life read through her evolving author names, see Odell, *Helen Hunt Jackson (H.H.)*.

2. Quoted in Nevins, "Sentimentalist vs. Realist," 281.

3. Dorris, Introduction, ix, xvii.

4. This exchange is cited by both Rolle and Dorris. Each follow Jackson's lead in privileging the novel over the essay in terms of social impact, but Rolle prefers the essay.

5. Mathes, *Indian Reform Letters*, 81. Mathes argues that the failure of the novel to elicit direct reform is a result of the statistically fewer Native Americans than slaves and of the different time period than Stowe's *Uncle Tom's Cabin*.

6. Quoted in Mathes, *Indian Reform Legacy*, 203

7. Tompkins, *Sentimental Designs*, 124.

8. Ibid., 126.

9. I take this phrase from a representative review that dismisses the novel as a "failure" in yoking sentimentalism and the "modern realistic novel." See Tourgée, "Study in Civilization."

10. Mathes, *Indian Reform Legacy*, 82.

11. Ibid., 83.

12. Sara Hubbard, "Helen Hunt Jackson," 109–10.

13. Quoted in Mathes, *Indian Reform Legacy*, 338.

14. See Alémán; DeLyser; Mathes, *Indian Reform Legacy*; Moylan; Polanich; Sandos; and Stevens. Thank you to Angeline Henrickson for compiling some of this research.

15. Phillips, *Helen Hunt Jackson*, 259.

16. Mathes, *Indian Reform Legacy*, 37. While Mathes does not dwell on the reception of *A Century of Dishonor*, she tracks Jackson's personal disillusionment in the face of the poor reception of the novel (76–94). Mathes's thorough chronicling of substantial correspondence to government officials on behalf of Indians further demonstrates Jackson's resolution that the American conscience lay in the power of the government as the official representative of "the people." Phillips's treatment of *Century* is relatively cursory in its chronological survey of Jackson's reform activities leading up to the publication of *Ramona* (230–35). See also Moylan for a chronology of the reprintings of *Ramona* and its attendant erasure of Indian reform.

17. Higginson, "Literature as Art," 25. Higginson adds, "Except for the ballot for woman,—a contest which is thus far advancing very peaceably,—there seems nothing left which need be absolutely fought for; no great influence to keep us from a commonplace and perhaps debasing success" (21).

18. Anderson, *Imagined Communities*, 16. For a response that looks at "reimagining" nations, see Bhabha, *The Location of Culture*.

19. Review of *Century of Dishonor*, 152.

20. Ibid., 152.

21. Seelye, Introduction, 2. This 1885 edition is enlarged from the original 1881 edition with an appendix on the needs of the Mission Indians of California.

22. Ward, "Everybody's Protest Novel," 174.

23. Steinbeck translated "Their Blood Is Strong" (1938), his journalistic account of migrant farm labor in California during the Great Depression, into his popular novel *The Grapes of Wrath* (1940). Many other celebrated writers of the period pursued journalistic endeavors, such as Hughes's work with *The Chicago Defender* and his history of the NAACP, *Fight for Freedom* (1962).

24. Decker turns to the essay on Watts because Pynchon's journalistic account of "the refuse produced by the August 1965 Watts riots is especially revealing for what it can tell us about the status of the Tristero in *Lot 49*." Decker, "The Enigma His Efforts Had Created," 29–30.

25. Pynchon, "Journey into the Mind of Watts." Like Jackson, Pynchon works among multiple genres while writing about racial exclusion, social disorder, and the politics of violence. Rather than chronicle the *withdrawal* from official lines of communication in the Republic (the U.S. mail) as in *The Crying of Lot 49*, in his essay Pynchon uses his privileged access to national print venues to attempt to understand—and communicate—the mind of Watts to a readership unable to comprehend the meaning of the race riots. Pynchon instructs his readers, "Far from a sickness, violence may be an attempt to communicate" (84).

26. See Fishkin, *From Fact to Fiction*, for an examination of the journalism careers of many celebrated American novelists.

27. Johnson, "The Dilemma of the Negro Author," 93. For Johnson, the answer was clear: "And now, instead of black America and white America as separate or alternating audiences, what about the combination of the two into one? That, I believe, is the only way out" (97).

28. Thurman, "Negro Poets and Their Poetry," 101.

29. Als, "In Black and White," viii.

30. Wright, "Blueprint for Negro Writing," 194.

31. See Wright, "Between Laughter and Tears."

32. Baldwin, *Notes of a Native Son*.

33. Britt, "Watershed of Negro Protest Literature," 4. Britt wishes to save Wright's novels from the fate of being overly topical by arguing for their ability to endure beyond "special courses in American social problems" (4).

34. Hassan, "The Novel of Outrage."

35. Foote, "James Baldwin's Holler Books."

36. Bell, "Roth & Baldwin," 109. For other examples of appraisals of Baldwin's protest fiction and drama after his public rebuke of Wright's influence see Brustein, "Everybody's Protest Play" and Burks, "James Baldwin's Protest Novel."

37. Ibid., 109.

38. In 1963, Kenneth B. Clark described these three leaders as "the voice of Negro Protest" in the wake of Baldwin's rise to fame after his essay *The Fire Next Time*.

39. See Berlant on the transverse phenomenon: a privatized body going public.

40. Tompkins, 125.

41. Spillers, "Changing the Letter."

42. Spillers argues, "After *Uncle Tom's Cabin*, one needs a drink. Reed provides it" (33).

43. Ikard, "Love Jones."

44. Itagaki, "Transgressing Race and Community."

45. Danielle Allen, "Ellison and the Tragicomedy of Citizenship," 57.

46. See DeKoven, *Utopia Limited*. DeKoven argues that in the American 1960s modernist ambivalence and anxieties about fragmentation began to shift toward a postmodernist sensibility that embraces and celebrates such a necessarily locational subjectivity.

47. Jackson sent copies to other influential figures, including literary elites such as Thomas Wentworth Higginson and notable clergymen (Phillips 234).

48. Reported in Rolle, xiv. If Rolle is correct, Jackson may have sent congressmen a copy of the second edition. Phillips notes that the first edition was bound in brown cloth with another embossed epigraph: "When one of the Spartan kings pronounced that commonwealth happy which was bounded by the sword and spear, Pompey, correcting him, said: 'Yea, rather that commonwealth is truly happy which is on every side bounded with justice.'" (234).

49. Tompkins, 190.

50. For surveys of these emergent fields see Gillman, Rowe, Schueller, and Singh and Schmidt. For a survey of what she calls the "transnational turn" in American Studies, see Fishkin's 2004 ASA Presidential Address in "Crossroads of Culture."

51. Kaplan, "Nation, Region, and Empire."

52. Phillips, *Helen Hunt Jackson*, 39.

53. See David Luis-Brown, Gonzales, and Jacobs.

54. See Samuels, *The Culture of Sentiment*.

55. For a discussion of the relationship between universalist national citizenship and imperialism, especially under a doctrine of expansionist citizenship, see Balibar, *We, The People of Europe?*, esp. 56–58.

56. Irwin, "*Ramona* and Postnationalist American Studies."

57. Martí's strategy, according to Irwin, fails because the novel irrevocably translates the potentially postnational mestiza culture and region into a squarely American novel in the protest tradition of Stowe's black and white world. As evidence, Irwin cites Ramona's blue eyes and the popularity of the novel despite no real redress of the political problems in the Mexican borderlands. Dorris also traces the increasing whitening of the protagonist couple in *Ramona*'s U.S. reception. Irwin follows the tradition of quickly dismissing Jackson's protest essay as prelude to a critique of the novel.

58. On white writers imagining Native American characters, see Senier, *Voices of American Indian Assimilation and Resistance*; and Sherry L. Smith, *Reimagining Indians*.

59. Jackson, *Ramona*, 106. Further citations given in text.

CHAPTER FOUR

I thank the staff of the Schomburg Center of the New York Public Libraries for their assistance. Research for this chapter was partially supported by Grant No. FY2005-2 from the Humanities/Social Sciences Research Committee at Idaho State University, Pocatello, Idaho.

NOTES TO CHAPTER FOUR

1. Baldwin, "The Price May Be Too High," D9.

2. Ibid., D9.

3. Ibid., D9.

4. For articles that explore race spokesmanship during Baldwin's early career, see Coles, Hernton, Jacobson, Redding, Simmons, and Tuttleton.

5. Meriwether, "Fiery Voice of Negro Revolt," 3.

6. Ibid., 7.

7. Warren, *Who Speaks?*

8. Gross, "Interview," 24.

9. See Joshua L. Miller, Tóibín, Wallace, and Wood.

10. Relyea, *Outsider Citizens*.

11. Porter, *Stealing the Fire*.

12. DeKoven, *Utopia Limited*, 234.

13. Ibid., 233.

14. Baldwin, "Everybody's Protest Novel," 38.

15. Baldwin, "Truth," 1.

16. Ibid., 38.

17. Kenan, *James Baldwin*, 18.

18. Hughes, "From Harlem to Paris," 9.

19. Howe, "Black Boys," 267.

20. Clarke, "Alienation," 351

21. Strong, "Notes on James Baldwin," 168.

22. Karrer, "Discursive Strategies in Baldwin's Essays."

23. Rusk, "Selfhood and Strategy."

24. Cunningham, 199.

25. Baldwin, *No Name in the Street*, 481. Further citation given in text.

26. "Black Scholar," 36.

27. Collier, "Thematic Patterns," 135.

28. Ford, "Walls Do a Prison Make," 125.

29. Ford, "Search for Identity," 128.

30. Hobart Jarret and Gayle ("Dialectic") also place Baldwin in line with Emerson.

31. Ford, "Evolution," 85, 103.

32. Dickstein, "Wright, Baldwin, Cleaver," 124." See also Dickstein, "Black Writing."

33. Dickstein, "Wright, Baldwin, Cleaver," 120.

34. See, for example, Nichols, "New Calvinism"; and Strout, "Portent of Millenium."

35. Levin, "Baldwin's Autobiographical Essay," 239.

36. See, for example, Aman, "James Baldwin."

37. See Michael Anderson; Bonofsky; Charles Newman; Porter, "Baldwin and the 'Mighty' Henry James" in *Stealing the Fire*; and Powers. James's influence is widely noted in Baldwin's biographies. See James Campbell, 70; Kenan, 70; Leeming, 253–55; and Weatherby, 84–86, 178–79.

38. Pratt, "The Literary Ghetto," 266.

39. Ibid., 267.

40. Standley, "The Artist," 18.

41. Ibid., 19.

42. Ibid., 22.

43. Stein, *Native Sons*, 13.

44. Ibid., 15.

45. Hicks, "Commitment," 9.

46. See also Flint, "Not Ideas but Life."

47. Hicks, "Commitment," 9.

48. Maloff, "Two Baldwins," 15.

49. Ibid., 16.

50. Thomas Jarrett, "Search for Identity," 87.

51. Ibid., 87–88.

52. Spingarn, 87.

53. Cox and Jones, "After the Tranquilized Fifties," 118, 115.

54. Malcolm, "The Author in Search of Himself," 323.

55. Coles, "Baldwin's Burden"; and Coles, "James Baldwin Back Home," respectively.

56. See, for example, Beaufly, and Whitehead Jackson.

57. Brower, "Of Nothing But Facts," 613.

58. Bonofsky, "The Negro Writer and Commitment."

59. Stevenson, "The Activists," 238.

60. Baldwin, *Nobody Knows My Name*. Further citations given in text. The essay originally appeared in 1958 as "A Hard Kind of Courage" on assignment from *Harper's* magazine.

61. Kenan, 77.

62. Wills, "Uses of Coincidence," 234.

63. Dupee, "James Baldwin and 'The Man,'" 12.

64. Dance, "You Can't Go Home Again," 81, 87. On Baldwin's connection—or lack thereof—to place and expatriation, see also Daniels, Darsey, Power, Schatt, Bryan Washington, Edward Watson, and David Wright.

65. Harper, "Art of Propaganda," 138.

66. Gross, *Transition*, 21.

67. Ibid., 21.

68. On Baldwin's identity, see especially Bigsby, B. B. Jones, Keller, Klein, Pratt, and Vandyke for analyses of Baldwin's relationship to his audience, or constituencies.

69. Bluefarb, "A Problem of Identity."

70. West, "Tip-Toeing."

71. Watkins, "An Appreciation," 117.

72. DeKoven, *Utopia*, 237, 235. DeKoven argues that Baldwin's shifting pronouns are both a rhetorical technique and a political possibility specific to the sixties moment.

73. Schroth, "James Baldwin's Search," 289.

74. Mowe and Nobles, "Message for White America."

75. Gross, "Day of Wrath," 79.

76. Gross, "World of James Baldwin," 139.

77. Spender, "Voice of a Revolution," 256, 257.

78. Root, "It's a Wasteland," 1354.

79. Dwyer, "I *Know* about Negroes and the Poor," 517.

80. Patterson, "The Essay of James Baldwin," 37.

81. Ibid., 32.

82. Ibid., 38.

83. Golden, "A Comment," 145.

84. Als, "The Enemy Within," 78.

85. For analyses of Baldwin's rejection by Black Power, especially following Eldredge Cleaver's homophobic attack in *Soul on Ice* (1969), see Field, Reid-Pharr, and Thomas.

86. Abdul, "Negro Artists," 22.

87. Neal, "The Black Writer's Role," 10.

88. Ibid., 10, 18. Eventually, Neal helped found the Black Arts movement with fellow writer LeRoi Jones, soon to be known as Amiri Baraka.

89. Baldwin, *Price of the Ticket*, 673–74. Further citations given in text.

90. Southwick, "James Baldwin's Jeremiad," 362.

91. Dupee, 11, 12.

92. Jacobson, 498.

93. Elkoff, "Everybody Knows His Name," 59.

94. Morrison, "The Angriest Young Man," 25.

95. Hentoff, "The Price of Fame."

96. The May 24, 1963, meeting at Robert F. Kennedy's apartment is well documented in Baldwin biographies (Campbell, 163–71; Eckman, 182–83; Kenan, 107–13; Leeming, 22–26; Porter; and Weatherby, 219–28). For many, the meeting signaled an impasse rift between white liberals and African Americans around Civil Rights issues.

97. Clark, *Negro Protest*, 13.

98. "Races," 25.

99. Ibid., 26.

100. Schroth, 288.

101. Ibid., 288.

102. For more on connections to white Hollywood women, see Gaines, "'Green Like Me.'"

103. Baldwin, *The Devil Finds Work*, 34. Further citations given in text.

104. Coombs, 6.

105. Ibid., 7.

106. Lee, "Critical Review," 84.

107. Allan Morrison, 23.

108. Ibid., 24.

109. Leaks, "I Know His Name," 105.

110. Ibid., 104.

111. See also, Larry X; Cleaver.

112. Anderson, "Trapped," 13.

113. Ibid., 13.

114. McClusky, *Black World*, 51.

115. Ibid., 51.

116. Puzo, "Cardboard Lovers," 155.

117. Howe, "At Ease in the Apocalypse," 104, 98.

118. Baker, "Embattled Craftsman."

119. Shayon, "T. V. and Radio," 35.

120. Finn, "The Identity of James Baldwin," 116.

121. Ibid., 113–14.

122. Geraldine Murphy, "Subversive Anti-Stalinsim," 1021.

123. Michael Anderson, 14.

124. Gross, "Day of Wrath," 79.

125. Watkins, "The Fire Next Time This Time," 17.

126. Finn, "Vision," 447.

127. Watkins, "The Fire Next Time This Time," 17, 18.

128. Wright, "African American Tensions," 445.

129. Hall, Interview, 22.

130. Featherstone, "Blues for Mister Baldwin," 36.

131. Balliet, "Wrong Pulpit," 69.

132. Balliet's phrase.

133. Anderson, "The Co-Opted Voice," 289.

134. See Dudziak, *Cold War Civil Rights*. Like Dudziak, many argue that American ideals of freedom and democracy exported during the Cold War are threatened by, and therefore inextricably linked to, domestic challenges to ideals of fairness and equality coming out of Civil Rights.

135. Banks, "James Baldwin's Rage."

136. Bawer, "Race and Art," 22.

137. McBride, *James Baldwin Now*.

138. Reid-Pharr places Baldwin's gay novel *Giovanni's Room* (1956) in conversation with Cleaver's virulent homophobic attack to explore the panic that "twentieth-century black male narrators are in danger of being homosexualized." Reid-Pharr, "Tearing the Goat's Flesh," 160. Thomas argues that Baldwin's gay work has been underemphasized in "a certain revisionist impeachment" as a result of the "jargon of authenticity" in black culture and letters. Thomas, "'Ain't Nothing Like the Real Thing,'" 56. Field places debates about Baldwin's ambiguous sexuality in an identitarian literary tradition of Langston Hughes, Bruce Nugent, Wallace Thurman, and Claude McKay, rather than Eldridge Cleaver. Field, "Looking for Jimmy Baldwin."

139. McBride constructs an entire field of black queer studies by placing Baldwin at the head of his genealogy (*Why I Hate*). In these and similar projects, many look at Baldwin's late essay "Here Be Dragons" (1985), originally in *Playboy*, as Baldwin's much anticipated statement on gay politics and identity. Addison Gayle came to Baldwin's defense before Cleaver's attacks to argue, "The day is quite distant when Negroes will be found engaging in sit-ins for the rights of homosexuals." Gayle, "Defense," 205. For more treatments of Baldwin's sexual politics, see also DeGout, Henderson, Cora Kaplan, Ohi, and Shin and Judson.

140. See Harris, DeGout, Henderson, Kaplan, and Ongiri. See Norman, "Crossing" for an analysis of women's liberation claims to Baldwin.

141. See, for example, Balfour, Nabers, and Pemberton.

142. "James Baldwin: Writer of Black America," A1.

143. "We Carry Him," 1. Troupe collected these elegies with other reflections by boldfaced names.

144. Als, "The Enemy Within," 72.

145. Ibid., 77.

146. Dailey; Dworkin; Gates, "The Welcome Table"; Cora Kaplan; Rich, "Split at the Root," *On Lies, Secrets, and Silence*; Rodriguez; and West.

CHAPTER FIVE

1. Lorde, "An Open Letter to Mary Daly," *Sister Outsider*, 66.

2. Rich, "Notes Toward a Politics of Location," *Blood, Bread, and Poetry*, 210. Further citations given in text.

3. This is by now a familiar narrative. For an influential early example, see Evans, *Personal Politics*.

4. Breines explores the tensions between black and white women in feminism (*The Trouble Between Us*) and Roth explores the differing feminist histories of black, white, and chicana women (*Separate Roads to Feminism*). Breines recounts, "The promise of the early sixties shaped me and others of my generation of whites. I have not easily let go of a humanistic, universal, racially integrated sisterhood and brotherhood ideal where, hand in hand, we create a benign and just world, a vision I took from the civil rights movement. And, for many of us, the new left, socialism, and Marxism reinforced a universalism that the early civil rights movement embodied" ("What's Love" 1096).

5. DeKoven, *Utopia Limited*, esp. 249–69, 288–91.

6. Ibid., 250–51.

7. See, for example, Susan Field's work on Lorde's connection to Ralph Emerson.

8. See Kemp for a recent example.

9. For recent examples, see Elizabeth Alexander, Olson, and Steele.

10. For recent examples, see Morris, Walk, and Wu.

11. Lorde, "Poetry Is Not a Luxury," *Sister Outsider*, 36. Further citations given in text.

12. Joeres, "Passionate Essay," 157.

13. Ibid., 157.

14. Ibid., 358.

15. See, for example, Ratcliffe.

16. Joeres, "Passionate Essay," 156.

17. Ibid., 157.

18. Recchio, 271.

19. Walker, *In Search*, 138. Further citations given in text.

20. Wall, "On Freedom," 291; and *Worrying the Line*, 211.

21. Allan, "A Voice of One's Own," 131.

22. Ibid., 137.

23. Ibid., 144. Allan refers to Walker's engagement with DuBois, but the point can be generalized.

24. Wall, *Worrying*, 217.

25. Ibid., 218.

26. Lyon, 176.

27. Shulman, "Agreement," 219.

28. Shulman, "Disagreement," 290.

29. *Up from Under*, August–September 1970; *Redbook*, August 1971; *Life*, 28 April 1972.

30. Shulman describes Norman Mailer's nationally published assault on feminism using the "Marriage Agreement" as a straw position, and the pernicious and often fraudulent references to her agreement as a "Contract" in the ensuing national discussion (ibid., 294–99). Shulman argues that "Contract" renders the feminist critique of marriage as "adversarial and legal" instead of potentially "amicable and voluntary" (297).

31. Cooper, *Voice*, 31.

32. Hansberry, "The Negro Writer," 131.

33. NYRF, "Politics of the Ego," 443. Further citations given in text.

34. See Armstrong; Baxandall; Breines, *The Trouble Between Us* and "What's Love"; Evans, "Re-viewing" and *Tidal Wave*; Guy-Sheftall; Jennifer Nelson; Roberts; Roth; Springer; and Thompson, *Living for the Revolution* and "Third Wave."

35. Quoted in Joreen, "Trashing," 94.

36. Phelan, "Reciting the Citation of Others," 16 (emphasis in the original).

37. This section draws heavily on my review of *Heartbreak* in *Women's Studies*.

38. Dworkin, *Heartbreak*, xiii. Further citations given in text.

39. Mailer, "The White Negro," 339. Further citations given in text.

40. Hansberry, "The Negro Writer," 134.

41. Combahee River Collective, *Statement*, 9. I will cite from the *Freedom Organizing Series'* pamphlet reprint. Further citations given in text.

42. For an extendend analysis of this document and identity politics, see my "Publishing History." This section draws heavily from that article.

43. Friedman, "Locational Feminism." For Friedman, the Second Wave (1960s-1970s) adopts a "prevailing rhetoric of awakening, revelation, and rebirth" whereas

the Third Wave (1980s-1990s) uses a "rhetoric of location, multipositionality, and migration" (18). Similarly, the *Statement's* circulation evidences continuity between "waves."

44. For more on women's liberation anthologies, see my "Black Women in *Sisterhood*."

45. Smith, Foreword, 7.

46. Ibid., 5.

47. See Crenshaw, and Collins. McCall identifies intersectionality as the methodology of feminism itself. Crenshaw and Collins cite the *Statement* as foundational.

48. Friedman, "Locational Feminism."

49. Chang, "Last Past the Post," 72.

CHAPTER SIX

1. Postcolonial concerns and ideas now permeate American literary studies, as evidenced by scores of recent work that proposes transnational approaches to American literatures. Key examples include Kaplan and Pease, Singh and Schmidt, Scheuller, and Madsen.

2. Arendt, *The Origins of Totalitarianism*.

3. Gillman, "The New Newest Thing," 196.

4. Guerrero et al., "The U.S. from Inside and Out," 3.

5. Jordan, *Soldier*, 248–49.

6. George H. W. Bush, State of the Union Address.

7. Jordan, *Technical Difficulties*, 198. Further citations given in text.

8. Joeres, "Passionate Essay," 158 (emphasis in original).

9. Ibid., 159.

10. For more on Jordan as racial spokesperson, see MacPhail, "New Black Intellectuals."

11. Philip Metress, "Performing 'Righteous Certainty,'" 186.

12. Marsh, "'Come Together.'"

13. Accomando, "Exposing the Lie." See also, Coleman, "Narrating Nation."

14. Marsh, 29.

15. Joeres, 15.

16. Kymlicka, "Citizenship in an Era of Globalization," 119.

17. Beyond work by Appiah; Benhabib; Mohanty, *Feminism without Borders*; and Nussbaum, "Patriotism and Cosmopolitanism" and "Women's Education," see also Appadurai; Edwards; and Ong.

18. See John Campbell, and Kymlicka. Kymlicka values transnational organizations such as Greenpeace, but points out that "the only forum in which genuine democracy occurs is within national boundaries" (124). Kymlicka further notes that "globalization is undoubtedly producing a new civil society, but it has not yet produced anything we can recognize as transnational democratic citizenship" (124).

19. Godfrey and Unger, *The Shifting Foundations of Modern Nation-States*, 2.

20. For a recent sampling, see Gamble and Wright; Godfrey and Unger; Paul, Ikenberry, and Hall; and Roy.

21. See Jenkins and Cox, "Bringing Human Rights Home."

22. Cheah and Robbins, *Cosmopolitics*.

23. See Appiah; Archibugi; Gilroy; and Nussbaum, "Patriotism and Cosmopolitanism" and "Women's Education."

24. Friedman, "Locational Politics."

25. Alexander; and Shohat and Stam.

26. See Domna Stanton's 2005 MLA Presidential Address.

27. Brubaker, *Ethnicity without Groups*.

28. Mohanty, *Feminism without Borders*. Mohanty, who famously critiqued "Western feminism" for effectively colonizing third-world women in "Under Western Eyes," considers the vast changes in feminist scholarship and the academy that arose in response to her and other's critiques of Eurocentrism. Mohanty is skeptical of feminist-as-tourist and feminist-as-explorer models that still read global subjects through western or colonial lenses. Mohanty turns to anti-globalization work for a viable transnational politics.

29. See Balibar, *We, the People of Europe?*

30. Messmer, "Toward a Declaration of Interdependence," 51.

31. Bérubé, "American Studies without Exceptions," 104.

32. Ibid., 105.

33. Nussbaum, "Patriotism and Cosmopolitanism," 15. Nussbaum examines Tagore's novel *The Home and the World*.

34. Ibid., 17.

35. Silko, "Border Patrol," 1.

36. Comfort, "Becoming a Writerly Self."

37. Mittlefehldt, 204.

38. Ibid., 200.

39. Morrison, "Roundtable," 716.

40. Ibid., 716.

41. Benhabib, *The Rights of Others*, 1. Benhabib seeks "disaggregated citizenship" outside, across, or beyond national citizenship and its outdated territorial definitions.

CONCLUSION

1. DuBois, *Souls of Black Folk*, 2.

2. DuBois's later work engages an explicitly transnational politics culminating in his renunciation of the U.S. nation-state, as signified by his Ghanaian citizenship in 1963. For more on DuBois's relation to the transnational and the United States, see Gilroy, *The Black Atlantic* and *Against Race*, esp. 288.

3. Atkins, *Tracing the Essay*, 149.

4. Lorde, *Cancer Journals*, 23.

5. For a study of the reception of *Silent Spring*, see Coit Murphy, *What a Book Can Do*.

6. Finley Campbell, "More Notes," 96.

7. Ibid., 97.

8. For more on cross-identity connections, especially with white women, see Gaines, "Green Like Me" and Norman, "Crossing Identitarian Lines" and "The Threat of Historical Irrelevance."

9. Gilroy, *Against Race*, 2.

10. Rich, "When We Dead Awaken: Writing as Re-Vision," *On Lies, Secrets, and Silence*.

11. Moon and Davidson, *Subjects and Citizens*, esp. 1–3.

BIBLIOGRAPHY

Abdul, Raoul. "Negro Artists, Writers Using Talents to Spur the Struggle for Liberation." *Muhammad Speaks* 19 Nov. 1965: 22.

Accomando, Christina. "Exposing the Lie of Neutrality: June Jordan's *Affirmative Acts.*" Grebowicz and Kinloch 33–48.

Adorno, T. W. "The Essay as Form." 1958. Trans. Bob Hullot-Kentor and Frederic Will. *New German Critique* 32 (1984): 151–71.

Alarcón, Norma "The Theoretical Subject(s) of *This Bridge Called My Back* and Anglo-American Feminism." Anzaldúa, *Making Face, Making Soul* 356–79.

Alémán, Jesse. "Historical Amnesia and the Vanishing Mestiza: The Problem of Race in *Squatter and the Don* and *Ramona.*" *Aztlán* 27.1 (2002): 59–93.

Alexander, Elizabeth. "'Coming Out Blackened and Whole': Fragmentation and Reintegration in Lorde's *Zami* and *The Cancer Journals.*" *Skin Deep, Spirit Strong: The Black Female Body.* Ed. Kimberly Wallace-Sanders. Ann Arbor: U of Michigan P, 2002. 218–36.

Alexander, M. Jacqui. "Remembering *This Bridge,* Remembering Ourselves." *Sing, Whisper, Shout, Pray! Feminist Visions for a Just World.* Eds. M. Jacqui Alexander et al. Fort Bragg, CA: EdgeWork Books, 2003. 611–39.

Allan, Tuzyline Jita. "A Voice of One's Own: Implications of Impersonality in the Essays of Virginia Woolf and Alice Walker." Joeres and Mittman 131–50.

Allen, Danielle. "Ellison and the Tragicomedy of Citizenship." *Raritan* 23.3 (2004): 56–74.

Als, Hilton. "In Black and White." Introduction. *If He Hollers Let Him Go.* By Chester Himes. New York: Thunder's Mouth Press, 2002. vii–xx.

———. "The Enemy Within: The Making and Unmaking of James Baldwin." *New Yorker* 16 Feb. 1998: 72–80.

Aman, Harry. "James Baldwin." *Encyclopedia of the Essay.* London: Fitzroy Dearborn, 1997. 51–54.

"America: The Idea, the Literature." *PMLA* 118.1 (2003).

Anderson, Benedict. *Imagined Communities: Reflections on the Origin and Spread of Nationalism*. London: Verso, 1983.

Anderson, David R. "The Co-Opted Voice: Politics, History, and Self-Expression in James Baldwin's 'Journey to Atlanta.'" *CLA Journal* 42.3 (1999): 273–89.

Anderson, Michael. "Trapped Inside James Baldwin." Rev. of *James Baldwin: Early Novels and Stories*, ed. Toni Morrison, and *James Baldwin: Collected Essays*, ed. Toni Morrison. *New York Times Book Review* 29 Mar. 1998: 13–14.

Anzaldúa, Gloria. "Hacienda Caras, Una Entrada." Introduction. *Making Face, Making Soul: Haciendo Caras, Creative and Critical Perspectives by Women of Color*. Ed. Gloria Anzaldúa. San Francisco: Aunt Lute Foundation Books, 1990. xv–xxviii.

———. "Speaking in Tongues." Moraga and Anzaldúa 165–73.

———, ed. *This Bridge We Call Home: Radical Visions for Transformation*. New York: Routledge, 2002.

Appadurai, Arjun, ed. *Globalization*. Durham, NC: Duke UP, 2001.

Appiah, Kwame Anthony. *Cosmopolitanism: Ethics in a World of Strangers*. New York: Norton, 2006.

Archibugi, Daniele. *Debating Cosmopolitics*. London: Verso, 2003.

Arendt, Hannah. *The Origins of Totalitarianism*. New York: Harcourt Brace, 1951.

Armitage, David. "The Declaration of Independence and International Law." *William and Mary Quarterly* 59.1 (2002): 39–64.

Armstrong, Elisabeth. *The Retreat from Organization: U.S. Feminism Reconceptualized*. Albany: State U of New York P, 2002.

Atkins, Douglass. *Estranging the Familiar: Toward a Revitalized Critical Writing*. Athens and London: U of Georgia P, 1992.

———. *Tracing the Essay: Through Experience to Truth*. Athens: U of Georgia P, 2005.

Awkward, Michael. "A Black Man's Place(s) in Black Feminist Criticism." Blount and Cunningham 3–26.

Bacon, Jacqueline. "'Do You Understand Your Own Language?': Revolutionary *Topoi* in the Rhetoric of African-American Abolitionists." *Rhetoric Society Quarterly* 28.2 (1998): 55–75.

Baker, Houston A., Jr. "The Embattled Craftsman: An Essay on James Baldwin." 1977. Rpt. in Standley and Burt 62–77.

Baldwin, James. *Another Country*. New York: Dial, 1960.

———. "As Much Truth as One Can Bear." *New York Times Book Review* 14 Jan. 1962: 1, 38.

———. *Blues for Mister Charlie*. New York: Dial, 1964.

———. *The Devil Finds Work*. New York: Dial, 1976.

———. *The Evidence of Things Not Seen*. New York: Holt, Rinehart and Winston, 1985.

———. *The Fire Next Time*. New York: Dial, 1963.

———. *Nobody Knows My Name: More Notes of a Native Son*. New York: Dial, 1961.

———. *No Name in the Street*. New York: Dial, 1972.

———. *Notes of a Native Son*. 1955. New York: Beacon Press, 1984.

———. *One Day, When I Was Lost: A Scenario Based on Alex Haley's* The Autobiography of Malcolm X. 1972. New York: Dell, 1992.

———. "The Price May Be Too High." *New York Times* 2 Feb. 1969: D9.

———. *The Price of the Ticket: Collected Non-Fiction, 1948–1985*. New York: St. Martin's, 1985.

Baldwin, James, and Margaret Mead. *A Rap on Race*. Philadelphia: J. B. Lippincott, 1971.

Baldwin, James, and Nikki Giovanni. *A Dialogue*. Philadelphia: J. B. Lippincott, 1973.

Balfour, Katharine Lawrence. *The Evidence of Things Not Said: James Baldwin and the Promise of American Democracy*. Ithaca, NY: Cornell UP, 2001.

Balibar, Etienne. *We, the People of Europe? Reflections on Transnational Citizenship*. Princeton, NJ: Princeton UP, 2003.

Balliet, Whitney. "Wrong Pulpit." *The New Yorker* 4 Aug. 1962: 69–70.

Bambara, Toni Cade. *Those Bones Are Not My Child*. New York: Pantheon, 1999.

Banks, William H., Jr. Letter. "James Baldwin's Rage." *New York Times* 17 Sept. 2004.

Baraka, Amiri. "Jimmy!" *James Baldwin: The Legacy*. Ed. Quincy Troupe. New York: Simon & Schuster, 1989. 127–34.

Barry, Lawrence E. "The Indian in a Cultural Trap." 1965. Treat 284–94.

Baumgardner, Jennifer, and Amy Richards. *Manifesta: Young Women, Feminism, and the Future*. New York: Farrar, Strauss and Giroux, 2000.

Bawer, Bruce. "Race and Art: The Career of James Baldwin." *New Criterion* 10.3 (1991): 16–26.

Baxandall, Rosalyn. "Re-visioning the Women's Liberation Movement's Narrative: Early Second Wave African American Feminists." *Feminist Studies* 27.1 (2001): 225–45.

Baxandall, Rosalyn, and Linda Gordon, eds. *Dear Sisters: Dispatches from the Women's Liberation Movement*. New York: Perseus, 2000.

Beaufly, James. "James Baldwin: The Struggle for Identity." *Journal of Sociology* 17 (1966): 107–21.

Becker, Carl. *The Declaration of Independence: A Study in the History of Political Ideas*. New York: Knopf, 1922.

Bell, Pearl K. "Roth & Baldwin: Coming Home." *Commentary* 68.6 (1979). Rpt. in *James Baldwin: Modern Critical Views*. Ed. Harold Bloom. New York: Chelsea House, 1986. 109–12.

Benhabib, Seyla. *The Rights of Others: Aliens, Resident, and Citizens*. London: Cambridge UP, 2004.

Bennett, Paula. *Poets in the Public Sphere: The Emancipatory Project of American Women's Poetry, 1800–1900*. Princeton, NJ: Princeton UP, 2003.

Benson, Thomas W., ed. *American Rhetoric: Context and Criticism*. Carbondale: Southern Illinois UP, 1989.

Bercovitch, Sacvan. *The American Jeremiad*. Madison: U of Wisconsin P, 1978.

Berlant, Lauren. *The Queen of America Goes to Washington: Essays on Sex and Citizenship*. Durham: U of North Carolina P, 1997.

Bérubé, Michael. "American Studies without Exceptions." *PMLA* 118.1 (2003): 103–13.

Bhabha, Homi K. *The Location of Culture*. London: Routledge, 1994.

Bigsby, C. W. E. "The Divided Mind of James Baldwin." 1979. Bloom 113–30.

"The *Black Scholar* Interviews James Baldwin." *Black Scholar* 5.4 (1973–1974): 33–42.

Bloom, Harold. *James Baldwin: Modern Critical Views*. New York: Chelsea House, 1986.

Blount, Marcellus, and George P. Cunningham, eds. *Representing Black Men*. New York: Routledge, 1996.

Bluefarb, Sam. "James's Baldwin's 'Previous Condition': A Problem of Identification." *Negro American Literature Forum* 31 (1969): 26–29.

Bonofsky, Philip. "The Negro Writer and Commitment." *Mainstream* 15 (1962): 16–22.

Bosniak, Linda. "Citizenship." *The Oxford Handbook of Legal Studies*. Eds. Peter Can and Mark Tushnet. New York: Oxford UP, 2003. 183–201.

Bread and Roses. "Declaration of Women's Independence." 1970. Baxandall and Gordon 45–47.

———. Outreach leaflet. 1970. Baxandall and Gordon 35.

Breines, Wini. Rev. of *Going South: Jewish Women in the Civil Rights Movement* by Debra L. Schultz and *Deep in Our Hearts: Nine White Women in the Freedom Movement* by Constance Curry et al. *Signs* 30.2 (2005): 1670–74.

———. *The Trouble Between Us: An Uneasy History of White and Black Women in the Feminist Movement*. New York: Oxford UP, 2006.

———. "What's Love Got to Do with It?: White Women, Black Women, and Feminism in the Movement Years." *Signs* 27.4 (2002): 1095–1134.

Breitman, George, ed. *Malcolm X Speaks: Selected Speeches and Statements*. 1965. New York: Grove Weidenfeld, 1989.

Brickhouse, Anna. *Transamerican Literary Relations and the Nineteenth-Century Public Sphere*. New York: Cambridge UP, 2004.

"Brief Description." *The Evidence of Things Not Seen*. Tipped-in page of uncorrected proof. New York: Holt, Rinehart and Winston, 1985. Private collection of Brian Norman.

Britt, David. "*Native Son*: Watershed of Negro Protest Literature." *Negro American Literature Forum* 1.1 (1967): 4–5.

Brooks, A. Russell. "James Baldwin as Poet-Prophet." O'Daniel 126–34.

Brower, Brock. "Of Nothing But Facts." *American Scholar* 33 (1964): 613–18.

Brown, Wesley, and Amy Ling, eds. *Imagining America: Stories from the Promised Land*. New York: Persea, 2002.

Brubaker, Rogers. *Ethnicity without Groups*. Cambridge: Harvard UP, 2004.

Brustein, Robert. "Everybody's Protest Play." *New Republic* 16 May 1964: 35–37.

Burks, Mary Fair. "James Baldwin's Protest Novel: *If Beale Street Could Talk*." *Negro American Literature Forum* 10 (1976): 83–87.

Bush, George H. W. State of the Union Address. 28 Jan. 1992. <http://www.c-span.org/executive/stateoftheunion.asp>.

Butrym, Alexander, ed. *Essays on the Essay: Redefining the Genre*. Athens: U of Georgia P, 1989.

Byerman, Keith. *Remembering the Past in Contemporary African American Fiction*. Chapel Hill: U of North Carolina P, 2005.

Callahan, John F., ed. *The Collected Essays of Ralph Ellison*. New York: Modern Library, 1995.

Campbell, Finley. "More Notes of a Native Son." Rev. of *Nobody Knows My Name*. *Phylon* 23 (1962): 96–97.

Campbell, James. *Talking at the Gates: A Life of James Baldwin*. New York: Viking, 1991.

Campbell, John L. "States, Politics, and Globalization: Why Institutions Still Matter." Paul, Ikenberry, and Hall 234–59.

Carby, Hazel. *Race Men*. Cambridge: Harvard UP, 1998.

———. *Reconstructing Womanhood: The Emergence of the Afro-American Woman Novelist*. New York: Oxford UP, 1987.

"A Century of Dishonor." Rev. of *Century of Dishonor*. *The Nation* 32 (1881): 152.

Chang, Elaine K. "Last Past the Post: Theory, Futurity, Feminism." DeKoven, *Feminist Locations* 60–74.

Cheah, Phengh, and Bruce Robbins, eds. *Cosmopolitics: Thinking and Feeling Beyond the Nation*. Minneapolis: U of Minnesota P, 1998.

Clark, Glenn. *Personality in Essay Writing*. New York: Ray Long & Richard R. Smith, 1932.

Clark, Keith. *Black Manhood in James Baldwin, Ernest J. Gaines, and August Wilson.* Urbana: U of Illinois P, 2002.

Clark, Kenneth B. *The Negro Protest: James Baldwin, Malcolm X, Martin Luther King Talk with Kenneth B. Clark.* Boston: Beacon Press, 1963.

Clarke, John Henrik. "The Alienation of James Baldwin." *Black Expression.* Ed. Addison Gayle. New York: Weybright and Talley, 1969. 350–53.

Cleaver, Eldrige. *Soul on Ice.* New York: Dell, 1968. 97–111.

Coit Murphy, Patricia. *What a Book Can Do: The Publication and Reception of Silent Spring.* Amherst: U of Massachusetts P, 2005.

Coleman, Ramona. "Narrating Nation: Exploring the Space of Americanness and the Place of African American Women through the Works of June Jordan." Kinloch and Grebowicz 49–65.

Coles, Robert. "Baldwin's Burden." *Partisan Review* 31 (1964): 41–56.

———. "James Baldwin Back Home." *New York Times Book Review* 31 July 1977: 1, 22–24.

Collier, Eugenia W. "Thematic Patterns in Baldwin's Essays." *Black World* 21.8 (1972): 28–34. Rpt. in O'Daniel, *James Baldwin: A Critical Evaluation* 135–42.

Collier-Thomas, Bettye, and V. P. Franklin. *Sisters in the Struggle: African American Women in the Civil Rights-Black Power Movement.* New York: New York UP, 2001.

Collins, Patricia Hill. *Black Feminist Thought: Knowledge, Consciousness, and the Politics of Empowerment.* New York: Routledge, 1990.

Combahee River Collective. "Black Feminist Statement." 1977. See the appendix for a bibliography of printings.

———. *Eleven Black Women: Why Did They Die?* Cambridge, MA: The Collective, 1980.

Comfort, Juanita Rogers. "Becoming a Writerly Self: College Writers Engaging Black Feminist Essays." *College Composition and Communication* 51.4 (2000): 540–59.

Coombs, Orde. "The Devil Finds Work." *New York Times Book Review* 2 May 1976: 6–7.

Cooper, Anna Julia. *A Voice from the South: By a Black Woman of the South.* 1892. New York: Oxford UP, 1988.

Corber, Robert J. "Everybody Knew His Name: Reassessing James Baldwin." Rev. of *James Baldwin Now*, ed. Dwight McBride, and *Re-Viewing James Baldwin*, ed. Quentin Miller. *Contemporary Literature* 42.1 (2001): 166–75.

Cowles, Henry D. Letter to George W. Wickersham, United States Attorney General. 15 May 1909. *Emma Goldman Papers: A Microfilm Collection.* Alexandria, VA: Chadwyck-Healey, 1991–1993. Reel 56.

Cox, C. B., and A. R. Jones. "After the Tranquilized Fifties: Notes on Sylvia Plath and James Baldwin." *Critical Quarterly* 6 (1964): 107–22.

Crane, Gregg. *Race, Citizenship, and Law in American Literature*. New York: Cambridge UP, 2003.

Crenshaw, Kimberlé. "Mapping the Margins: Intersectionality, Identity Politics, and Violence Against Women of Color." *The Public Nature of Private Violence*. Eds. Martha Albertson Fineman and Rixanne Mykitiuk. New York: Routledge 1994. 93–118.

Crow, Barbara A. *Radical Feminism: A Documentary Reader*. New York: New York UP, 2000.

Cunningham, James. "Public and Private Rhetorical Modes in the Essays of James Baldwin." Butrym 192–204.

Curthoys, Jean. *Feminist Amnesia: The Wake of Women's Liberation*. New York: Routledge, 1997.

Dailey, Peter. "Jimmy." *American Scholar* (1994): 102–10.

Dance, Daryl C. "You Can't Go Home Again: James Baldwin and the South." *CLA Journal* 18 (1974): 81–90.

Daniels, Mark R. "Estrangement, Betrayal and Atonement: The Political Theory of James Baldwin." *Studies in Black Literature* 7 (1976): 10–13.

Darsey, James. "Baldwin's Cosmopolitan Loneliness." McBride, *James Baldwin Now* 187–207.

Davidson, Cathy. *Revolution and the Word: The Rise of the Novel in America*. New York: Oxford UP, 1985.

Davis, Angela. *Women, Race & Class*. 1981. New York: Vintage, 1983.

Davis, Flora. *Moving the Mountain: The Women's Movement in America Since 1960*. Urbana: U of Illinois P, 1999.

Decker, Jeffrey Louis. "'The Enigma His Efforts Had Created': Thomas Pynchon and the Legacy of America." *Thomas Pynchon Notes* 28–29 (1991): 27–42.

DeGout, Yasmin. "Dividing the Mind: Contradictory Portraits of Homoerotic Love in *Giovanni's Room*." *African American Review* 26.3 (1992): 425–35.

———. "'Masculinity' and (Im)maturity: 'The Man Child' and Other Stories in Baldwin's Gender Studies Enterprise." Quentin Miller 128–53.

DeKoven, Marianne, ed. *Feminist Locations: Global and Local, Theory and Practice*. New Brunswick, NJ: Rutgers UP, 2001.

———. *Utopia Limited: The Sixties and the Emergence of the Postmodern*. Durham, NC: Duke UP, 2004.

Deloria, Vine, Jr. "From the Archives—December 2, 1504." 1965. Treat 295–96.

———. "Missionaries and the Religious Vacuum." 1969. Treat 22–30.

———. "The Missionary in a Cultural Trap." 1965. Treat 284–94.

DeLyser, Dydia. "Ramona Memories: Tourist Practices and Placing the Past in Southern California." *Annals of the Association of American Geographers* 93.4 (2003): 886–908.

———. *Ramona Memories: Tourism and the Shaping of Southern California.* Minneapolis: U of Minnesota P, 2005.

———. "Recovering Social Memories of the Past: The 1884 Novel Ramona and Tourist Practices." *Social and Cultural Geography* 5.3 (2004):483–496.

DeMott, Benjamin. "James Baldwin on the Sixties: Acts and Revelations." 1972. Rpt. in Kinnamon 155–62.

Dickstein, Morris. "The Black Aesthetic in White America." *Partisan Review* 38 (1971): 376–95.

———. "Black Writing and Black Nationalism: Four Generations." *Gates of Eden: American Cultures in the Sixties.* 1977. Cambridge: Harvard UP, 1997. 154–82.

———. "Wright, Baldwin, Cleaver." *New Leader* 38 (1971): 117–24.

DiLeo, Jeffrey R., ed. *On Anthologies: Politics and Pedagogy.* Lincoln: U of Nebraska P, 2004.

Docherty, Thomas. *Aesthetic Democracy.* Palo Alto, CA: Stanford UP, 2006.

Doreski, C. K. *Writing America Black: Race Rhetoric in the Public Sphere.* Cambridge: Cambridge UP, 1998.

Dorris, Michael. Introduction. *Ramona.* Helen Hunt Jackson. New York: Penguin Books, 1988. v–xviii.

Douglass, Frederick. "What to the Slave Is the Fourth of July?" Printed as "Oration, Delivered in Corinthian Hall, Rochester, July 5th, 1852." *The Oxford Frederick Douglass Reader.* Ed. William L. Andrews. New York: Oxford UP, 1996. 108–30.

Drinnon, Richard. "Harking Back to the Future." Introduction to *Anarchism and Other Essays by Emma Goldman.* New York: Dover, 1969. v–xiv.

Drinnon, Richard, and Anna Maria, eds. *Nowhere at Home: Letters from Exile of Emma Goldman and Alexander Berkman.* New York: Schocken, 1975.

DuBois, W. E. B. *The Souls of Black Folk.* 1903. *W.E.B. DuBois: Writings.* New York: Library of America, 1986. 357–548.

Dudziak, Mary L. *Cold War Civil Rights: Race and the Image of American Democracy.* Princeton, NJ: Princeton UP, 2002.

Dupee, F. W. "James Baldwin and the 'Man.'" *New York Times Review of Books* 1.1 (1963): 1–2. Rpt. in Kinnamon 11–15.

DuPlessis, Rachel Blau, and Ann Snitow, eds. *The Feminist Memoir Project: Voices from Women's Liberation.* New York: Three Rivers Press, 1998.

Dworkin, Andrea. *Heartbreak.* New York: Basic Books, 2002.

Dwyer, Robert J. "I *Know* about Negroes and the Poor." *National Review* 17 Dec. 1963: 517–21.

Early, Gerald, ed. *Speech & Power, Volume 2: The African-American Essay and Its Content from Polemics to Pulpit.* Hopewell, NJ: Ecco Press, 1993.

Echols, Alice. *Daring to Be Bad: Radical Feminism in America, 1967–1975.* Minneapolis: U of Minnesota P, 1989.

———. "'Nothing Distant About It': Women's Liberation and Sixties Radicalism." 1991, 1994. *Shaky Ground: The Sixties and Its Aftershocks*. New York: Columbia UP, 2002. 75–94.

Eckman, Fern Marja. *The Furious Passage of James Baldwin*. New York: M. Evans & Company, 1966.

Edelman, Lee. *Homographesis: Essays in Gay Literary and Cultural Theory*. New York: Routledge, 1994.

Edwards, Brent Hayes. *The Practice of Diaspora: Literature, Translation, and the Rise of Black Internationalism*. Cambridge: Harvard UP, 2003.

Ehrenreich, Barbara. *The Hearts of Men: American Dreams and the Flight from Commitment*. Garden City, NY: Anchor Books, 1983.

———. *Nickel and Dimed: On (Not) Getting By in America*. New York: Henry Holt, 2001.

Elkoff, Marvin. "Everybody Knows His Name." *Esquire* Aug. 1964: 59–64; 120–23.

Ellison, Ralph. "Change the Joke and Slip the Yoke." 1958. Callahan 100–12.

———. "Richard Wright's Blues." 1945. Callahan 128–44.

Emerson, Amanda. "From Equivalence to Equity: The Management of an American Myth." *differences* 14.2 (2003): 78–105.

Epstein, Barbara. "Ambivalence about Feminism." DuPlessis and Snitow 124–48.

Evans, Sara. *Personal Politics: The Roots of Women's Liberation in the Civil Right Movement and the New Left*. New York: Knopf, 1979.

———. "Re-Viewing the Second Wave." *Feminist Studies* 28.2 (2002): 259–67.

———. *Tidal Wave*. New York: Free Press, 2003.

Falk, Candace. "Emma Goldman: Passion, Politics, and the Theatrics of Free Expression." *Women's History Review* 11.2 (2002): 11–26.

———. *Love, Anarchy, and Emma Goldman*. New York: Holt, Reinhart and Winston, 1984.

Falk, Candace, ed. *Emma Goldman: A Documentary History of the American Years; Volume 1: Made for America, 1890–1901*. Berkeley: U of California P, 2003.

———. *Emma Goldman: A Documentary History of the American Years; Volume 2: Making Speech Free, 1902–1909*. Berkeley: U of California P, 2003.

———. *Emma Goldman: A Guide to Her Life and Documentary Sources*. Alexandria, VA: Chadwyck-Healey, 1995.

———. Interview. July 21, 2005.

Featherstone, Joseph. "Blues for Mr. Baldwin." *New Republic* 27 Nov. 1965: 34–36.

Field, Douglass. "Looking for Jimmy Baldwin: Sex, Privacy and Black Nationalist Fervor." *Callaloo* 27.2 (2004): 457–80.

Field, Susan. "Ralph Waldo Emerson and Audre Lorde on Loss." *American Transcendental Quarterly* 19.1 (2005): 5–22.

Finn, James. "The Identity of James Baldwin." Rev. of *Another Country*, by James Baldwin. *Commonweal* 26 Oct. 1962: 113–16.

———. "James Baldwin's Vision." *Commonweal* 26 July 1963: 447–49.

Firestone, Shulamith. *The Dialectic of Sex: The Case for Feminist Revolution*. New York: William Morrow, 1970

———, ed. *Notes from the Second Year*. New York: Radical Feminism, 1970.

Fischer, Karin. "Colleges Would Be Required to Teach the Constitution Under Provision Tucked into Spending Bill." *The Chronicle of Higher Education* 3 Dec. 2004.

———. "Education Department Issues Rules on How Colleges May Comply with New 'Constitution Day' Requirement." *The Chronicle of Higher Education* 25 May 2005.

Fishkin, Shelly Fisher. "Crossroads of Culture: The Transnational Turn in American Studies." *American Quarterly* 57.1 (2005): 17–58.

———. *From Fact to Fiction: Journalism and Imaginative Writing in America*. New York: Oxford UP, 2001.

Flint, Robert W. "Not Ideas but Life." Rev. of *Notes of a Native Son*, by James Baldwin. *Commentary* May 1956: 494–95.

Foner, Philip S., ed. *We, the Other People: Alternative Declarations of Independence by Labor Groups, Farmers, Woman's Rights Advocates, and Blacks, 1829–1975*. Urbana: U of Illinois P, 1976.

Foote, Dorothy. "James Baldwin's 'Holler Books.'" *CEA Critic* 25 (1963): 8.

Ford, Nick Aaron. "The Evolution of Baldwin as Essayist." O'Daniel 85–104.

———. "The Fire Next Time? A Critical Survey of Belles Lettres by and about Negroes Published in 1963." *Phylon* 25 (1964): 123–34.

———. "Search for Identity: A Critical Survey of Significant Belles-Lettres by and about Negroes Published in 1961." *Phylon* 23 (1962): 128–38.

———. "Walls Do a Prison Make: A Critical Survey of Significant Belles Lettres by and about Negroes Published in 1962." *Phylon* 24 (1963): 123–34.

Freeman, Jo (a.k.a. Joreen). "The Tyranny of Structurelessness." 1970. Baxandall and Gordon 73–75.

Friedman, Susan Stanford. "Locational Feminism: Gender, Cultural Geographies, and Geopolitical Literacy." DeKoven, *Feminist Locations* 13–36.

Gaines, Jane M. "'Green Like Me.'" *Hollywood Spectatorship: Changing Perceptions of Cinema Audiences*. Eds. Melvyn Stokes and Richard Maltby. London: British Film Institute, 2001. 105–120.

Gamble, Andrew, and Tony Wright. *Restating the State?* Malden, MA: Blackwell, 2004.

Garnet, Henry Highland. "An Address to the Slaves of the United States of America (Rejected by the National Convention, 1843.)." *Walker's Appeal and Garnet's Address to the Slaves of the United States of America*. 1848. Rpt. Nashville: James C. Winston, 1994.

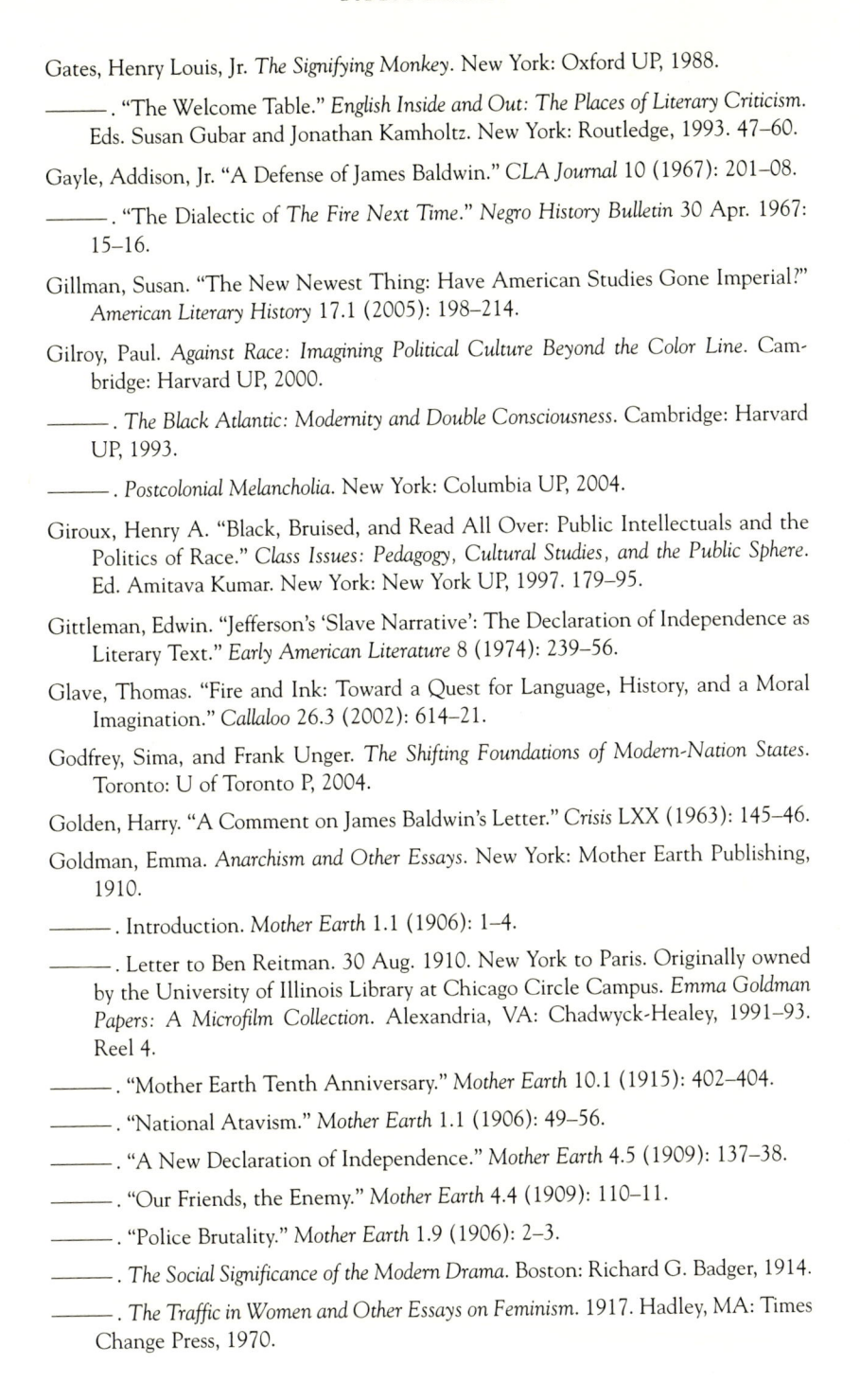

Gates, Henry Louis, Jr. *The Signifying Monkey.* New York: Oxford UP, 1988.

———. "The Welcome Table." *English Inside and Out: The Places of Literary Criticism.* Eds. Susan Gubar and Jonathan Kamholtz. New York: Routledge, 1993. 47–60.

Gayle, Addison, Jr. "A Defense of James Baldwin." *CLA Journal* 10 (1967): 201–08.

———. "The Dialectic of *The Fire Next Time.*" *Negro History Bulletin* 30 Apr. 1967: 15–16.

Gillman, Susan. "The New Newest Thing: Have American Studies Gone Imperial?" *American Literary History* 17.1 (2005): 198–214.

Gilroy, Paul. *Against Race: Imagining Political Culture Beyond the Color Line.* Cambridge: Harvard UP, 2000.

———. *The Black Atlantic: Modernity and Double Consciousness.* Cambridge: Harvard UP, 1993.

———. *Postcolonial Melancholia.* New York: Columbia UP, 2004.

Giroux, Henry A. "Black, Bruised, and Read All Over: Public Intellectuals and the Politics of Race." *Class Issues: Pedagogy, Cultural Studies, and the Public Sphere.* Ed. Amitava Kumar. New York: New York UP, 1997. 179–95.

Gittleman, Edwin. "Jefferson's 'Slave Narrative': The Declaration of Independence as Literary Text." *Early American Literature* 8 (1974): 239–56.

Glave, Thomas. "Fire and Ink: Toward a Quest for Language, History, and a Moral Imagination." *Callaloo* 26.3 (2002): 614–21.

Godfrey, Sima, and Frank Unger. *The Shifting Foundations of Modern-Nation States.* Toronto: U of Toronto P, 2004.

Golden, Harry. "A Comment on James Baldwin's Letter." *Crisis* LXX (1963): 145–46.

Goldman, Emma. *Anarchism and Other Essays.* New York: Mother Earth Publishing, 1910.

———. Introduction. *Mother Earth* 1.1 (1906): 1–4.

———. Letter to Ben Reitman. 30 Aug. 1910. New York to Paris. Originally owned by the University of Illinois Library at Chicago Circle Campus. *Emma Goldman Papers: A Microfilm Collection.* Alexandria, VA: Chadwyck-Healey, 1991–93. Reel 4.

———. "Mother Earth Tenth Anniversary." *Mother Earth* 10.1 (1915): 402–404.

———. "National Atavism." *Mother Earth* 1.1 (1906): 49–56.

———. "A New Declaration of Independence." *Mother Earth* 4.5 (1909): 137–38.

———. "Our Friends, the Enemy." *Mother Earth* 4.4 (1909): 110–11.

———. "Police Brutality." *Mother Earth* 1.9 (1906): 2–3.

———. *The Social Significance of the Modern Drama.* Boston: Richard G. Badger, 1914.

———. *The Traffic in Women and Other Essays on Feminism.* 1917. Hadley, MA: Times Change Press, 1970.

———. "The Tragedy at Buffalo." *Free Society* 6 Oct. 1901. Rpt. in Falk, *Volume 2* 471–78.

———. "The Tragedy of Woman's Emancipation." *Mother Earth* 1.1 (1906): 9–18.

Gonzales, John M. "The Warp of Whiteness: Domesticity and Empire in Helen Hunt Jackson's *Ramona*." *ALH* 16.3 (2004): 437–65.

Good, Graham. Introduction. *Encyclopedia of the Essay*. London: Fitzroy Dearbon, 1997. xix–xxi.

———. *The Observing Self: Rediscovering the Essay*. New York: Routledge, 1988.

Govindarajan, Shweta. "Criticism Puts Citizenship Oath Revision on Hold; Conservatives Pan Immigration Officials' Modernization of the Long-used Pledge," *Los Angeles Times* 19 Sept. 2003, sec. 1: 13.

Granger, Bruce. *American Essay Serials from Franklin to Irving*. Knoxville: U of Tennessee P, 1978.

Grasso, Linda. *The Artistry of Anger: Black and White Women's Literature in America, 1820–1860*. Chapel Hill: U of North Carolina P, 2002.

Grebowicz, Margret, and Verlie Kinloch, eds. *Still Seeking an Attitude: Critical Reflections on the Work of June Jordan*. Lanham, MD: Lexington Books, 2004.

Griffin, Farah Jasmine. *"Who Set You Flowin'?": The African American Migration Narrative*. New York: Oxford UP, 1995.

Grimes, Jane. "Green Like Me" *Hollywood Spectatorship: Changing Perceptions of Cinema Audiences*. Eds. Melvyn Stokes and Richard Maltby. London: British Film Institute, 2001. 105–20.

Gross, John. "Day of Wrath." *New Statesman* 19 July 1963: 79–80.

Gross, Theodore L. "James Baldwin." Interview. *Transition* 8.4 [41] (1972): 20–24.

———. "The World of James Baldwin." *Critique* 7.2 (1965): 139–49.

Guerrero, Ed, Elaine Kim, and Alvina Quintana. "The United States from Inside and Out: Transnational American Studies." Call for papers. *ASA Newsletter* 28.3 (2005): 1–4.

Guy-Sheftall, Beverly. "Response from a 'Second Waver' to Kimberly Springer's 'Third Wave Black Feminism?'" *Signs* 27.4 (2002): 1091–94.

Haefner, Joel. "Unfathering the Essay: Resistance and Intergeniality in the Essay Genre." *Prose Studies* 12 (1989): 259–73.

Hagopian, John V. "James Baldwin: The Black and the Red-White-and-Blue." *Five Black Writers: Essays on Wright, Ellison, Baldwin, Hughes, and LeRoi Jones*. Ed. Donald B. Gibson. New York: New York UP, 1970. 159–64.

Hall, John. "Interview with Baldwin." *Transatlantic Review* 37–38 (1970–1971): 5–14.

Hall, Michael. "The Emergence of the Essay and the Idea of Discovery." Butrym 73–91.

Hamilton, Kristie. *America's Sketchbook: The Cultural Life of a Nineteenth-Century Literary Genre*. Athens: Ohio UP, 1998.

Handy, W. C. *E Pluribus Unum: Nineteenth-Century American Literature and the Constitutional Paradox*. Iowa City: U of Iowa P, 2005.

Hansberry, Lorraine. "The Negro Writer and His Roots: Toward a New Romanticism." 1959, 1981. Early 129–41.

Haraway, Donna. "Ecce Homo, Ain't (Ar'n't) I a Woman, and Inappropriate/d Others: The Human in a Post-Humanist Landscape." *Feminists Theorize the Political*. Eds. Judith Butler and Joan W. Scott. New York: Routledge, 1992. 86–100.

Harding, Sandra. "Rethinking Standpoint Epistemology: What Is 'Strong Objectivity'?" *The Centennial Review* 36.3 (1992): 437–70.

Hardison, O. B., Jr. "Binding Proteus: An Essay on the Essay." Butyrm 11–28.

Hariman, Robert. "Afterword: Relocating the Art of Public Address." Benson 163–84.

Harper, Howard M., Jr. "James Baldwin—Art of Propaganda." In his *Desperate Faith: A Study of Bellow, Salinger, Mailer, Baldwin, and Updike*. Chapell Hill: U of North Carolina P, 1967. 137–61.

Harris, Trudier. *Black Women in the Fiction of James Baldwin*. Knoxville: U of Tennessee P, 1985.

Hassan, Ihab. "The Novel of Outrage: A Minority Voice in Postwar American Fiction." *American Scholar* 34 (1965): 239–53.

Henderson, Gwendolyn Mae. "James Baldwin: Expatriation, Homosexual Panic, and Man's Estate" *Callaloo* 23.1 (2000): 313–27

Henry, David. "Garrison at Philadelphia: The 'Declaration of Sentiments' as Instrumental Rhetoric." Benson 113–29.

Hentoff, Nat. "'It's Terrifying,' James Baldwin: The Price of Fame." Interview by Nat Hentoff. *New York Herald Tribune Books* 16 June 1963.

The Heritage Foundation. *First They Attacked the Pledge, Now the Oath*. 10 Sept. 2003. <http://www.heritage.org/Research/HomelandDefense/meeseletter.cfm>.

Hernton, Calvin C. "The Blood of the Lamb: The Ordeal of James Baldwin." *White Papers for White Americans*. New York: Doubleday, 1966. 105–21.

———. "A Fiery Baptism." 1970. Kinnamon 109–19.

Hicks, Granville. "Commitment Without Compromise." Rev. of *Nobody Knows My Name*, by James Baldwin. *Saturday Review* 1 July 1961: 9.

———. "A Gun in the Hand of a Hater." *Saturday Review* 2 May 1964: 27–28.

Higginson, Thomas Wentworth. "Literature as an Art." 1867. *Atlantic Essays*. Boston: J. R. Osgood and Company, 1874. 25–47.

Himes, Chester. *If He Hollers Let Him Go*. 1945. New York: Thunder's Mouth Press, 2002.

———. "Negro Martyrs Are Needed." 1943. Early 307–11.

Hinks, Peter P. *To Awaken My Afflicted Brethren: David Walker and the Problem of Antebellum Slave Resistance*. University Park: Pennsylvania State UP, 1997.

Hoffman, George. *Montaigne's Career*. New York: Oxford UP, 1999.

Holton, Sandra Stanley. "'To Educate Women into Rebellion': Elizabeth Cady Stanton and the Creation of a Transatlantic Network of Radical Suffragists." *The American Historical Review* 99.4 (1994): 1112–36.

Honig, Bonnie. *Democracy and the Foreigner*. Princeton, NJ: Princeton UP, 2001.

Howard-Pitney, David. *The Afro-American Jeremiad*. Philadelphia: Temple UP, 1990.

Howe, Irving "Black Boys and Native Sons." *Dissent* 10 (1963): 353–68.

———. "James Baldwin: At Ease in the Apocalypse." 1968. Rpt. in Kinnamon 96–108.

Howell, Wilbur Samuel. "The Declaration of Independence: Some Adventures with America's Political Masterpiece." *The Quarterly Journal of Speech* 62.3 (1976): 221–33.

Hubbard, Dolan. *The Sermon and the African American Literary Imagination*. Columbia: U of Missouri P, 1994.

Hubbard, Sara. "Helen Hunt Jackson." *Dial* 6 (1885): 109–10.

Huberman, Leo. *We, the People*. London: Victor Gallancz, 1940.

Hughes, Langston. "Emmett Till, Mississippi, and Congressional Investigations." 1955. Rpt. in Fight for Freedom *and Other Writings on Civil Rights: The Collected Works of Langston Hughes, Volume 10*. Ed. Christopher C. De Santis. Columbia: U of Missouri P, 2001. 248–51.

———. *Fight for Freedom*. 1962. Ed. Christopher C. De Santis, Fight For Freedom *and Other Writings on Civil Rights: The Collected Works of Langston Hughes, Volume 10*. Columbia: U of Missouri P, 2001.

———. "From Harlem to Paris." 1956. Kinnamon 9–10.

———. "The Negro Artist and the Racial Mountain." 1925. Early 88–91.

Hull, Gloria T., Patricia Bell Scott, and Barbara Smith, eds. *All the Women Are White, All the Men Are Black, But Some of Us Are Brave: Women' Studies*. New York: The Feminist Press, 1982.

Huneker, James. "A Sentimental Rebellion." *Visionaries*. New York: Charles Scribner & Sons, 1916. 227–48.

Hutcheon, Linda. *A Poetics of Postmodernism: History, Theory, Fiction*. New York: Routledge, 1988.

Huxman, Susan Schultz. "Perfecting the Rhetorical Vision of Women's Rights: Elizabeth Cady Stanton, Anna Howard Shaw, and Carrie Chapman Catt." *Women's Studies in Communication* 23.3 (2000): 307–36.

Ikard, David. "Love Jones: A Black *Male* Feminist Critique of Chester Himes's *If He Hollers Let Him Go*." *African American Review* 36.2 (2002): 299–310.

Irwin, Robert McKee. "*Ramona* and Postnationalist American Studies: On 'Our America' and the Mexican Borderlands." *American Quarterly* 55.4 (2003): 539–68.

BIBLIOGRAPHY

Ishay, Micheline R. *The History of Human Rights: From Ancient Times to the Globalization Era.* Berkeley: U of California P, 2004.

Itagaki, Lynn M. "Transgressing Race and Community in Chester Himes's *If He Hollers Let Him Go.*" *African American Review* 37.1 (2003): 65–80.

Jackson, Helen Hunt. *A Century of Dishonor: A Sketch of the United States Government's Dealing with Some of the Indian Tribes.* 1881. Rpt. New York: Harper Torchbooks, 1965.

——. *Ramona.* 1884. New York: Penguin Books, 1988.

Jackson, Jocelyn Whitehead. "The Problem of Identity in Selected Early Essays of James Baldwin." 1978. Rpt. in Standley and Burt 250–66.

Jackson, Virginia. *Dickinson's Misery: A Theory of Lyric Reading.* Princeton, NJ: Princeton UP, 2005.

Jacobs, Margaret. "Mixed-Bloods, Mestizas, and Pintos: Race, Gender, and Claims to Whiteness in Helen Hunt Jackson's *Ramona* and María Amparo Ruiz de Burton's *Who Would Have Thought It?*" *Western American Literature* 36 (2001): 212–31.

Jacobson, Dan. "James Baldwin as Spokesman." *Commentary* 32 (1961): 497–502.

"James Baldwin: Writer of Black America." Obituary for James Baldwin. *Times* 2 Dec. 1987: A1, D27.

Jarrett, Hobart. "From a Region in My Mind: The Essays of James Baldwin." O'Daniel 105–25.

Jarrett, Thomas D. "Search for Identity." *Phylon* 17 (1956): 87–88.

Jehlen, Myra, and Michael Warner, eds. *The English Literatures of America: 1500–1800.* New York: Routledge, 1997.

Jenkins, Alan, and Larry Cox. "Bringing Human Rights Home." *The Nation* 27 June 2005: 27–29.

Joeres, Ruth-Ellen Boetcher, "The Passionate Essay: Radical Feminist Essays." Joeres and Mittman 151–71.

Joeres, Ruth-Ellen Boetcher, and Elizabeth Mittman, eds. *The Politics of the Essay: Feminist Perspectives.* Bloomington: Indiana UP, 1993.

Johnson, James Weldon. "The Dilemma of the Negro Author." 1928. Early 92–97.

Jones, B. B. "James Baldwin: The Struggle for Identity." *British Journal of Sociology* XVII (1966): 107–21.

Jones, LeRoi. *Home: Social Essays by LeRoi Jones.* New York: William Morrow, 1966.

Jordan, June. *Affirmative Acts: Political Essays.* New York: Doubleday, 1998.

——. *Civil Wars: Political Essays.* Boston: South End Press, 1981.

——. *On Call: Political Essays.* Boston: South End Press, 1985.

——. *Passion.* Boston: Beacon Press, 1980.

——. *Soldier: A Poet's Childhood.* New York: Basic Books, 2000.

———. *Some of Us Did Not Die: New and Selected Essays of June Jordan.* New York: Perseus, 2002.

———. *Technical Difficulties: African American Notes on the State of the Union.* New York: Pantheon, 1992.

Joreen, "Trashing: The Dark Side of Sisterhood." *Ms.* (April 1976): 49–51, 92–98.

Kaplan, Amy. "Nation, Region, and Empire." *The Columbia History of the American Novel.* Ed. Emory Elliott. New York: Columbia UP, 1991. 240–66.

Kaplan, Amy, and Donald Pease. *Cultures of United States Imperialism.* Durham, NC: Duke UP, 1994.

Kaplan, Cora. "'A Cavern Opened in My Mind': The Poetics of Homosexuality and the Politics of Race in James Baldwin." Blount and Cunningham 27–54.

Kauffman, Lane. "The Skewed Path: Essaying as Unmethodical Method." Butrym 221–40.

Karrer, Wolfgang. "Discursive Strategies in James Baldwin's Essays." *James Baldwin: His Place in American Literary History and His Reception in Europe.* Ed. Jakob Köllhofer. Frankfurt am Main & Bern: 1987. 113–28.

Keller, Joseph. "Black Writing and the White Critic." *Negro American Literature Forum* 3 (1970): 103–10.

Kelley, Mary. *Private Woman, Public Stage: Literary Domesticity in Nineteenth-Century America.* 1984. Chapel Hill: U of North Carolina P, 2002.

Kemp, Yakina B. "Writing Power: Identity Complexities and the Exotic Erotic in Audre Lorde's Writing." *Studies in the Literary Imagination* 37.2 (2004): 21–36.

Kenan, Randall. *James Baldwin.* New York: Chelsea House, 1994.

Kerber, Linda Keller. *No Constitutional Right to Be Ladies: Women and the Obligations of Citizenship.* New York: Farrar, Strauss and Giroux, 1998.

Ketchum, Michael G. *Transparent Designs: Reading, Performance, and Form in the Spectator Papers.* Athens: U of Georgia P, 1985.

Kim, Kichung. "Wright, the Protest Novel, and Baldwin's Faith." *CLA Journal* 17 (1974): 387–96.

King, Martin Luther, Jr. "Letter from Birmingham City Jail." 1963. *A Testament of Hope: The Essential Writings and Speeches of Martin Luther King, Jr.* Ed. James M. Washington. San Francisco: HarperCollins, 1986. 289–302.

Kinloch, Valerie, and Margret Grebowicz, eds. *Still Seeking an Attitude: Critical Reflections on the Work of June Jordan.* Lanham, MD: Rowman & Littlefield, 2004.

Kinnamon, Kenneth, ed. *James Baldwin: A Collection of Critical Essays.* Englewood Cliffs, NJ: Prentice-Hall, 1974.

Kirklighter, Cristina. *Traversing the Democratic Borders of the Essay.* Albany: State U of New York P, 2002.

Klein, Marcus. "James Baldwin: A Question of Identity." *After Alienation: American Novels in Mid-Century.* New York: World Publishing Co., 1962. Rpt. in Bloom 17–36.

Kravetz, Diane. "Consciousness-Raising Groups in the 1970's." *Psychology of Women Quarterly* 3.2 (1978): 168–86.

Kymlicka, Will. "Citizenship in an Era of Globalization." *Democracy's Edges*. Eds. Ian Shapiro and Casiano Hacker-Cordon. Cambridge: Cambridge UP, 1999. 112–33.

Larry, 5X. "Baldwin 'Baptised' in Fire This Time." *Muhammad Speaks* 23 Feb. 1973: 25.

Leaks, Sylvester. "James Baldwin—I Know His Name." *Freedomways* 3 (1963): 102–05.

Lee, Erika. *At America's Gates: Chinese Immigration During the Exclusion Era, 1882–1943*. Chapel Hill: U of North Carolina P, 2003.

Lee, Robert A. "A Critical Review: James Baldwin: The Devil Finds Work." *Negro American Literature Forum* 10 (1976): 84–85.

Leeming, David. *James Baldwin: A Biography*. New York: Penguin, 1994.

Leon, Barbara. "Separate to Integrate." *Feminist Revolution*. New York: Random House, 1978. 152–57.

Levin, David. "Baldwin's Autobiographical Essay: the Problem of Negro Identity." *The Massachusetts Review* 5 (1964): 239–47.

Lim, Shirley Geok-Lin, ed. "Where in the World Is Transnational Feminism?" Special Issue of *Tulsa Studies in Women's Literature* 23.1 (2004): 7–12.

Loeffelholz, Mary. "Posing the Woman Citizen: The Contradictions of Stanton's Feminism." *Genders* 7 (1990): 87–98.

Lopate, Phillip. *The Art of the Personal Essay: An Anthology from the Classical Era to the Present*. New York: Doubleday, 1994.

Lorde, Audre. *The Cancer Journals*. Argyle, NY: Spinsters, Ink., 1980.

———. *Sister Outsider: Essays and Speeches*. Trumansburg, NY: The Crossing Press, 1984.

Lottman, Herbert R. "It's Hard to Be James Baldwin: An Interview." 1972. Rpt. in *Black Times: Voices of the National Community* (Menlo Park, CA) 2.12 (1972): 10.

Lubiano, Wahneema, ed. *The House That Race Built: Black Americans, U.S. Terrain*. New York: Pantheon, 1997.

Lucas, Stephen E. "Justifying America: The Declaration of Independence as a Rhetorical Document." Benson 67–130.

———. "The Rhetorical Ancestry of the Declaration of Independence." *Rhetoric and Public Affairs* 1.2 (1998): 143–84.

Luis-Brown, David. "'White Slaves' and the 'Arrogant *Mestiza*': Reconfiguring Whiteness in *The Squatter and the Don* and *Ramona*." *American Literature* 69 (1997): 813–39.

Lukacs, George. "On the Nature and Form of the Essay: A Letter to Leo Popper." (1910) *Soul and Form*. Trans. Anna Bostock. Cambridge: MIT Press, 1974. 1–18.

Lyon, Janet. *Manifestoes: Provocations of the Modern*. Ithaca, NY: Cornell UP, 1999.

MacPhail, Scott. "June Jordan and the New Black Intellectuals." *African American Review* 33.1 (1999): 57–71.

Madsen, Deborah L. *Beyond Borders: American Literature and Post-colonial Theory.* London: Pluto Press, 2003.

Mailer, Norman. "The White Negro: Superficial Reflections on the Hipster." 1957. *Advertisements for Myself.* New York: G. Putnam's Sons, 1959. 337–58.

Malcolm, Donald. "The Author in Search of Himself." Rev. of *Nobody Knows My Name*, by James Baldwin. *The New Yorker* 25 Nov. 1961: 233–34.

Maloff, Saul. "The Two Baldwins." Rev. of *Another Country*, by James Baldwin. *The Nation* 14 July 1962: 15–16.

Mankiller, Wilma, Gwendolyn Mink, Marysa Navarro, Barbara Smith, and Gloria Steinem, eds. *The Reader's Companion to U.S. Women's History.* Boston: Houghton Mifflin, 1998.

Marsh, Nicky. "'This Is the Only Time to Come Together': June Jordan's Publics and the Possibility of Democracy." Grebowicz and Kinloch 15–32.

Mathes, Valerie Sherer. *Helen Hunt Jackson and Her Indian Reform Legacy.* Austin: U of Texas P, 1990.

———. *The Indian Reform Letters of Helen Hunt Jackson, 1879–1885.* Norman: U of Oklahoma P, 1998.

Matterson, Stephen. "Shaped by Reader: The Slave Narratives of Frederick Douglass and Harriet Jacobs." *Soft Canons: American Women Writers and Masculine Tradition.* Ed. Karen L. Kilcup. Iowa City: U of Iowa P, 1999. 82–98.

McBride, Dwight A. "Can the Queen Speak? Racial Essentialism, Sexuality and the Problem of Authority." *Callaloo* 21.2 (1998): 363–79.

———, ed. *James Baldwin Now.* New York: New York UP, 1999.

———. "Straight Black Studies: On African American Studies, James Baldwin, and Black Queer Studies." *Black Queer Studies.* Eds. E. Patrick Johnson and Mae G. Henderson. Durham, NC: Duke UP, 2005. 68–89.

———. *Why I Hate Abercrombie & Fitch: Race and Sexuality in America.* New York: New York UP, 2005.

McBride, Dwight A., and Jennifer Devere Brody. Introduction to "Plum Nelly: New Essays in Black Queer Studies." *Callaloo* 23.1 (2000): 286–88.

McCall, Leslie. "The Complexity of Intersectionality." *Signs* 30.3 (2005): 1771–800.

McClusky, John. "'If Beale Street Could Talk.'" *Black World* 24 (1974): 51–52, 88–91.

McDougal, Russell. "Capricornia: Recovering the Imaginative Vision of a Polemical Novel." *Australian Literary Studies* 10.1 (1988): 67–78.

McNeil, Genna Rae. "From the Kennedy Commission to the Combahee Collective: Black Feminist Organizing, 1960–80." *African American Women in the Civil Rights–Black Power Movement.* Eds. Bettye Collier-Thomas and V. P. Franklin. New York: New York UP, 2001.

Meriwether, L. M. "James Baldwin: Fiery Voice of Negro Revolt." *Negro Digest* [*The Black World*] Aug. 1963: 3–7.

Messer-Davidow, Ellen. *Disciplining Feminism: How Women's Studies Transformed the Academy and Was Transformed By It*. Durham, NC: Duke UP, 2002.

Messmer, Marietta. "Toward a Declaration of Interdependence; or, Interrogating the Boundaries in Twentieth-Century Histories of North American Literature." *PMLA* 118.1 (2003): 41–55.

Metress, Christopher. "Langston Hughes's 'Mississippi—1955': A Note on Revisions and an Appeal for Reconsideration." *African American Review* 37.1 (2003): 139–48.

———. "'No Justice, No Peace': The Figure of Emmett Till in African American Literature." *MELUS* 28.1 (2003): 87–103.

Metress, Christopher, and Harriet Pollack, eds. *Emmett Till in Literary Memory and Imagination*. Baton Rouge: Louisiana State UP, forthcoming.

Metress, Philip. "Performing 'Righteous Certainty': The Shifting Poetic Address of June Jordan's War Resistance Poetry." Kinloch & Grebowicz 175–88.

Meyer, Doris. *Reinterpreting the Spanish American Essay: Women Writers of the Nineteenth and Twentieth Centuries*. Austin: U of Texas P, 1995.

Miller, Diane Helene. "From One Voice a Chorus: Elizabeth Cady Stanton's 1860 Address to the New York State Legislature." *Women's Studies in Communication* 22.2 (1999): 152–89.

Miller, Joshua L. "The Discovery of What It Means to Be a Witness: James Baldwin's Dialectics of Difference." McBride, *James Baldwin Now* 331–59.

Miller, Quentin, ed. *Re-Viewing James Baldwin: Things Not Seen*. Philadelphia: Temple UP, 2000.

Mills, Charles. *The Racial Contract*. Ithaca, NY: Cornell UP, 1999.

Mishra, Pramod K. "'[A]ll the World Was America': The Transatlantic (Post)Coloniality of John Locke, William Bartram, and the Declaration of Independence." *The New Centennial Review* 2.1 (2002): 213–58.

Mittlefehldt, Pamela Klass. "'A Weaponry of Choice': Black American Women Writers and the Essay." Joeres and Mittman 196–208.

Mohanty, Chandra Tolpade. *Feminism without Borders: Decolonizing Theory, Practicing Solidarity*. Durham, NC: Duke UP, 2003.

———. "*Under Western Eyes* Revisited: Feminist Solidarity through Anticapitalist Struggles." *Signs* 28.2 (2003): 499–536.

Monk, Craig. "Emma Goldman, Mother Earth, and the Little Magazine Impulse." *The Only Efficient Instrument: American Women Writers & the Periodical, 1837–1916*. Eds. Aleta Feinsod Cane and Susan Alves. Iowa City: U of Iowa P, 2001. 113–25.

Moon, Michael, and Cathy Davidson. *Subjects and Citizens: Nation, Race, and Gender from* Oronooko *to Anita Hill*. Durham, NC: Duke UP, 1995.

Moraga, Cherríe. Foreword to *This Bridge Called My Back: Writings by Radical Women of Color*. Latham, NY: Kitchen Table: Women of Color Press, 1983. No page numbers.

Moraga, Cherríe, and Gloria Anzaldúa, eds. *This Bridge Called My Back: Writings by Radical Women of Color*. 1981. Latham, NY: Kitchen Table: Women of Color Press, 1983.

Morgan, Robin, ed. *Sisterhood Is Global: The International Women's Movement Anthology*. 1984. New York: The Feminist Press, 1996.

———, ed. *Sisterhood Is Powerful: An Anthology of Writings from the Women's Liberation Movement*. New York: Vintage, 1970.

Morris, Margaret. "Audre Lorde: Textual Authority and the Embodied Self." *Frontiers: A Journal of Women's Studies* 23.1 (2002): 168–88.

Morrison, Allan. "The Angriest Young Man." *Ebony* Oct. 1961: 23–30.

Morrison, Toni. *Playing in the Dark: Whiteness and the Literary Imagination*. New York: Vintage, 1992.

Morrison, Toni, Gayatri Chakravorty Spivak, and Ngahuia Te Awekotuku. "Roundtable on the Future of the Humanities in a Fragmented World." *PMLA* 120.3 (2005): 715–23.

Mowe, Gregory, and W. Scott Nobles. "James Baldwin's Message for White America." *Quarterly Journal of Speech* 58.2 (1972): 142–51.

Moylan, Michele. "Materiality as Performance: The Forming of Helen Hunt Jackson's *Ramona*." *Reading Books: Essays on the Material Text and Literature in America*. Eds. Michele Moylan and Lane Stiles. Amherst: U of Massachusetts P, 1996. 223–27.

Murphy, Dean E. "Old Words on War Stirring a New Dispute at Berkeley." *New York Times* 14 Jan. 2003, late ed.: A1.

Murphy, Geraldine. "Subversive Anti-Stalinism: Race and Sexuality in the Early Essays of James Baldwin." *ELH* 63 (1996): 1021–46.

Nabers, Deak. "Past Using: James Baldwin and Civil Rights Law in the 1960s." *Yale Journal of Criticism* 18.2 (2005): 221–42.

Neal, Lawrence P. "The Black Writers' Role: James Baldwin." *Liberator* 6 (1966): 10–11, 18.

Nelson, Jennifer. *Women of Color and the Reproductive Rights Movement*. New York: New York UP, 2003.

Nelson, Richard. "Patriots for the American Land." *Patriotism and the American Land*. Barrington, MA: The Orion Society, 2002. 1–21.

Nevins, Allan. "Helen Hunt Jackson, Sentimentalist vs. Realist." *American Scholar* 10 (1941): 269–85.

New York Radical Feminists (NYRF). "Politics of the Ego: A Manifesto for New York Radical Feminists." 1969. *Rebirth of Feminism*. Eds. Judith Hole and Ellen Levine. New York: Quadrangle Books, 1971. 442–45.

Newman, Charles. "The Lesson of the Master: Henry James and James Baldwin." 1966. Kinnamon 52–65.

Newman, Louise Michele. *White Women's Rights: The Racial Origins of Feminism in the United States.* New York: Oxford UP, 1999.

Newman, Richard. *Pamphlets of Protest: An Anthology of Early African-American Protest Literature, 1790–1860.* New York: Routledge, 2000.

Ngai, Mae. *Impossible Subjects: Illegal Aliens and the Making of Modern America.* Princeton, NJ: Princeton UP, 2003.

Nichols, Charles H. "New Calvinism." Rev. of *Giovanni's Room*, by James Baldwin. *Commentary* Jan. 1957: 94–96.

Nicholson, Linda, ed. *The Second Wave: A Reader in Feminist Theory.* New York: Routledge, 1997.

Noriega, Chon A., and Wendy Belcher, eds. *I Am Aztlán: The Personal Essay in Chicano Studies.* Los Angeles: UCLA Chicano Studies Research Center Press, 2004.

Norman, Brian. "The Addressed and the Redressed: Helen Hunt Jackson's Protest Essay and the U.S. Protest Novel Tradition," *Canadian Review of American Studies* 37.1 (2007): 111–34.

———. "Allegiance and Renunciation at the Border," *M/C—a journal of media and culture* 7.2 (2004). <http://www.media-culture.org.au/0403/04–allegiance.html>.

———. "Baldwin's Unifying Polemic: Racial Segregation, Moral Integration, and the Polarizing Figure of Emmett Till." Metress and Pollack: forthcoming.

———. "The Consciousness-Raising Document, Feminist Anthologies, and Black Women in *Sisterhood Is Powerful.*" *Frontiers* 37.3 (2006): 38–64.

———. "Crossing Identitarian Lines: Women's Liberation and James Baldwin's Early Essays." *Women's Studies: An Interdisciplinary Journal* 35.3 (2006): 241–64.

———. "Duplicity, Purity, and Policitized Morality: *Go Tell It On the Mountain* and the Emergence of the Civil Rights Movement." *James Baldwin's Go Tell It on the Mountain: Historical and Critical Essays.* Ed. Carol Henderson. Westport, CT: Greenwood, 2006. 13–28.

———. "June Jordan." *An Encyclopedia of African American Literature.* Ed. J. David Macey Jr. and Hans A. Ostrom. Westport, CT: Greenwood, 2005. 900–03.

———. "Reading a 'Closet Screenplay': Hollywood, James Baldwin's Malcolms, and the Threat of Historical Irrelevance," *African American Review* 39.1–2 (2005): 103–18.

———. Rev. of *Heartbreak: A Political Memoir of a Militant Feminist*, by Andrea Dworkin. *Women's Studies* 32.7 (2003): 889–92.

———. "'We' in Redux: The Publishing History of the Combahee River Collective's *A Black Feminist Statement* (1977)." *differences* 18.2 (2007): forthcoming.

Nussbaum, Martha. "Patriotism and Cosmopolitanism." *For Love of Country.* Ed. Joshua Cohen. Boston: Beacon Press, 1996. 3–17.

———. "Women's Education: A Global Challenge." *Signs* 29.2 (2004): 325–55.

Obaldia, Claire de. *The Essayistic Spirit: Literature, Modern Criticism, and the Essay.* Oxford: Oxford UP, 1995.

Occom, Samson. "A Sermon Preached by Samson Occom." 1772. *The English Literatures of America: 1500–1800.* Jehlen and Warner 643–59.

O'Daniel, Thurman. *James Baldwin: A Critical Evaluation.* Washington, DC: Howard UP, 1977.

Odell, Ruth. *Helen Hunt Jackson (H.H.).* London: D. Appleton-Century Company, 1939.

Ohi, Kevin. "'I'm Not the Boy You Want': Sexuality, 'Race,' and Thwarted Revelation in Baldwin's *Another Country.*" *African American Review* 33.2 (1999): 260–81.

O'Leary, R. D. *The Essay.* New York: Thomas Y Crowell, 1928.

Olson, Lester. "On the Margins of Rhetoric: Audre Lorde Transforming Silence into Language and Action." *Quarterly Journal of Speech* 83.1 (1997): 49–70.

O'Neill, John. *Essaying Montaigne: A Study of the Renaissance Institution of Reading and Writing.* Liverpool: U of Liverpool P, 2001.

Ong, Aihwa. *Flexible Citizenship: The Cultural Logics of Transnationality.* Durham, NC: Duke UP, 1999.

Ongiri, Amy. "We Are Family: Miscegenation, Black Nationalism, Black Masculinity, and the Black Gay Cultural Imagination." *Race-ing Representation: Voice, History, and Sexuality.* Eds. Kostas Myrsiades and Linda Myrsiades. Lanham, MD: Rowman & Littlefield, 1998. 231–46.

Patriotism and the American Land. Barrington, MA: The Orion Society, 2002.

Patterson, H. Orlando. "The Essays of James Baldwin." *New Left Review* 26 (1964): 31–38.

Paul, T. V., G. John Ikenberry, and John A. Hall. *The Nation-State in Question.* Princeton, NJ: Princeton UP, 2003.

Pemberton, Gayle. "A Sentimental Journey: James Baldwin and the Thomas-Hill Hearings." *Race-ing Justice, En-gendering Power: Essays on Anita Hill, Clarence Thomas, and the Construction of Social Reality.* Ed. Toni Morrison. New York: Pantheon, 1992. 172–99.

Perry, Patsy Brewington. "*One Day When I Was Lost*: Baldwin's Unfulfilled Obligation." Collected in *James Baldwin: A Critical Evaluation.* Ed. Therman B. O'Daniel. Washington, DC: Howard UP, 1977. 213–27, notes 238–40.

Phelan, Peggy. "Reciting the Citation of Others; or, A Second Introduction." *Acting Out: Feminist Performances.* Eds. Lynda Hart and Peggy Phelan. Ann Arbor: U of Michigan P, 1993. 13–31.

Phillips, Kate. *Helen Hunt Jackson: A Literary Life.* Berkeley: U of California P, 2003.

Pocock, J. G. A. "The Ideal of Citizenship since Classical Times." *The Citizenship Debates.* Ed. Gershon Shafir. Minneapolis: U of Minnesota P, 1998. 31–41.

Polanich, Judith K. "Ramona's Baskets: Romance and Reality." *American Indian Culture and Research Journal* 21.3 (1997): 145–62.

Porter, Dorothy. *Negro Protest Pamphlets*. New York: Arno Press, 1969.

Porter, Horace. *Stealing the Fire*. Middletown, CT: Wesleyan UP, 1989.

Power, Peter Kerry. "The Treacherous Body: Isolation, Confession, and Community in James Baldwin." *American Literature* 77.4 (2005): 787–813.

Powers, Lyall H. "Henry James and James Baldwin: The Complex Figure." *Modern Fiction Studies* 30.4 (1984): 651–67.

Pratt, Louis H. "James Baldwin and the 'Literary Ghetto.'" *CLA Journal* 20 (1976): 262–72.

Puzo, Mario. "His Cardboard Lovers." *New York Times Book Review* 23 June 1968: 5, 34.

Pynchon, Thomas. *The Crying of Lot 49*. 1965. New York: HarperPerennial, 1986.

———. "A Journey into the Mind of Watts." *New York Times Magazine* 12 June 1966: 34–5, 78, 80–82, 84.

"Races." *Time Magazine* 17 May 1963: 23–27.

Radford-Hill, Sheila. "Keepin' It Real: A Generational Commentary on Kimberly Springer's 'Third Wave Black Feminsm?'" *Signs* 27.4 (2002): 1083–90.

Ratcliffe, Krista L. *Anglo-American Feminist Challenges to the Rhetorical Traditions: Virginia Woolf, Mary Daly, and Adrienne Rich*. Carbondale: Southern Illinois UP, 1995.

Recchio, Thomas E. "A Dialogic Approach to the Essay." Butrym 271–88.

Redding, Saunders. "The Problems of the Negro Writer." *The Massachusetts Review* 6 (1964–1965): 57–70.

Redstockings, "Manifesto." Mimeographed position paper, 1969. Baxandall and Gordon 90–91.

Reed, Ishmael. *Flight to Canada*. New York: Random House, 1976.

Reed, T. V. *The Art of Protest: Culture and Activism from the Civil Rights Movement to the Streets of Seattle*. Minneapolis: U of Minnesota P, 2005.

Reid-Pharr, Robert. "Tearing the Goat's Flesh: Crisis, Abjection, and Homosexuality in the Production of a Late-Twentieth-Century Black Masculinity." *Novel Gazing: Queer Readings in Fiction*. Ed. Eve Kosofsky Sedgwick. Durham, NC: Duke UP, 1997. 353–76.

Relyea, Sarah. *Outsider Citizens: The Remaking of Postwar Identity in Wright, Beauvoir, and Baldwin*. New York: Routledge, 2006.

Renker, Elizabeth M. "'Declaration-Men' and the Rhetoric of Self-Presentation." *Early American Literature* 24 (1989): 120–34.

Rich, Adrienne. *Blood, Bread, and Poetry: Selected Prose 1979–1985*. New York: Norton, 1986.

———. *On Lies, Secrets, and Silence*. New York: Norton, 1979.

———. *What Is Found There: Notebooks on Poetry and Politics*. New York: Norton, 1993.

Roberts, Dorothy. *Killing the Black Body: Race, Reproduction, and the Meaning of Liberty*. New York: Random House, 1997.

Rodriguez, Richard. *Brown: The Last Discovery of America*. New York: Viking, 2002.

Rolle, Andrew F. Introduction. *A Century of Dishonor: The Early Crusade for Indian Reform*. New York: Harper Torchbooks, 1965. i–xx.

Root, Robert. "It's a Wasteland." Rev. of *Another Country*, by James Baldwin. *Christian Century* 79 (1962): 1354–55.

Roth, Benita. *Separate Roads to Feminism: Black, Chicana, and White Feminist Movements in America's Second Wave*. New York: Cambridge UP, 2004.

Rowe, John Carlos. *Post-Nationalist American Studies*. Berkeley: U of California P, 2000.

Roy, Arundhati. "Do Turkeys Enjoy Thanksgiving?" *An Ordinary Person's Guide to Empire*. Boston: South End Press, 2004.

Rusk, Lauren. "Selfhood and Strategy in *Notes of a Native Son*." McBride, *James Baldwin Now!* 360–92.

Samuels, Shirley, ed. *The Culture of Sentiment: Race, Gender, and Sentimentality in Nineteenth-Century America*. New York: Oxford UP, 1992.

Sandos, James A. "Historic Preservation and Historical Facts: Helen Hunt Jackson, Rancho Camulos, and Ramona." *California History* 77.3 (1998): 168–85, 197–99.

Sarachild, Kathie. "Consciousness-Raising: A Radical Weapon." Notes for speech for the First National Conference of Stewardesses for Women's Rights in New York City, 12 March 1973. *Feminist Revolution*. New York: Random House, 1978. 144–50.

Schatt, Stanley. "You Must Go Home Again: Today's Afro-American Expatriate Writers." *Negro American Literature Forum* 7 (1973): 80–82.

Scheuller, Malini Johar. "Postcolonial American Studies," *ALH* 16.1 (2004): 162–75.

Schueller, Malini Johar, and Edward Watts, eds. *Messy Beginnings: Postcoloniality and Early American Studies*. New Brunswick, NJ: Rutgers UP, 2003.

Schlosser, Eric. *Fast Food Nation: The Dark Side of the All-American Meal*. Boston: Houghton Mifflin, 2001.

Schroth, Raymond A. "James Baldwin's Search." *Catholic World* Feb. 1964: 288–94.

Scott, Darieck. "Jungle Fever? Black Gay Identity Politics, White Dick, and the Utopian Bedroom." *GLQ* 1.3 (1994): 299–321.

Scott, Lynn Orilla. *James Baldwin's Later Fiction*. East Lansing: Michigan State UP, 2002.

Seelye, Thomas H. Introduction. *A Century of Dishonour*. Helen Hunt Jackson. Boston: Roberts Brothers, 1885.

Senier, Siobhan. *Voices of American Indian Assimilation and Resistance: Helen Hunt Jackson, Sarah Winnemucca, and Victoria Howard.* Norman: U of Oklahoma P, 1993.

Shayon, Robert Lewis. "T.V. and Radio." Rev. of an interview with James Baldwin. *Saturday Review* 24 Feb. 1962: 35.

Shin, Barbara, and Andrew Judson. "Beneath the Black Aesthetic: James Baldwin's Primer of Black American Masculinity." *African American Review* 32.2 (1998): 247–61.

Shklar, Judith. *American Citizenship and the Quest for Inclusion.* Cambridge: Harvard UP, 1991.

Shohat, Ella, and Robert Stam, eds. *Multiculturalism, Postcoloniality, and Transnational Media.* New Brunswick, NJ: Rutgers UP, 2003.

Shulman, Alix Kates. "Emma Goldman's Feminism: A Re-appraisal." Introduction to the new edition of *Red Emma Speaks: An Emma Goldman Reader.* 1972. New York: Schocken, 1983. 3–20.

———. "A Marriage Agreement." 1970. Baxandall and Gordon 218–20.

———. "A Marriage Disagreement, or Marriage by Other Means." DuPlessis and Snitow 284–303.

Silko, Leslie Marmon. "The Border Patrol State." *Tucson Weekly* 26 Sept. 1996.

Simmons, Harvey G. "James Baldwin and the Negro Conundrum." *Antioch Review* 23 (1963): 250–60.

Singh, Amrijit, and Peter Schmidt, eds. *Postcolonial Theory and the United States.* Jackson: UP of Mississippi, 2000.

Smith, Andrea. "Native American Feminism, Sovereignty, and Social Change." *Feminist Studies* 31.1 (2005): 116–32.

Smith, Barbara. Foreword. "The Combahee River Collective Statement: Black Feminist Organizing in the Seventies and Eighties." *Freedom Organizing Series #1.* Latham, NY: Kitchen Table: Women of Color Press, 1986.

———. "'Feisty Characters' and 'Other People's Causes': Memories of White Racism and U.S. Feminism." DuPlessis and Snitow 477–81.

———, ed. *Home Girls: A Black Feminist Anthology.* Albany, NY: Kitchen Table: Women of Color Press, 1983.

———. "Toward a Black Feminist Criticism." 1977. Ed. Elaine Showalter. *The New Feminist Criticism: Essays on Women, Literature and Theory.* New York: Pantheon, 1995. 168–85.

Smith, Rogers M. *Civic Ideals: Conflicting Visions of Citizenship in U.S. History.* New Haven, CT: Yale UP, 1997.

———. *Stories of Peoplehood: The Politics and Morals of Political Membership.* New York: Cambridge UP, 2003.

Smith, Sherry L. *Reimagining Indians: Native Americans Through Anglo-Eyes, 1880–1940.* New York: Oxford UP, 2000.

Smith, Valerie. "Introduction." *Incidents in the Life of a Slave Girl*. By Harriet Jacobs (Linda Brent). Rpt. New York: Oxford UP, 1988. xxvii–xl.

Smith, William Raymond. "The Rhetoric of the Declaration of Independence." *College English* 26.4 (1965): 306–09.

Snyder, John. *Prospects of Power: Tragedy, Satire, the Essay, and the Theory of Genre*. Louisville: U of Kentucky P, 1991.

Sollors, Werner, ed. *Multilingual America: Transnationalism, Ethnicity, and the Languages of American Literature*. New York: New York UP, 1998.

Solomon, Martha. *Emma Goldman*. Boston: Twayne, 1984.

———. "Ideology as Rhetorical Constraint: The Anarchist Agitation of 'Red Emma' Goldman." *Quarterly Journal Speech* 74 (1988): 184–200.

Southwick, Albert B. "James Baldwin's Jeremiad; or, Baldwin Gone Awry." *The Christian Century* 24 Mar. 1965: 362–64.

Spellmeyer, Kurt. "A Common Ground: The Essay in the Academy." Butrym 253–70.

Spender, Stephen. "James Baldwin: Voice of a Revolution." *Partisan Review* 30 (1963): 256–60.

Spillers, Hortense. "Changing the Letter: The Yokes, the Jokes of Discourse, or, Mrs. Stowe, Mr. Reed." *Slavery and the Literary Imagination*. Ed. Deborah McDowell and Arnold Rampersad. Baltimore: Johns Hopkins UP, 1989. 25–61.

Spingarn, Arthur B. "Notes of a Native Son." *Crisis* 63 (Feb. 1956): 87.

Spooner, Lysander. "No Treason. No. II. The Constitution." 1867. Rpt. in *The Right Wing Individualist Tradition in America*. New York: Arno Press, 1972.

Springer, Kimberly. *Living for the Revolution: Black Feminist Organizations*. Durham, NC: Duke UP, 2005.

———. "Third Wave Black Feminism?" *Signs* 27.4 (2002): 1059–82.

Stabb, Martin. *The Dissenting Voice: The New Essay of Spanish America, 1960–1985*. Austin: U of Texas P, 1994.

Standley, Fred L. "James Baldwin: The Artist as Incorrigible Disturber of the Peace." *Southern Humanities Review* 4 (1970): 18–30.

Standley, Fred L., and Nancy V. Burt, eds. *Critical Essays on James Baldwin*. Boston: G. K. Hall, 1988.

Standley, Fred L., and Louis H. Pratt, eds. *Conversations with James Baldwin*. Jackson: UP of Mississippi, 1989.

Stanton, Domna. "On Rooted Cosmpolitanism." *PMLA* 121.3 (2006): 627–40.

Stanton, Elizabeth Cady et al. "A Declaration of Sentiments." 1848. Rpt. in *Available Means: An Anthology of Women's Rhetoric(s)*. Ed. Joy Ritchie and Kate Ronald. Pittsburgh: U of Pittsburgh P, 2001. 138–42.

Starr, Thomas. "Separated at Birth: Text and Context of the Declaration of Independence." *Proceedings of the American Antiquarian Society* 110.1 (2000): 153–99.

Steele, Cassie. "Drawing Strength from Our Mothers: Tapping the Roots of Black Women's History." *Mother Matters: Motherhood as Discourse and Practice*. Ed. Andrea O'Reilly. Toronto: Association for the Research on Mothering, 2004. 154–64.

Stein, Sol. *Native Sons*. New York: Ballantine, 2004.

Stevens, Errol Wayne. "Helen Hunt Jackson's *Ramona*: Social Prolems Novel as a Tourist Guide." *California History* 77.3 (1998): 158–67, 196–97.

Stevenson, David L. "The Activists." *Daedalus* 92 (1963): 238–49.

Stowe, Harriet Beecher. *Uncle Tom's Cabin; or, Life Among the Lowly*. 1852.

Strange, Lisa S., and Robert S. Brown. "The Bicycle, Women's Rights, and Elizabeth Cady Stanton." *Women's Studies* 31 (2002): 609–26.

Strauss, Andrew et al. *Debating Cosmopolitics*. London: Verso, 2003.

Strong, Augusta. "Notes on James Baldwin." *Freedomways* 2 (1962): 167–71.

Strout, Cushing. "*Uncle Tom's Cabin* and the Portent of Millenium." *Yale Review* 57 (1968): 375–85.

Students for a Democratic Society. "The Port Huron Statement." 1962. Mimeographed at 1608 W. Madison St., Chicago, third printing, 1966.

Sundquist, Eric J. "Realism and Regionalism." In *The Columbia History of the American Novel*. Ed. Emory Elliott. New York: Columbia UP, 1991. 501–24.

———, ed. *To Wake the Nations: Race in the Making of American Literature*. New York: Belknap, 1994.

Thomas, Kendall. "'Ain't Nothin' Like the Real Thing': Black Masculinity, Gay Sexuality, and the Jargon of Authenticity." Blount and Cunningham 55–69.

Thomas, Piri. *Down These Mean Streets*. 1967. New York: Vintage, 1997.

Thompson, Becky. "Multiracial Feminism: Recasting the Chronology of Second Wave Feminism." *Feminist Studies* 28.2 (2002): 337–60.

Thoreau, Henry David. "Resistance to Civil Government." 1849. *Walden and Resistance to Civil Government*. Ed. William Rossi. New York: Norton, 1992. 226–45.

Thurman, Wallace. "Negro Poets and their Poetry." 1928. Early 98–107.

Tóibín, Colm. "The Last Witness." *London Review of Books* 20 Sept. 2001: 15–20.

Tompkins, Jane. *Sensational Designs*. New York: Oxford UP, 1985.

Tourgée, Albion W. "A Study in Civilization." *North American Review* 143 (3): 1886; 246–61.

Treat, James, ed. *For This Land: Writings on Religion in America*. Vine Deloria, Jr. New York: Rotuledge: 1999.

Trodd, Zoe, ed. *American Protest Literature*. Cambridge: Harvard UP, 2006.

Troupe, Quincy. *James Baldwin: The Legacy*. New York: Simon & Schuster, 1989.

Turner, Darwin T. "James Baldwin and the Dilemma of the Black Dramatist." O'Daniel 189–94.

Tuttleton, James W. "The Negro Writer as Spokesman." *The Black American Writer.* Ed. C. W. E. Bigsby. Deland, FL: Everett/Edwards, 1969. 245–59.

United States. White House. Press Release. "Citizenship Day and Constitution Week, 2002: A Proclamation." 16 Sept. 2002. <http://www.whitehouse.gov>.

———. White House. Press Release. "Citizenship Day and Constitution Week, 2003: A Proclamation." 17 Sept. 2003. <http://www.whitehouse.gov>.

———. White House. Press Release. "Citizenship Day and Constitution Week, 2004: A Proclamation." 17 Sept. 2004. <http://www.whitehouse.gov>.

———. White House. Press Release. "Loyalty Day, 2004: A Proclamation." 30 Apr. 2004. <http://www.whitehouse.gov>.

Vandyke, Patricia. "Choosing One's Side with Care: The Liberating Repartee." *Perspectives on Contemporary Literature* (Louisville, KY) 1.1 (1975): 105–17.

Vidal, Gore. *Dreaming War: Blood for Oil and the Cheney–Bush Junta.* New York: Thunder's Mouth Press, 2002.

———. "Police Brutality." 1961. Rpt. in *United States: Essays 1952–1992.* New York: Random House, 1993. 553–57.

Wald, Priscilla. *Constituting Americans: Cultural Anxiety and Narrative Form.* Durham, NC: Duke UP, 1995.

Walk, Lori. "Audre Lorde's Life Writing: The Politics of Location." *Women's Studies: An Interdisciplinary Journal* 32.7 (2003): 815–34.

Walker, Alice. *In Search of Our Mothers' Gardens: Womanist Prose.* New York: Harcourt Brace, 1983.

———. *Living by the Word: Selected Writings, 1973–1987.* Orlando, FL: Harcourt Brace Jovanovich, 1988.

Walker, David. "Walker's Appeal." *Walker's Appeal and Garnet's Address to the Slaves of the United States of America.* 1848. Rpt. Nashville: James C. Winston, 1994.

Wall, Cheryl. "On Freedom and the Will to Adorn." *Aesthetics & Ideology.* Ed. George Levine. New Brunswick, NJ: Rutgers UP, 1994. 283–303.

———. *Worrying the Line: Black Women Writers, Lineage, and Literary Tradition.* Chapel Hill: U of North Carolina P, 2005.

Wallace, Maurice. "On Being a Witness." *Black Queer Studies.* Ed. E. Patrick Johson and Mae G. Henderson. Durham, NC: Duke UP, 2005. 276–88.

Wallace, Michelle. *Black Macho and the Myth of the Superwoman.* New York: Dial, 1979.

———. "To Hell and Back: On the Road with Black Feminism in the 1960s and 1970s." DuPlessis and Snitow 426–42.

Walzer, Michael. "Pluralism: A Political Perspective." 1980. *What It Means to Be an American: Essays on the American Experience.* New York: Marsilio, 1996. 53–80.

Ware, Celestine. "The Relationship of Black Women to the Women's Liberation Movement." 1970. Crow 98–112.

Warner, Michael. *Letters of the Republic: Publication and the Public Sphere in Eighteenth-Century America.* Cambridge: Harvard UP, 1990.

———. *Publics and Counter-Publics.* New York: Zone Publications, 2002.

Warren, Robert Penn. *Who Speaks for the Negro?* New York: Random House, 1965.

Washington, Bryan. *The Politics of Exile: Ideology in Henry James, F. Scott Fitzgerald, and James Baldwin.* Boston: Northeastern UP, 1995.

Washington, Mary Helen. "Introduction." *A Voice from the South.* Anna Julia Cooper. New York: Oxford UP, 1988. xxvii–liv.

Watkins, Mel. "An Appreciation." *James Baldwin: The Legacy.* Ed. Quincy Troupe. New York: Simon & Schuster, 1989. 107–23.

———. "The Fire Next Time This Time." Rev. of *No Name in the Street. New York Times Book Review* 28 May 1972: 17–18.

Watson, Edward A. "The Novels and Essays of James Baldwin: Case-Book of a 'Lover's War' with the United States." *Queen's Quarterly* 72 (1965): 385–402.

Watson, Martha Solomon. "The Dynamics of Intertextuality: Re-Reading the Declaration of Independence." Benson 91–111.

Weatherby, W. J. *James Baldwin: Artist on Fire.* New York: Donald Fine, 1989.

"'We Carry Him With Us': James Baldwin: His Voice Remembered." *New York Times Book Review* 20 Dec. 1987: 1, 27, 29–30.

Weiner, Mark. *Black Trials: Citizenship from the Beginning of Slavery to the End of Caste.* New York: Knopf, 2004.

Weixlmann, Joe. "Staged Segregation: Baldwin's *Blues for Mister Charlie* and O'Neill's *All God's Chillun Got Wings.*" *Black American Literature Forum* 11.1 (1977): 35–36.

West, Stan. "Tip-Toeing on the Tightrope: A Personal Essay on Black Writer Ambivalence." *African American Review* 32.2 (1998): 285–91.

Wexler, Alice. *Emma Goldman in Exile: From the Russian Revolution to the Spanish Civil War.* Boston: Beacon Press, 1989.

———. *Emma Goldman: An Intimate Life.* New York: Pantheon, 1984.

Whitman, Walt. "Democratic Vistas." 1871. *Prose Works.* Ed. Floyd Stovall. New York: New York UP, 1964. 361–425.

Williams, Terry Tempest. "One Patriot." *Patriotism and the American Land.* Barrington, MA: The Orion Society, 2002. 37–58.

Willis, Ellen. Foreword. Echols, *Daring to Be Bad* vii–xv.

Wills, Antony A. "The Uses of Coincidence in 'Notes of a Native Son.'" *Negro American Literature Forum* 8.3 (1974): 397–406.

Wolfe, Alan. "The New Pamphleteers." *New York Times Book Review* 11 July 2004: 12–13.

Wood, Joe. "Witness for the Persecution: James Baldwin in Black and White." *Village Voice Literary Supplement* July 1989: 14–16.

Wright, David. "No Hiding Place: Exile 'Underground' in James Baldwin's 'This Morning, This Evening, So Soon.'" *CLA Journal* 42.4 (1999): 445–61.

Wright, Derek. "African-American Tensions in Black Writing of the 1960s." *Journal of Black Studies* 19.4 (1989): 442–58.

Wright, Richard. "Between Laughter and Tears." *New Masses* 5 Oct. 1937: 22, 25.

———. *Black Boy*. 1945. New York: HarperPerennial, 1998.

———. "Blueprint for Negro Writing." 1937. *Richard Wright Reader*. Eds. Ellen Wright and Michael Fabre. New York: Harper & Row, 1978. 194–204.

———. "How 'Bigger' Was Born." Introduction to *Native Son*. 1940. New York: Harper & Row, 1987. vii–xxxiv.

———. *Native Son*. 1940. New York: Harper & Row, 1987.

Wu, Cynthia. "Marked Bodies, Marking Time: Reclaiming the Warrior in Audre Lorde's *The Cancer Journals*." *A/B: Auto/Biography Studies* 17.2 (2002): 245–61.

Yardley, Jonathan. "The Writer and the Preacher." 1985. Rpt. in Standley and Burt 240–43.

Young, Iris Marion. "The Logic of Masculinist Protection: Reflections on the Current Security State," *Signs* 29.1 (2003): 1–26.

Zaeske, Susan. *Signatures of Citizenship: Petitioning, Antislavery, and Women's Political Identity*. Chapel Hill: U of North Carolina P, 2003.

Zinn, Howard. *Declarations of Independence: Cross-Examining American Ideology*. New York: HarperPerennial, 1990.

INDEX

abolitionism, 2, 23–24, 27–28, 33–35, 46, 49–50, 74, 80
Addison, Joseph, 11, 31
Adorno, Theodor, 15, 29–30, 37
Africa, 14, 24, 34, 90, 100, 110, 147
African American: culture, 14, 16, 155; essay, 11, 14; experience, 19, 32, 35, 96, 110, 114, 144; literary traditions, 11, 13, 42, 80–81, 88, 101, 112, 120, 124; relation to whites, 34, 88, 93, 98, 134; relation to U.S. democracy, 7, 15, 26, 33–34, 40, 42, 43, 74, 88, 134, 141–45; studies, 3
alien citizenship, 143, 162n16
Als, Hilton, 81, 103, 111, 115
American Indians, 9, 20, 21–22, 35–37, 44–46, 49, 67, 71–79, 83–86, 127, 152; and assimilation, 79, 184–89; and citizenship, 74–75, 78–79, 152; and Declaration of Independence, 44–46, 49, 67. *See also* Deloria, Vine, Jr.; Jackson, Helen Hunt; Occom, Samson
American Revolution, 41–45, 144; as ideal, 51, 61, 168n49; as rhetoric, 43. *See also* Declaration of Independence
American Studies Association, 140
anarchism, 50–63, 69, 168n49
anecdotal, essays as, 9, 15, 92–93, 100, 108, 125–26, 132, 144, 146, 148
Anderson, Benedict, 24, 79, 164n35
Angelou, Maya, 114

anthology as form, 118, 120, 136, 182n44
anti-immigration *See* immigrants
anti-feminism. *See* feminism
anti-racism. *See* racism and anti-racism
anti-slavery. *See* abolition
anti-war. *See* war
Anzaldúa, Gloria, 38, 121, 152
Appiah, Kwama Anthony, 149–50
Arendt, Hannah, 140
artist-advocates, 3–4, 8–11, 16, 39–40, 71–72, 79–91, 101–11, 155–57
Atkins, G. Douglass, 1, 11, 14, 15, 17, 27, 29, 119–23, 156
Atlanta child murders, 30, 165n52

Bacon, Francis, 15, 22
Bakhtin, Mikhail, 122
Baldwin, James, 1, 2, 7, 9, 28–30, 40, 81–82, 87–115, 89, 135, 138, 139, 146, 151–52, 156–68; *Another Country*, 111; and black nationalism, 92, 103, 110, 114; *Blues for Mister Charlie*, 91, 101, 107–8; and civil rights, 29–30, 82, 87–91; *The Devil Finds Work*, 94, 108–9; "Everybody's Protest Novel," 81, 90, 95; *The Evidence of Things Not Seen*, 29–30; *The Fire Next Time*, 1, 9, 88, 92–94, 99–105, 108–12, 138, 158; *Giovanni's Room*, 110, 179n138; *Go Tell it on the Mountain*, 110; and Harlem, 7, 98,

215

Baldwin, James (continued)
  100, 113; *If Beale Street Could Talk*,
  110; as master essayist, 1, 8–9, 15,
  87–100; as media celebrity, 105–6;
  No Name in the Street, 94, 109, 112;
  Nobody Knows My Name, 98, 101,
  106–7; *Notes of a Native Son*, 88, 91,
  95–96, 99, 113; perceived artistic
  decline, 9, 89, 109, 112; and Richard
  Wright, 81, 91, 95; as spokesperson,
  9, 87–89, 93, 96, 104–11, 117, 157;
  Tell Me How the Train's Been Gone,
  110
Balkanization. See identity politics
Bambara, Toni Cade, 152, 165
Baraka, Amiri/LeRoi Jones, 40, 115, 165n52
beat movement, 133–34
Benhabib, Seyla, 153
Bercovitch, 162n18
Bhabha, Homi, 44
Bill of Rights, re-visions of, 64, 144
Black Arts, 153, 177n88
Black Elk, 127–28
black liberation. See Black Nationalism; Black Power, Civil Rights movement, pan-Africanism
Black Nationalism, 34, 92, 103, 110, 114. See also Black Power
Black Power, 87, 96, 108, 114, 117, 126, 135. See also Black Nationalism
borderlands (Southwest), 85–86, 174n57
borders: identitarian, 4, 10–11, 34, 64, 110, 123, 125, 141, 148, 157; national, 3–10, 54, 74, 78–79, 113, 139–53
Bosniak, Linda, 7
Brando, Marlon, 89
Bread and Roses, 63–69
Bush, George H. W., 19, 142
Bush, George W., 5, 32, 162n16
Butrym, Alexander, 11, 16
Byerman, Keith, 42, 137, 166n4

capitalism, 54, 57–58, 130, 135, 150–51
Carby, Hazel, 14, 48
Carson, Rachel, 3, 156

Chicago Defender, 25, 31, 172n23. See also Hughes, Langston
cinema. See film; Hollywood
citizenship, 4–12, 23–24, 28, 36–39, 47, 54–56, 74, 85–86, 121, 134, 143–58; as allegiance, 4–5, 58; cosmopolitan, 10, 150–51; definitions of, 7, 68, 162n16; as formal status, 7, 24, 56, 68, 72, 79, 85, 139; partial, 6–8, 56, 75, 142–46; second class, 7, 26, 81, 86, 134, 163n34
Citizenship Day, 4–5, 161n8
"civic myths," 6, 34
civil disobedience, 20, 133
Civil Rights movement, 12, 20, 26, 29–30, 82, 87–119, 124–27, 133, 135, 141, 180n4; and James Baldwin; 29–30, 87–119; and Martin Luther King, Jr., 20, 126–27; and Alice Walker, 124–27
Clarke, Cheryl, 136
Cleaver, Eldridge, 114, 177n85, 179n138–39
collective authorship, 45, 57, 167n22, 128–31, 134–37
collectivity, 1–6, 17–24, 44, 57, 67, 92–93, 108, 117–38, 141, 146; and anti-collectivity, 69, 118, 132–34
colonialism, 22, 35–37, 67, 183n28
color line, 14–16, 147, 155, 157. See also DuBois, W.E.B.
Columbus, Christopher, 36
Combahee River Collective, 10, 134–37, 159–60
complicitous critique, 54
Congress on Racial Equality (CORE), 135
Congress, U.S., 72–78, 84–85
constative events, 131
Constitution Day, 162n12
conversation, essays as, 25, 117–38
Cooper, Anna Julia, 25–26, 121, 129, 153
cosmopolitanism, 5, 10, 67, 149–51
cosmopolitics, 150
Crisis, 81, 97, 103
Cunningham, James, 28–29, 93–95

Declaration of Human Rights, 149, 151
Declaration of Independence, 2, 12, 14, 15, 28, 34, 41–45, 138, 151, 168n49; as literary document, 42, 45; revisions of, 35, 41–42, 45–70, 144
DeKoven, Marianne, 90, 95, 102, 117, 119, 174n46
Deloria, Vine, Jr., 35–37, 152
democracy: as American tradition, 4–10, 32, 34, 98, 167n4; essay as, 18, 23, 27; as ideal, 19, 26, 33, 40, 42, 83, 118–19, 143, 146; as language, 28, 34, 38, 141, 144–47; as promise, 2–3, 7, 12, 32, 73–79, 83–86, 139–43, 158; as state apparatus, 2, 34, 39, 63, 140–53, 183n18
deportation, 5, 55, 169n57
dialogue, essays as, 15, 20, 27, 117–30
diaspora, 5, 24
Dickstein, Morris, 95
digressive, essays as, 15, 38, 94, 109
divestment, as protest strategy, 12, 18–20, 28, 57, 123, 132–33, 146
double consciousness, 155
Douglass, Frederick, 2, 27–29, 35, 45
DuBois, W. E. B., 8, 14–16, 123, 144, 155–56, 184n2
Dworkin, Andrea, 125, 132–33

Early, Gerald, 11, 14
Ebony, 105, 109
Ehrenreich, Barbara, 83, 157
Eliot, T. S., 15
Ellison, Ralph Waldo, 22, 32, 83, 112
"embodied truth," 119–23. *See also* Atkins, G. Douglass
Emerson, Ralph Waldo, 11, 15, 22–23, 32, 95, 122
ephemeral, in essays, 2, 9, 29–30, 61, 146, 155
epistolary tradition, 121
e pluribus unum, 6, 44, 128
essay, and American oratory, 8, 13, 16–18, 21–24, 27–29, 33–34, 40, 45, 59, 83, 91, 104, 122, 152, 156; European origins, 13, 16–17, 22–24, 40, 83, 96, 106, 155–56; and Montaigne, 17, 21–23, 40, 98; and other national traditions, 11, 157; periodical essay, 11, 31, 165n56; personal essay, 2, 8–11, 13, 15, 17–22, 25–30, 39–40, 42, 45, 83, 92–93, 98, 106, 114–18, 148, 156; protest essay definition, 1–2, 13–40; protest essay tradition, 1, 13–40, 41, 60, 71, 87–89, 106, 117–19, 139–40, 143, 151–53, 155–58; and readership, 17–24, 37–39, 84–85, 89–90, 101–11, 114
exceptionalism, American, 54, 85, 106, 142
experience. *See* personal experience
European Union, 150

Falk, Candace, 55–56, 59–60, 62, 170n85
familial rhetoric, 46–49, 56, 66, 143–44
feminism, 25, 41–69, 114, 117–38, 139–53; and anti-feminism, 67, 82, 181n30; black, 18, 83, 118–21, 133–53; and essay, 11, 39, 152–53; First Wave, 45–50, 60, 63; liberal, 45–50, 65, 68; radical, 39, 50–68, 121–23, 130–31; second wave, 10, 60, 63–68, 118–38, 143; suffragism, 6, 45–50; third wave, 181–82n43; transnational, 57–59, 66–67, 139–53. *See also* women's liberation movement
film, 83, 94, 108. *See also* Hollywood
Foner, Philip, 43, 70
founding documents, 6, 8, 11, 33–45, 41–70, 112, 118, 139, 144
Freedomways, 93, 109
Friedman, Susan Stanford, 136, 137

Gandhi, Mohatma, 133
Garnet, Henry Highland, 17, 23–24, 34, 38, 130
Garvey, Marcus, 6
Gates, Henry Louis, Jr., 42, 47, 111. *See also* signifying
Gilroy, Paul, 157

INDEX

Goldman, Emma, 5, 8, 41–42, 50–63, 55, 69, 152; and *Boston Globe*, 62; as essayist, 59–62, 170n83; *Mother Earth*, 50–54, 57–62, 168n168, 169n64; "New Declaration of Independence," 41, 50–51, 52–53, 57, 61; as orator, 59–62; and police surveillance, 55–56, 169n59; "The Traffic in Women," 51; and U.S. citizenship, 5, 54–56, 58,169n57, 169n75
Good, Graham, 14, 16
Gordimer, Nadine, 157
Gordon, Linda, 65–68
gothic, 4
Grasso, Linda, 11
group rights, 7, 47, 156

Habermas, Jürgen, 3
Hall, Michael, 22, 27
Hansberry, Lorraine, 71, 123, 129, 133–34
Haraway, Donna, 48
Harlem Renaissance, 81
Heritage Foundation, The, 5
Higginson, Thomas Wentworth, 79, 172n17
Himes, Chester, 81, 83
Hiroshima, 146
Hollywood, 94, 108
holocaust, 94
Homeland Security, Department of, 5
homophobia, 109, 114, 135, 179n138
Honig, Bonnie, 4, 7
House Unamerican Activities Committee (HUAC), 26
Hughes, Langston, 16, 25–27, 30–31, 39, 87, 88, 91–92
human rights, 7, 56, 67, 140, 146–53. See also Declaration of Human Rights
Hurston, Zora Neale, 38–39, 81, 124–25, 127
Hutcheon, Linda, 54
hypocrisy, state, 3, 8, 24–29, 31–37, 42, 51, 68, 101, 118, 133, 147, 150

identity politics, 4, 117–38, 140, 146. See also borders: identitarian

immigrants, 4–5, 38, 44, 54–56, 142–47, 167n11, 168n48
imperialism, 22, 32, 38, 50, 67, 85–86, 136–50, 161n8, 174n55
Indian reform movement, 73–75, 78–79, 86, 171n5, 172n16
individualism, 10, 12, 16, 18–21, 23, 27, 42, 47, 66, 69, 83, 120, 128–37, 150, 156; and the essay, 2, 4, 16–21, 23
integration, 1, 9, 82, 92–94, 98–104, 107–15
internationalism. *See* transnationalism; cosmopolitanism
International Women's Day, 66
intersectionality, 137, 182n47

Jackson, Helen Hunt, 9, 71–79, 83–86, 139, 141; and assimilation, 75, 79, 85–86, 174n57; *A Century of Dishonor*, 72–79, 83–86; and citizenship, 72–73, 74, 78–79; and Indian Reform, 72–78, 172n16; and José Martí, 86; and nation-state, 83–86, 139, 141; as New Englander, 73, 75, 83, 85–86; as partial citizen, 75, 78, 85–86; *Ramona*, 74–77, 85–86; Ramona myth, 74; and Harriet Beecher Stowe, 74, 80, 174n57; strategy of shame, 73–79, 141; and Southwest, 73, 85; and U.S. Congress, 72, 75, 84, 174n48
Jacobs, Harriet, 46
jail, 18–21
James, Henry, 96, 106
Jefferson, Thomas, 20, 31, 33, 43, 45, 51
jeremiad, 11, 40, 77, 93, 164n20
Jim Crow, 15, 26, 98–100, 109, 143
Joeres, Ruth-Ellen Boetcher, 38, 39, 118, 120, 122, 142, 145, 152
Johnson, James Weldon, 81
Jordan, June, 10, 18–20, 38, 40, 123, 126, 139–53, 157; and black feminism, 140–43, 152; *Civil Wars*, 40, 141; and language policy, 144–45; and nationalism, 143–49; as partial citizen, 139–40; and State of the

Union, 140–43; relation to Thoreau, 18–20; *Soldier*, 140–41; *Technical Difficulties*, 18–20, 38, 141–49; and transnationalism, 140, 145–53
journalism, 29–31, 40, 83, 165n56; essayists as journalists, 30, 80, 172n23–24, 173n26; as influence on protest essay, 1, 9, 29–31, 38, 73, 80, 157

Kenan, Randall, 91, 99
Kennedy, Robert F., 105, 178n96
King, Martin Luther, Jr., 18, 20–21, 82, 110, 126–27, 147
Kirklighter, Cristina, 11, 22, 29, 152
Kushner, Tony, 62
Kymlicka, Will, 149, 183n18

latino essay tradition, 11, 18, 22, 152
lesbians: and rights, 119; and separatism, 125; and visibility, 135–36; black lesbians, 136–37, 156
Lopate, Philip, 11, 17, 27
Lorde, Audre, 10, 39, 70, 117–21, 123, 147, 152, 156; *Cancer Journals*, 119, 156; "Open Letter to Mary Daly," 118; "Poetry Is Not a Luxury," 119–20
Loyalty Day, 162n16
Lubiano, Wahneema, 3
Lukacs, George, 15, 37
lynching, 25–26, 39, 82, 98

Mailer, Norman, 20, 106–7, 133–34, 181n30
Malamud, Bernard, 98
Malcolm X, 21, 82, 107, 123, 147
manifest destiny, 145–47
manifesto, 10, 11, 35, 38, 40, 66, 128–29, 131–33, 135–38
March on Washington, 89, 127
marriage, 64–65, 129–30
Martí, José, 86, 174n57
Marxism, 64–65, 119, 180n4
McBride, Dwight, 114
McCarthy, Joseph, 26
Mencken, H. L., 31, 59

Mills, Charles, 3
miscegenation, 75, 86
missionaries, 36–37
modernism, 80, 174n46
modernity, 3, 12, 51, 128, 130, 140
Mohammad, Elijah, 92
Mohanty, Chandra Tolpade, 150, 183n28
Montaigne, Michel de, 8, 11, 15, 17, 21–23, 27, 31–32, 40, 98, 145–46, 165n44; and orality, 22; and personal essay, 17, 21–23, 40, 98
Morrison, Toni, 1, 3, 8, 114, 153, 163n34
Mother Earth, 50–54, 57–62, 168n168, 169n64
Moynihan, Daniel Patrick, 144
Muhammad Speaks, 103
multiculturalism, 3, 85, 114, 119, 139–53. *See also* identity politics; pluralism

NAACP, 31
National Black Feminist Organization (NBFO), 135
National Organization for Women (NOW), 64, 68, 132
nation-state, 22, 41–70, 83–86, 101, 139–53, 158
Native Americans. *See* American Indians
nativism, 54–57, 141
naturalization, 4–6, 58, 143, 170n83
natural rights, 7, 18, 21, 24, 44, 51, 56, 73, 140
Neal, Lawrence, 103, 177n88
Nelson, Richard, 6
New Left, 65, 102–3, 117–19, 132, 180n4
New World, 22, 35–37
New Yorker, 93, 97–98, 103, 111
New York Radical Feminists (NYRF), 130–31
New York Times, 80, 87, 90–91, 98, 99, 104, 110, 112, 112–14
"not-we," 6, 43–49, 57
Nussbaum, Martha, 151

Oath of Citizenship (also: Oath of Allegiance), 4–6, 58, 68
Obaldia, Cheryl de, 14–16
Occom, Samson, 21–24, 72
O'Connor, Flannery, 124
open-ended (essays as), 15–16, 29–30, 37–39, 50, 90, 92, 122, 124, 145
open letter, 20, 120, 125
oratory (American political), 8, 13, 16–18, 21–24, 27, 33, 40, 45, 83, 91, 122, 152, 156

Paine, Thomas, 3, 18, 45, 51
Palestine, 148
pan-Africanism, 90
parody, as protest strategy, 82
partial citizen, 6–8, 41, 47, 133–34, 139, 158, 163n24; James Baldwin as, 93; definition of, 7, 139; Frederick Douglass as, 28; Henry Highland Garnet as, 24; Emma Goldman as, 56; Helen Hunt Jackson as, 75, 78, 85–86; June Jordan as, 139–42
patriotism, 3–4, 6, 51, 54–57, 63, 67–69, 141, 144, 151–52, 162n16
pamphleteering, 3, 11, 18, 34, 40, 54, 62, 64, 69, 95
Percy, Walker, 98
personal essay. *See* essay
personal experience, 1–3, 31–37, 91–100, 119–28, 158; in the essay, 12, 14–15, 17–18, 89, 91–100, 106, 108–9, 119–29, 135–37, 140–43, 158; as representative experience, 1–3, 14–18, 28, 31–37, 108–9, 114, 146–48, 156; as source of authority, 8–10, 25, 29, 31–37, 54, 61, 99, 117
Phelan, Peggy, 132
Phylon, 95, 97, 157
pluralism, 44, 85, 136, 143, 151. *See also* multiculturalism
Poetry for the People, 140
polemical, 2, 9, 38, 40, 43, 51, 57, 96, 101, 104, 113, 132, 147
police brutality, 26, 31, 51
Port Huron Statement, 35, 37, 133

postcolonialism, 85, 138, 146–49, 157, 182n1
postmodernism, 36, 80, 83, 174n46
Price, H. (Commissioner of Indian Affairs), 76–77
private sphere, 44, 48–50, 72, 93, 106
Progressive, The, 93
protest essay. *See* essay
protest novel, 1, 4, 9, 11, 12, 72, 75, 79–83, 90–91, 95–96, 98
provisional, essays as, 38, 121–23, 131, 136, 141, 147, 155
public sphere, 11, 19, 23, 44, 48–50, 72, 83, 85, 153
Puzo, Mario, 110
Pynchon, Thomas, 80, 172n24

queer studies, 114, 179n139

"race men," 14, 110
racial segregation, 20, 98–100, 131, 143, 157
racism and anti-racism, 19–21, 24–39, 56, 63–64, 72–74, 79, 81, 87–115, 117–30, 133–38, 139–54, 156–58; and feminism, 59, 63–64, 117–30, 133–38, 139–54
Ramona. *See under* Jackson, Helen Hunt
Ramona myth, 74–75. *See also* Jackson, Helen Hunt
rape, 19
Reconstruction, 14, 16, 25, 32–33, 78–80, 113
reconstruction romance, 75, 78
Redstockings, 129
Reed, Ishmael, 82–83
Reed, T. V., 12, 41
Reitman, Ben, 61
religious rhetoric, 22, 28, 36, 48, 51, 93, 105, 158
re-vision. *See under* Rich, Adrienne
Rich, Adrienne, 10, 39, 111, 117–19, 120–23, 157; re-vision, 8, 42, 45–70, 157
rights. *See* Civil Rights movement; democracy; group rights; human rights; natural rights

Roosevelt, Theodore, 58
Roth, Philip, 82
Roy, Arundhati, 157

Sarah Lawrence College, 124
Schlosser, Eric, 83, 157
Segregation. *See* racial segregation
self-determination, 1, 60, 62, 117, 125–26, 138, 156; feminist, 130–31, 134–37; racial, 82, 88, 94, 100, 103, 114, 157. *See also* Black Nationalism; integration; separatism
Seneca Falls Convention, 41, 45, 49
separate spheres (doctrine of), 49–50, 72
separatism, 1, 63–65, 92, 107, 109, 112, 114, 125, 136, 150, 156
sermon, 11, 21–22, 40, 74, 93, 111, 164n20
Shklar, Judith, 3, 162n10, 163n34
Shulman, Alix Kates, 60, 62–63, 129, 181n30
signifying, 8, 42, 126. *See also* Gates, Henry Louis, Jr.
silence (as form of oppression), 25–28, 58, 120, 121, 152, 156
Silko, Leslie Marmon, 152
sisterhood, 10, 63–67, 117–38, 156. *See also* feminism; women's liberation movement
slave narrative, 27, 45
slavery, 2–3, 13, 17, 19–20, 24, 27–29, 33–35, 43, 45–46, 49, 67, 93, 95, 104, 133, 163n34, 167n11, 171n5; as metaphor, 45, 57; as subject position, 27, 93, 104
Smith, Barbara, 123, 125, 135, 137
Smith, Rogers M., 6, 34
Solanas, Valerie, 129
Souls of Black Folk, The, 14–16, 155–56. *See also* DuBois, W. E. B.
Spacks, Patricia Meyer, 125
Spectator, The, 31
speeches (political), 2, 21, 24, 27, 34, 40, 60–62, 105, 110, 117, 122, 124, 156; as essays, 23, 59, 117, 122, 126, 156; as rhetorical mode, 45, 57, 100, 147

Spellmeyer, Kurt, 27
Spender, Stephen, 102
spokespersonship, 14, 73, 84, 88–89, 104–11, 142, 182n10
Spooner, Lysander, 69
Stanton, Elizabeth Cady, 45–50, 69
State of the Union Address, 140–41; revisions of, 140–49
Statute of Liberty, 143, 146
Steele, Richard, 11, 31
Stein, Sol, 96–97
Steinbeck, John, 80, 172n23
Stowe, Harriet Beecher, 46, 74, 80, 82–83, 90, 95, 171n5, 174n57
Student Nonviolent Coordinating Committee (SNCC), 65, 119, 135
Students for a Democratic Society (SDS), 35, 37, 118
"subject politics," 119

Tax, Meredith, 65–68
taxes, 18, 26
third world politics, 67, 119, 121, 183n28
third world women, 121, 183n28
This Bridge Called My Back, 118, 120–21, 123
Thomas, Piri, 82
Thoreau, Henry David, 6, 11, 12, 13–15, 18–20, 23, 28, 59, 96, 122, 127, 133; as blueprint for protest, 6, 18–19, 28
Till, Emmett, 25–26, 39, 82, 107
Time, 105, 107
Tompkins, Jane, 74, 82–83
transnationalism, 10–11, 50, 57–59, 66–67, 85, 121, 139–53, 182n1, 183n18, 184n2
treason, 4, 58, 69
Trodd, Zoe, 162n18
Truth, Sojourner, 48, 123, 125, 145, 152
Tubman, Harriet, 134, 145

Uncle Tom's Cabin, 74–75, 80–81, 95, 171n5. *See also* Stowe, Harriet Beecher
United Nations, 145, 149, 151, 153

universalism. *See* collective; democracy; human rights; natural rights; sisterhood; utopian aspirations
U.S. Constitution, 5, 33–34, 54, 58, 69, 144, 148; re-visions of, 34–35, 69, 143–44, 148
utopian aspirations, 12, 117–19, 128, 131, 136–38, 174n46

Vidal, Gore, 2, 18, 31–33, 35; "Democratic Vistas," 32–33; "Police Brutality," 31
voting, 1, 8, 26, 32, 172n17

Wages for Housework, 64–65
Walker, Alice, 2, 8–10, 23–24, 16, 38–39, 117–18, 124–30, 137–38; as essayist, 8, 16, 123–28, 153; *In Search of Our Mothers' Gardens*, 38–39, 123–27; *Living by the Word*, 127–28
Walker, David, 31, 33–34, 43
Wall, Cheryl, 16, 124
Walzer, Michael, 44
war, 5, 13, 33, 37, 68, 147, 161n7–8, 163n16, 170n85, 179n134; and antiwar, 18, 65, 119; Civil War, 33, 69; Cold War, 35, 106, 113, 161n6; Mexican-American War, 18; race war, 107; as rhetoric, 24, 45; War on Ignorance, 37; War on Poverty, 36–37; World War II, 133, 140
Ward, Jerry, 16, 79
Warner, Michael, 21, 23, 163n29
Washington, Booker T., 15
Washington, D.C., 75, 85–86, 89
Washington, Mary Helen, 25
Watson, Martha Solomon, 47, 59
Watts riots, 80, 172n24
Wheatley, Phyllis, 81, 124
White, E. B., 15, 18
whiteness, 16, 78, 85–86, 87, 102, 106, 134
Whitman, Walt, 32–33, 98, 118
Williams, Terry Tempest, 3
Women's International Terrorist Conspiracy from Hell (WITCH), 60
women's liberation movement, 6, 8, 12, 41–42, 60, 62–68, 117–38, 119n140. *See also* feminism
Woolf, Virginia, 15, 121, 123–26, 165n39
Wright, Richard, 32, 81–82, 90, 92, 101, 124, 173n33, 172n36; "Blueprint for Negro Writing," 81; *Native Son*, 81; as protest novelist, 81–82, 90, 95

Zinn, Howard, 62, 68
Zitkala-Sa, 152